Practical Psychology for Primary Teachers

RYSJ

For Allan, Robert and Samuel with my love

Practical Psychology for Primary Teachers

Putting Theory into Practice in the Classroom

Rhona Stainthorp

The Falmer Press
(A Member of the Taylor & Francis Group)
London • New York • Philadelphia

UK   The Falmer Press, Falmer House, Barcombe, Lewes,
            East Sussex, BN8 5DL

USA   The Falmer Press, Taylor & Francis Inc., 242 Cherry Street,
            Philadelphia, PA 19106-1906

First published 1989

British Library Cataloguing in Publication Data

Stainthorp, Rhona
    Practical psychology for primary teachers.
    1.   Primary schools. Students. Cognitive development
    I.   Title
    370.15′2

    ISBN 1–85000–561–3
    ISBN 1–85000–562–1

Jacket design by Caroline Archer

Typeset 10½ on 13 Garamond by
Chapterhouse, The Cloisters, Formby L37 3PX

Printed in Great Britain by Taylor & Francis (Printers) Ltd, Basingstoke.

Contents

List of Figures and Tables

Figures

Tables

Acknowledgments

The author wishes to thank the following publishers for permission to reproduce material in this book.

NFER-Nelson for the excerpt from Sheridan, M. (1973) *'From birth to five years; Children's developmental progress'*. Reprinted in table 2.1 by permission of NFER-Nelson.

HOLT, REINHART & WINSTON, Inc. for the figure 'A Spectrogram of the words, heed, head and who'd as spoken in a British accent (speaker: Peter Ladefoged, Feb 16, 1973)' From Fromkin, V. and Rodman, R. (1988): *'An Introduction to language'*, 4th edition. Reprinted in figure 4.2 by permission of Holt Reinhart and Winston.

SCIENTIFIC AMERICAN, Inc for the figure by Alan Beechel from Atkinson, R. C. and Shiffrin, R. M. (1971): 'The control of short-term memory' *Scientific American*, **225**, 82–90. Reprinted as figure 6.1 by permission of Scientific American.

W. H. FREEMAN Inc. for the graph of the results of Keeney *et al.* (1967): 'Spontaneous and induced verbal rehearsal in a recall task' taken from Kail, R. (1979): *'The development of memory in children'*. Reprinted as figure 6.3 by permission of W. H. Freeman.

BASIL BLACKWELL Ltd. for the drawings similar to those used by Hughes, M. and Donaldson, M. (1983): 'The use of hiding games for studying coordination of viewpoints.' In Donaldson, M., Grieve, R. and Pratt, C. (1983): *'Early Childhood development and education'*. Used in figure 7.12 by permission of Basil Blackwell.

WILLIAM COLLINS SONS & CO. Ltd., for the excerpt from 'Children's Minds' Donaldson, M. (1979) Fontana. Reprinted by permission of William Collins Sons & Co.

LAWRENCE ERLBAUM ASSOCIATES Ltd., for the 'Model for both the direct and the phonically mediated recognition, comprehension and naming of written words.' and 'A model for both addressed and assembled spelling.' from Ellis, A. W. (1984): *'Reading writing and dyslexia: a cognitive analysis'*. Presented as figures 10.1 and 10.2 by permission of Lawrence Erlbaum Associates.

Also for 'The six-step model of skills in reading and writing acquisition.' from Frith, U. (1985): 'Beneath the surface of developmental dyslexia.' In Patterson, K., Marshall, J. and Coltheart, M. (1985): *'Surface Dyslexia'*. Presented as figure 10.3 by permission of Lawrence Erlbaum Associates.

The photographs of the children at Oaklands Infant School and the two views of the chairs were taken by Barbara Goodchild.

Preface

If teachers in training read in depth all the books that their tutors suggested, then it would probably take them ten years and not five to become qualified. As it is, all teachers now have to follow four years of academic/professional training followed by one year's probationary teaching before they are qualified. It is a very difficult task to read and assimilate all the relevant material and then to try to use it appropriately in classroom practice. This means that those of us who are involved in the training of teachers have a responsibility to make our own subjects as accessible as possible. The purpose of this book is to try to do just that.

I have decided to write this book because sufficient students and teacher colleagues have told me that they do find cognitive psychology very useful in their day to day teaching. Past students often suggest that they feel other teachers are at a disadvantage if they have not followed a psychology course during their training. With the changes in teaching courses demanded by the Department of Education and Science, the time that can be devoted to psychology during training is gradually being eroded. This means that psychologists need to present their material in such a way that its usefulness is explicit. After reading introductory applied books such as this, I hope that students and teachers will see the importance of cognitive psychology and so be moved to read the more complex theoretical research and make their own selection of useful material.

My own obsession with psychology came when I was teaching full time and studying at Birkbeck College in the evenings. I owe a debt of gratitude to the staff of the Psychology Department there during the years 1971–1974. I must also thank Klara Dormandy whose linguistics teaching at the Institute of Neurology and the National Hospitals College of Speech Sciences was and is outstanding. This work was started during a sojourn in Australia and I must thank Professor Day of the Psychology Department of Monash University for providing me with excellent accommodation. All my colleagues in the Psychology and Philosophy Department of Bulmershe College of Higher Education have provided continuous academic and emotional support but I must single out Josh Schwieso for his patience and tactful advice. It is usual to thank the patience of the typist of the manuscript, but I have to thank my personal computer. We have developed a great love-hate relationship this year and I doubt very much if this book could have been written without it. Finally, I have to thank Allan Quimby for everything.

Chapter 1

Introduction

Cognitive psychology deals with how we gain information about the world; how we transform this information in order to store it; and subsequently how we use this information to understand the world and communicate that understanding to other people.

Teaching, particularly primary teaching, is about developing children's understanding of and ability to communicate about the world. It is also about developing such particular skills as thinking and language, and the applied skills of reading, writing and mathematics in order to facilitate that understanding of the world.

It therefore seems obvious to a psychologist and educationalist that teachers need a knowledge of cognitive psychology in order to underpin their practice and to facilitate the development of the cognitive processes of the children in their charge. The problem for teachers is that they also need to have a knowledge of social psychology, sociology, classroom management, administration and all the curriculum subjects as well. Every teacher has to end up as a multi-professional. This is a tall order to expect of anyone. It then becomes the duty of those of us who train teachers to make our own particular academic areas accessible to teachers. It is very easy to say that teachers need to have a knowledge of cognitive psychology and then to expect them to go away and read the books that are written directly for psychology graduates, but this is not realistic. Teachers in training, and those practising already, have the right to expect that, initially, the psychologists will try to apply the material to help them to see the usefulness of using psychological theory to underpin and inform teaching practice. Once the connections have been made for you, it is so much easier to tackle the specialist material and expand your understanding.

This is the aim of this book. To introduce you to the subject matter of cognitive psychology and to make direct connections between the pure science and the applied active classroom experience. The chapters therefore are titled as they would be in any general psychology textbook — motor skill, perception, attention, memory, cognitive development and various aspects of language. However, in each instance there has been a conscious attempt made to show how a knowledge of each area can be applied directly to some aspect of teaching. This could be through developing greater insight into some aspect of how the children are functioning or through considering the effects on learning of what the teacher does or how the classroom is organized. With the advent of the Educational Reform Act (1988) teachers are going to have to be far more accountable to parents, governors and the world at large. We as a profession need to be able to justify our good practice and to back it up with objective research evidence.

One metaphor of human performance drawn from cognitive psychology whose influence can be seen to underpin much of the book is the concept of the human as a limited information processing system. We will consider this in depth in Chapter 5. If you watch a class of children all working away happily they will all be doing a number of things at once: maybe thinking and writing, listening, creating, throwing and catching, etc. Each of them has a capacity to process information, but for each of them this capacity is finite. Easy tasks will take up just a little capacity and leave spare capacity for other things. Difficult tasks will require a lot of capacity and require a great deal of focus to the exclusion of everything else. As new and difficult tasks become understood they become easier and so they themselves can be performed without taking up all the capacity. There will always be a three-way dynamic tension in teaching between providing enough new and difficult material to stimulate learning, providing enough con-solidation material to enable the tasks to become easy and yet not providing so much new material that the child has no way of coping. It is a very delicate path between too much and not enough.

This metaphor of limited capacity for processing information leads us in-evitably to a child centred approach to education. Each child is going to find new material more or less taxing depending on his or her level of processing ability. Even where the subject matter is the same for the whole class, the level of cognitive complexity of material will have to vary across the children. This expected range of ability is now clearly underlined in the education system with the advent of the National Curriculum. Though children's ages and number of years in school are used in developing progression, it is clearly stated that a range of achievement is to be expected within any one age group. 'For example, pupils at age 11, though typically achieving at around levels 3 to 5 might show attain-ment at anything from level 2 to level 6' (para. 3.17, *From Policy to Practice*, DES 1989). It must be clearly stated that this range of ability will be found across all children regardless of sex, social class, or ethnic group.

The National Curriculum will provide the focus for teaching in all schools, but, particularly in Primary Schools where cross curriculum topic work is so important, the choice of the material to be used and the way in which it will be used will be still the responsibility of the teachers. A knowledge of the cognitive abilities of children will enable teachers to make an informed choice about the appropriateness of material and the match of individual child to task. A diagnostic approach to children's abilities will enable teachers to recognize where some children need to have particular help to avoid possible failure and where other children need enrichment activities to avoid underachievement. Every primary teacher has to cope with this very wide spread of ability, but every primary teacher also knows that at times there are some children for whom particular help is needed. They will be able to make their own assessments of the particular needs and then discuss these with their colleagues in the Educational Psychological services and other support teams. Multidisciplinary decisions about children are always better when there is shared understanding and knowledge.

We begin in Chapter 2 by studying motor development and skill. All schools have to make provision for the physical education of children. This means that all primary teachers have responsibility for teaching and developing gross motor skills. PE is one of the 'other foundation subjects' within the National Curriculum. This means that all teachers need to have a knowledge of the development of physical skills, but also they need to see how the apparently 'physical' interacts very closely with the 'cognitive'. Turning to left and right, making large and small movements help language development and serial memory as much as motor control. The programme of study of PE is likely to be fairly non-specific, but in other areas of the curriculum the programmes of study and attainment targets require detailed knowledge of fine motor development. For example, by the end of the primary years (Year 6), the majority of children will be expected to write in a fluent cursive style. The onus is on the schools to teach an effective, efficient style of handwriting in the Infant and Junior years.

From motor performance we progress in Chapters 3 and 4 to what might be considered more mainstream cognitive psychology — perception in general with specific reference to visual processing and then auditory perception and hearing in particular. Knowledge of the processes of perception becomes important when we consider that children, as they progress through school, have to rely increasingly on two dimensional material in books. We cannot take it for granted that children will automatically be able to recognize figures and read maps and diagrams. Younger children will need highly representational material in order to distinguish the objects from the background. The sense of hearing is distinguished by being given a chapter all to itself because hearing loss is very much a hidden disability which can become handicapping if it goes undetected. Teachers may well be instrumental in recognizing when a child has a hearing problem and so they can act to prevent any cumulative deficit in progress occurring.

Chapter 5 deals with attention. An understanding of the development of attention and concentration capacities and the need for children to be able to focus attention in order to learn is essential if teachers are to be able to provide an effective learning environment. The model of the limited information processing system is explicitly developed in this chapter.

Any academic psychology library will have a major section on memory. If children cannot remember material then they can show no evidence of having learned. Chapter 6 provides an introduction to memory and in particular to the development of children's memory capacities. Research evidence shows us that at least during the Infant years (Years 1 and 2), children need to be helped to remember material explicitly because they have limited insights into how to remember. They may remember, incidently, what they had for their birthday but it may take much time and effort to enable them to remember the days of the week in order.

Memory, attention and perception all underpin the development of understanding of the world and the acquisition and use of concepts, in Chapter 7 we will study the work on the development of thinking and concepts. All teachers owe a debt of gratitude to Piaget for developing the notion of children being cognitively complex, but different from adults. However, though his work has been influential it is written in such a way as to daunt all but the most dedicated of researchers. Fortunately, we are able to approach his work through the more recent and relevant researches of Donaldson and her colleagues. She makes it very clear that teachers need to take account of cognitive development and the real world of children in order to make education meaningful to children. A knowledge of cognitive development becomes increasingly more important as teachers work under the umbrella of the National Curriculum. The match of the material within the curriculum to the children's own level of cognitive ability is the only way by which children will be able to progress and reach their true potential.

Underpinning much understanding of the curriculum, besides level of cognitive ability, is the children's comprehension and expressive language ability. In Chapter 8 we will consider the nature of language and language development and then widen this work in Chapter 9 to a discussion of the social aspects of language in use. Teachers are the people who are instrumental in promoting language development after the age of 5, so an understanding of the nature of language development would seem crucial. However, as the Kingman Report (HMSO 1988) made clear, beyond a knowledge of children's language, teachers need to have a more explicit linguistic knowledge in order to operate more effectively in the classroom. We all have an implicit knowledge of the form and functions of language. We are all competent language users, but, increasingly, it becomes necessary for teachers to develop their own explicit linguistic expertise.

All these discrete areas of cognition are covered in Chapters 2 to 9, but we end in Chapter 10 by using all of them to consider literacy. There is some mention of reading in every chapter. It is above all an example of an applied cognitive activity. One of the greatest achievements of all primary teachers is the development and sustaining of reading and writing. As we shall see, some children seem to learn to read almost in spite of being taught; however, most children learn to read *because* they have been taught. The understanding of the cognitive processes involved in the act of reading can help to make us more effective literacy teachers. Some children have the greatest difficulty in learning to read and write. When this happens, teachers can turn to the applied psychological literature to help them understand where the strengths and weaknesses of the children are. This will help them to develop a rational, tailor-made programme to help the children out of their difficulties.

The 1981 Education Act is gradually helping to change our views on the particular position of children with special educational needs. All teachers will be teaching children who have special educational needs. A few of these children will have been statemented under the Act, but the vast majority of them will be receiving their education in mainstream schools without ever having had a statement or review. Labelling the particular difficulty of the child is of much less value than making a diagnosis of the strengths and weaknesses of the children. This means that using knowledge of cognitive processing can be of particular value. In each chapter there will be mention of the need to take needs into account when considering the child from the perspective of, say, memory or attention or language. However, we must always remember that, though it is easier to compartmentalize the processes for the purposes of reading and writing about them, as teachers we always have to view the *whole* child.

Each chapter ends with a number of suggested readings. These are more specialist, but easily available books in the particular field. All of them, I hope, you will find challenging but well written. One of the most enjoyable general books on cognitive processing is Lindsay and Norman's *Human Information Processing*.

Finally, I think I should state my own prejudices. Above all else Psychology is fun. It can provide a very useful perspective on watching and promoting children's progress. It is a serious and respectable academic study in its own right, but because its focus is on human behaviour, inevitably other disciplines and applied professions, particularly teaching and education, need to use the results of psychological research. This book is meant to be introductory. It is a beginning and a series of signposts — so let us begin.

Chapter 2

Physical Development and Motor Skills

Introduction

There is a tendency, when applying psychology to education, to place slightly greater emphasis on the cognitive functioning of children than on their physical functioning. However, in reality we cannot divorce motor performance from cognitive acts. The two are inextricably intertwined. Many teachers are made acutely aware of the effects of motor skill learning right from the time the 5-year-old enters the classroom. For example, it is so much easier for children to operate in school if they can tie their own shoelaces and dress themselves with reasonable ease. Sometimes you will find that a child comes from a home where the parents have been very diligent in providing stimulating 'academic' experiences, but they have been content to dress and undress the child and supervise all the hygienic activities themselves. We have to recognize that children can be painfully slow at putting on their own clothes and it is often so much easier to do it for them. Nevertheless it is necessary for them to learn to be independent and to take some responsibility for themselves. The first PE lesson in the hall can be a very daunting experience. We tend to forget how small the children are and how huge the hall must seem. It must be even more daunting if you cannot get your clothes off, or if at the end of the lesson you cannot get back into them. Mind you, shoe manufacturers have colluded in the de-skilling of children by providing velcro fastenings which require far less skill than laces and buckles. This also means that teachers are forced to listen to twenty ripping sounds as an accompaniment to story time — but as far as school clothes are concerned ease of fastening should be the rule.

Teachers are concerned to develop the whole child and therefore they have to be conscious of providing good physical education and integrating their understanding of gross and fine motor skills into the whole integrated curriculum. It makes pragmatic sense for me as a writer and you as a reader to separate out the various cognitive activities, but we must constantly remind ourselves that all the activities form part of an integrated, interacting whole. Children whose physical development and motor coordination is good will be well liked by their peers. This will lead to high self esteem which will lead to enhanced school performance and social interactions which will lead to them being liked by their peers . . . and so it goes on.

But what do we mean by 'good' in this context? Children whose physical development is well in advance of their peers and whose genetic inheritance is one of above average height may well in fact experience considerable difficulty in the primary years. It is not easy for an 8-year-old to be taken for an 11-year-old. They may look three years older, but this may mean that people expect them to behave three years older which is basically unfair, because they will almost certainly not be socially, cognitively and emotionally an 11-year-old.

The plan for tackling this vast subject will be to present you with a description of the normal course of physical development, whilst constantly recognizing that children all vary from the expected pattern. We will then apply this knowledge to classroom practice, particularly in the domain of gross and fine motor skills.

Growth, Maturity and Development

It is always easier to define terms so that we have some shared meanings. The terms *growth, maturity* and *development* tend to be used interchangeably, but it will become clear that they really are not synonymous.

Growth basically means getting bigger. Hair grows, feet grow, chins grow, children grow taller — adults, alas, only grow fatter! Growth means that there is increase in size over time. In these terms, growth can only be applied to physical characteristics.

The height that each individual attains is determined by an interaction between genetic inheritance and environmental influences. The average adult male is taller than the average adult female and sons tend to be taller than their mothers, but across the sexes there is wide variability. Figure 2.1(a) shows you the extent of the range of heights across one primary class, which as you can see from Figure 2.1(b), does not bear a one-to-one relationship to age.

From birth onwards we tend to have our height measured. Health visitors will keep a watch on the growth of their clients to make sure that they are growing at an acceptable rate. It's not that there is anything intrinsically wrong with being small, but failure to grow may be an indication of an organic problem such as Growth Hormone Deficiency or it may indicate that the child is not receiving enough food. We now know, through the work of Dobbing (1973, 1974) that if children suffer from severe, prolonged malnutrition during the first two years of

Figure 2.1(a)   Oaklands Infant School, Top Infants in order of size.

Figure 2.1(b)   Oaklands Infant School, Top Infants in order of age.

The correlation between height and age for this group of infant children is 0.099. This means that there is no relationship between height and age here. The oldest child is a boy who is the third smallest in the class. He is 8 years old. The tallest girl is the sixth youngest and she is only six years old.

life then they will be permanently stunted. Not only that, but the brain too will not grow to its expected size. The cerebellum, which controls balance, will be differentially smaller. This will mean that the children may be clumsy. However, early, prolonged childhood malnutrition is only one of many causes of clumsiness. You must never assume that a child in your class who is clumsy has suffered from lack of food during the early years. The point about the example is to show you that there is a very real interaction between genetic inheritance and the environment in which the child grows up. We will return to the particular problem of clumsiness later on in the chapter.

Given a favourable environment, children will continue to grow throughout their primary years, but this growth will not necessarily be smooth. Children grow in fits and starts and girls tend to have a slightly smoother pattern of growth than boys. Children tend to grow quite rapidly during their first year and then the rate begins to slow down at about 3 or 4 and becomes fairly steady throughout the years up to puberty. With the onset of puberty, some children seem to shoot up almost overnight. If this book were being written a hundred years ago, puberty would have been of only academic interest to the primary teacher, but the age of onset of puberty has steadily dropped so that teachers in primary school now have to be able to understand the effects that puberty will have on their young pupils. Since in this section, we are confining ourselves to *growth* only, the aspect of puberty which concerns us is the adolescent growth spurt. On average, girls begin their adolescent growth spurt at about age 10 and boys at age 12. This means of course that some girls may have begun their growth spurt before they are 10, well down in the primary school. As we said earlier, being much bigger than your peers is not necessarily an advantage. It certainly is not an advantage if people make thoughtless remarks such as 'What a big girl she is!' and 'What are you feeding her on?' Even a teacher, capitalizing on height, by asking a girl to reach up for things because she is so tall, may be inadvertently drawing everyone's attention to her height and thus making her very self-conscious.

If growth is not smooth, then a sudden growth spurt may mean that a child, for a time, loses a sense of where the body is in space. We all live within our bodies and are aware of just how far our arms and legs can reach. As we shall see when we consider motor skill, this is important because we don't have to think in a conscious way about how far to move our arm to pick up a book on the table. We have perfect eye hand coordination and simply move our arm and hand smoothly to complete the task. However, if children have suddenly shot up, then it may be that they genuinely haven't come to a new awareness of how far to move their arms and instead of picking up the book, may knock it onto the ground. Such sudden clumsiness may be irritating for a teacher, but it can be profoundly confusing and embarrassing for the child — even more so if attention is drawn to the confusion.

Whereas growth simply implies getting bigger, maturity implies getting closer to the adult goal. There is also the evaluative meaning of maturity, but we will be using it here in its objective form. There are certain benchmarks which will define the level of physical maturity that a child has reached. Again, as with growth, these are genetically determined, but there is an interaction with the environment. Paediatricians will note the benchmarks when examining a child so that they can determine the level of physical maturity that a child has reached. It is possible in fact to be quite small, but yet still to be physically quite mature. The eruption of teeth is one of the benchmarks. Obviously, the eruption of milk teeth is one of the great moments for the parents, but the loss of the first milk tooth to make way for the permanent teeth is much more exciting for the child. Being the first child in the class to lose a tooth is a great sign of status. Actually losing it in the middle of story time is even better.

The onset of puberty is another sign of maturity. As we said above, teachers in primary schools must expect to cope with the effects of puberty in a sympathetic and practical manner. In girls, the onset of puberty, which generally follows a year after the adolescent growth spurt, is marked by the *menarche* (the first menstruation) and the appearance of the secondary sex characteristics of pubic hair and breasts. In boys the secondary sex characteristics are the growth of beard and pubic hair and the lowering of the voice. In both sexes, these very important changes are caused by the secretion of hormones. From about 7 years there is an increase in *oestrogen* (female hormones) and *androgen* (male hormones) in *both* sexes. The androgens are the hormones responsible for the adolescent growth spurt, the development of muscle, the activation of the sebaceous glands of the skin, the growth of the various patches of bodily hair and, specifically in boys, the lowering of the tone of voice. In girls there is a further increase in oestrogen level between around 9 to 11 until it reaches its adult levels. This is reponsible for the development of the genitals. The *testosterone* produced by the testes in boys results in the development of the male genitals.

Teachers have to handle menstruation very sensitively in the primary school. Obviously it has implications for PE and swimming lessons, but also little girls may experience severe discomfort and miss some days of school in an irregular fashion. Besides the obvious physical effects, the effects of hormone variation can lead to sharp changes in mood which need to be understood and coped with by the teachers. We have to remember that though sudden emotional lability may be problematic for the teacher in relation to discipline, it is much more confusing for the child who is experiencing the emotional surges.

Whilst there is the 'medical' benchmark side of maturity, the word also has an aspect which implies an adult-like quality in thought and behaviour. This is rather separate from the way we have been using it. It is, of course appropriate for us to talk about children who are socially mature in their dealings with other people and to use the term with a certain degree of approbation, but we have to remember that we are using it in a social context and not an objective context.

Lastly, we need to define development. This term is probably the most useful. It implies that there is change in organization and structure. Obviously development takes place over time so that, as well as changing, a child is getting older. However, children's capacities are not solely due to the passage of time, but because they are able to organize a response in a different way. In the arena of motor skill a child will be able to perform new activities because of changes in cognitive functioning and developments in physical skill. When we talked about growth, we said that it meant getting bigger. If we think of the body developing we recognize that a child does not just get taller, but the proportions and the organization of the body change.

At birth the head, which is a quarter of the baby's length, is approximately half the size it will be in adulthood. However, our grown-up heads are only about a twelfth of our total size. The body doesn't just grow, but its proportions change. Legs, which make up about 40 per cent of our total adult height, have increased 500 per cent since birth. Throwing a ball, or straddling a hurdle are much easier tasks when the body has reached adult-like proportions.

Externally, the body shows developmental changes, but internally there are developments as well and these are of major importance both physically and cognitively. Children are born with brains that are rather undeveloped. The brain is about a quarter its adult size. This means that there is a lot of brain development that has to go on after birth. Obviously, in terms of the sheer mechanics of the operation, the head could not be much bigger at birth without there being a much greater risk of brain damage. Thus we humans are born in a state of considerable brain immaturity in relation to other species. However, whilst this state of affairs leads to a much longer state of dependency, it also means there there is a much greater opportunity for brain development to take place within a knowable and stimulating environment.

At birth then, the brain has all of its *neurons* (nerve cells) present, but the complex connections are not fully developed. The *glial* cells which provide nutrition and the *myelin* sheath which eventually encases the *axons* (the nerve fibres) have yet to be formed. The glial cells are obviously crucial for further development of the brain, and Dobbing showed that there is massive development of these cells during the first two years of post-foetal life. This is why it is so important for children to receive adequate nutrition during these years. It seems to be the case that any deficiency during these years *cannot* be made up so that severe malnutrition can lead to the brain remaining permanently less complex.

Development — that is, integrated structural change — is important here. The *cerebral cortex* which controls so many of the activities that we identify as being human, such as motor skill, thinking, language, spatial abilities, etc., is underdeveloped at birth. There needs to be time for developmental change, growth and experience in order that these abilities can manifest themselves. However, very young babies can show quite sophisticated understanding of the environment, but it is just difficult for us to identify a way for them to express such understanding. The system is not yet working as an integrated whole.

We can see this with requirements for children to produce fine motor skill responses. The cerebral cortex is not finally connected up to the cerebellum until around 4 years. This means that the child may be able to understand the task requirements, but has not necessarily got the fine motor coordination to produce the response. Practice is important, but brain development also has to take place. We will return to this when we think about the fine motor skills of drawing and writing.

In terms of brain development, it is not just that the connections need to develop to make the brain more complex but the massive cerebral hemispheres have to take on their own distinct functions. Figure 2.2 shows a top view and a side view of the brain. You can see that there are two cerebral hemispheres.

In external appearance they appear to be roughly symmetrical but they do not perform the same functions in total. Motor control is *contralateral*. This means that, for motor activities, the *right* side of the body is controlled by the *left* cerebral hemisphere and the *left* side of the body is controlled by the *right* hemisphere. This more or less applies for the senses as well, although here the pattern is more complex. Both eyes are 'wired' up to both hemispheres. Stimulation caused by light entering both eyes from the left visual field is processed in the right hemisphere and from the right visual field in the left hemisphere. The ears too are connected to both hemispheres, but they have their strongest links with the contralateral hemisphere. Obviously it is important that the brain should be able to integrate experiences and actions so the two hemispheres are joined by a structure called the *corpus callosum* (Cowan, 1979).

This contralateral control of perception and movement does not apply to cognitive tasks. Here there appears to be hemispheric specialization. For the vast majority of people the *left* hemisphere controls language functioning and cognitive acts which are language based, whereas the *right* hemisphere controls musical and spatial abilities and also possibly emotion. Of course you can see that the corpus callosum is a crucial body since there are very few everyday activities that do not require the integration of a number of different cognitive processes and motor responses.

This *lateralization* of the hemispheres results in one hemisphere being said to be dominant over the other. About 91 per cent of the population are right-handed. They have greater fine and gross motor coordination of their right hand and foot. Remember, these members are controlled by the left motor cortex, and for these people, language too is controlled by the left hemisphere. Their left hemisphere is said to be dominant. What of the rest of the population who are left-handed or ambidextrous? The control of cognitive functioning in them is not just a mirror image of right-handers since 60 per cent of left-handers have language representation in the left hemisphere.

Figure 2.2   *Side and Top View of the Cerebral Cortex*

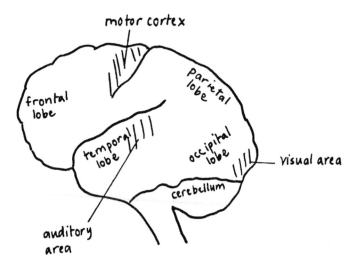

Side View of the Left Hemisphere

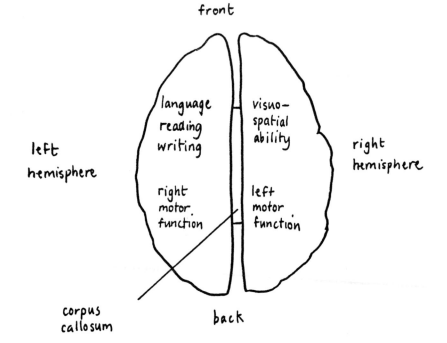

Top View

Being a left-hander myself I feel duty bound to point out that left-handedness is not of itself a problem. It only becomes a problem if the right-handed world does not make provision for left-handedness. Since we said the connections between the cerebellum and the cortex are not complete until around 4, children are not that skilled at fine motor tasks and generally do not begin to show hand preferences until around this time. It is most important that teachers do not make decisions for children about their handedness. It is so easy, thoughtlessly, to model right-handed skills and always put pencils and brushes in the right hand. Children should always be left to pick up implements themselves so that natural handedness can develop rather than being forced. Classroom organization should take account of handedness. A left-hander should always be on the *left* side of a right-hander when seated side by side so that their elbows do not get in the way of each other when they are writing. Once children are capable of using adult scissors, then the school should provide left-handed ones. Also, in all Craft, Design and Technology work, acknowledgment of the needs of the left-hander for suitable equipment should be met without any fuss.

The Normal Course of Motor Development

Table 2.1 shows a selection of the development of large movements and fine movements up to 5 years from Sheridan's Developmental Stages. This charts social, cognitive, linguistic and motor progress of pre-school children. Remember that the ages have to be treated with a certain degree of care for two reasons. Firstly, there is such a wide degree of normal variation amongst children and secondly, the context in which development is taking place has to be considered.

You will notice that at 4 years a child is said to be an expert rider of a tricycle. If you look around play areas and streets where children live you will see that there are very few tricycles, but that 4-year-olds are whizzing around on two wheelers. It is not the case that in the last twenty years, children have gained considerably in motor control over their parents' generation. What has happened is that technology has enabled children to show that they can balance and steer and ride on two wheels rather than three. When bicycles were originally invented they were for adults. They were used for leisure pursuits and as an effective means of transport. The bikes that children ride today are really just toys, albeit extremely expensive ones. Children can learn to ride them and have a great deal of fun on them, but the 4-year-old child could not use a bike as a genuine mode of transport. Bike riding shows us quite neatly how we have always to consider the whole situation and not just fragments of it. Four-year-olds can have the motor coordination and skill to enable them to ride bikes as skilfully as an adult, but those same children could not combine their motor skill with the ability to ride on a busy road. Schools generally do not provide cycling proficiency classes until children are in junior school. In fact the title of the classes is probably a misnomer since all

Table 2.1   Selection of some observed gross and fine motor skills

12 months:	Sits well on floor and for an indefinite time. Pulls to stand.
	Walks forward and sideways with one or both hands held.
	Picks up fine objects with neat pincer grasp between thumb and tip of index finger.
15 months:	Walks alone (usually) with uneven steps, feet wide apart, arms slightly flexed and held above head or at shoulder level for balance.
	Picks up string etc. with precise pincer grasp using either hand.
2 years:	Runs safely on whole foot, stopping and starting with ease.
	Walks into large ball when trying to kick it.
	Sits on small tricycle but cannot use the pedals.
3 years:	Walks alone upstairs with alternating feet and downstairs 2 feet to a step.
	Rides tricycle, using pedals, can steer it round wide corners.
	Can throw ball overhand and catch large ball on or between extended arms.
	Kicks ball forcibly.
	Threads large wooden beads on a lace.
	Copies circle (also letters VHT). Imitates cross.
4 years:	Expert rider of tricycle.
	Walks or runs alone up and down stairs one foot to step.
	Climbs ladders and trees.
	Holds pencil with good control in adult fashion.
	Draws a man with head, legs and trunk and (usually) arms and fingers.
5 years:	Runs lightly on toes.
	Skips on alternate feet.
	Copies square and (at $5\frac{1}{2}$) triangle (also letters VHTOXLACUY).

Source: Sheridan (1973) *From Birth to Five Years: Children's Developmental Progress.*

children attending them will be extremely proficient at the motor activity. What they have to learn is how to use that skill in the exceptionally complex situation of riding in traffic.

Though it is possible to list the expected development of children at various ages, we must always be conscious that there will be a great deal of normal variability between children. There are so many variables other than genetic inheritance that influence development, such as nutrition, childhood illness and nurturance, that the question as to what is 'normal' might seem impossible to answer. However we can observe that, though everyone develops at a slightly different rate, there are clearly overall trends which can be seen. Development is not totally idiosyncratic. There are underlying principles which control development among all humans.

Firstly, development occurs from top to tail. This is called *cephalocaudal* development (*kephale* — head; *cauda* — tail). This means that heads literally develop before trunks and arms and legs. Or, more importantly, it is the development of the brain which sets the pace for all other development. We saw this in the relative change in size of head and limbs, but more importantly we can see the effects of cephalocaudal development on muscular control. Babies learn to control their heads and necks long before they can walk. This motor control is all initiated from the brain. We walk with our brains! Obviously a child needs to be physically strong enough for the legs to support the body in motion, but the execution of the motor programme for walking is controlled by the motor cortex.

Cephalocaudal development is allied to *proximodistal* development. This means that development progresses form the centre of the body out to the extremities. Thus control of the shoulders comes before control of the arm muscles, and fine motor control of the hands comes later still.

Though in general we may be interested in the motor development of babies, this is not of direct concern to primary teachers. However, with increasing integration of children with special needs into mainstream schools some awareness of early development will be an advantage.

Gross Motor Skill

Unless there is a specific motor coordination problem, primary teachers will expect that children will be able to sit and stand and walk and run by the time they enter nursery school. These are gross motor skills; they relate to whole body movements.

Of course there is always an interaction with the environment. Having sufficient motor development and having the opportunity to exercise that skill may be two different things. Motor skills do not just happen because the brain is developing with the passage of time. They happen in a social context. Children have to be given the opportunity to practise their skills and to apply and adapt them to acquire new ones. With motor skill development we see a real interaction between physcial and cognitive readiness and environmental provision.

It is always necessary to remember the cognitive element that is evident in all motor behaviour. A child has to learn to adapt a motor action to a set of environmental circumstances; taking account of the feedback that occurs from the movement moment by moment. To learn to kick a stationary ball, children have to be aware of the position of their own bodies in space and in relation to the ball. They have to be able to remain balanced on one leg whilst swinging the other towards the ball. This requires a long series of complex 'calculations' because there are a whole series of fine adjustments needed in order to remain standing throughout the pendulum movement of the kicking leg. Then the reaction of the impact of the foot on the ball has to be anticipated so that the body remains upright when the foot meets the ball. Also the precise moment of impact has to be predicted or else the body will certainly end up on the floor. Indeed, with pre-school children, this often happens.

Prediction is a very important term when we are considering all skilled behaviour — and prediction is very much a cognitive act. If you watch slowed down action replays of Wimbledon or a test match you will be able to notice that the players seem to be able to position themselves correctly in order to play a shot, even before the ball is actually in motion towards them. This anticipation is not accidental. A skilled person can organize any action very early in the sequence so that the performance is smooth. 'Smooth' and 'skill' are two words that go together very clearly here.

Think about what happens when you go down an escalator. You approach the stairway in the full knowledge that it is moving at a constant speed. You take account of the fact that the treads are initially very shallow but then get deeper. You brace yourself to allow for the forward movement so that you are not thrown off balance . . . and then what happens if it turns out that it isn't working? All the movements are suddenly wrong and you have to do some instant readjustments. Next time it happens try to reconstruct how it feels.

I can give you another example from when you learnt to drive — that is, if you have. Initially you have to concentrate on the movements in the car: manipulating the pedals and turning the wheel. All this at the same time as taking account, through your visual feedback, of where the car is going. Novice drivers tend to focus a few feet from the bonnet of the car and make wild adjustments to the steering wheel. As you develop the skill, your movements become skilled and you are able to focus much further away from the car. Because of this you are able to anticipate future events and respond much more speedily but in a much more controlled and therefore safe manner.

All teachers would be well advised to set themselves the task of learning a new skill so that they can empathize with a few of the problems that children have to encounter. Always remembering, of course, that teachers have the advantage of a fully developed motor and cognitive system, if not the fluid body of a child.

Children entering primary schools will be at very different stages in their physical and motor development. Some children will have had pre-school swimming lessons, trampoline classes, ballet classes, football classes, etc. Some of them will have had none of these experiences. The task of the teacher is to help all children to develop their motor skills *to the best of their abilities*. This last phrase is important because there will be wide variations in ability both to move the body and to understand the task requirements.

Motor skill acquisition requires a combination of motor coordination and cognitive understanding of the task. What we have to aim for in acquiring a skill is that the motor programme that controls the activity becomes so automatic that we no longer appear to have to think about what we are doing. Such skilled behaviour obviously takes a lot of practice but needs teaching to back up the practice. All schools provide for physical education within their curriculum. This should never be just a chance for children to let off steam. They get plenty of that during playtime. The operative word in PE is 'education'. During a PE lesson the teacher will have planned the activities on which the children need to concentrate. This may involve practice of old skills, integrating a number of skills into a new activity or learning something entirely new. Throughout a PE lesson the children are being controlled rather than being free to do just as they want. They may have freedom of choice about the activities, but the teacher will have chosen the range of tasks with a particular purpose. The beauty of a really good PE lesson when children first enter school is that it will look effortless on the part of the teacher, and the children will be really enjoying themselves 'playing'. When this occurs, one knows that there has been a great deal of planning, thought and skill on the part of the teacher. As children get older, they will want to learn and to be taught new skills. Seeming to play will not be enough for them. Those who are really keen will demand the chance to develop their skills.

Planning a PE lesson requires that the teacher considers the organization of the apparatus very carefully. Choices of small apparatus do not present much of a problem. Recognizing the needs of some children to use bean bags when others can catch balls simply takes sensitive observation. Remembering the children's needs in relation to large apparatus also should not present a problem. However, it is possible to forget the differing needs of different age children when laying out the apparatus. With proper instruction, even 5-year-olds can move the apparatus to the correct position and height for their class. Heights and types of apparatus have to be matched to the height and developing abilities of the children. There can be no excuse for getting out the apparatus in the morning and leaving it out all day for all ages without any change. If that happens, and sadly it still does in some schools, the children are at best playing but at worst are in physical danger.

Again the word 'development' here is important. During the primary years there is a gradual honing of skill and the ability to adapt similar motor activities to different games. The change is not one of kind but of degree. Quite young children can be quite skilled at catching if they have to catch a big light ball or a reasonably large bean bag. Four-year-olds, however, will find it difficult to catch a rounders ball or a cricket ball. The task of the teacher is to provide the equipment necessary to succeed and perfect a skill. We can watch the skill of tennis players at Wimbledon and hear about young players who began by using their fathers' heavy racquets, but we know that pre-school children in general do not have the coordination or the strength necessary to be skilled ball players. However, they can develop the skill of hitting a ball to a predicted place by using light weight plastic racquets and foam balls.

We must recognize that, though many of the activities involved with gross motor skill are on the surface *physical* activities, they require a high level of cognitive awareness. It is not the case that children who are less intelligent will have the compensation of being skilled at games. A child who is well coordinated may or may not have the ability to think ahead sufficiently to be a skilled games player. All sports obviously require natural physical ability, but that by itself is not enough. Really skilled performance requires much practice and an ability to organize a response very quickly and accurately.

Children in primary schools are not all going to win Wimbledon, but all children in primary schools do need the chance to develop their gross motor skills for a number of reasons, not least their health and their enjoyment. We can also see that PE lessons provide an excellent medium for precision language development, listening, and memory skills. Listening to instructions to make sequences of movements and retaining them long enough to perform the sequence is a very powerful language experience.

Fine Motor Skills

Just as children will be at different stages in their gross motor development when they enter school, they will also show a wide variability in their fine motor skills. These involve eye hand coordination and fine adjustments of the hands. As with gross motor skill, there will be an interaction between the developmental pattern and the environmental opportunities.

Let us take paper cutting as an example here. If you watch a group of 5-year-olds cutting paper with scissors you will see children with various stages of skill. Some children will be able to manipulate the scissors and turn the paper so that they produce a smooth edge. Others will be able to cut with the scissors, but their ability to manipulate the paper at the same time will be limited so they will be able to cut out but only be capable of producing a jagged edge. Others will barely be able to hold the scissors. However, a single observation by teachers is not enough. The child who can barely hold the scissors may be a skilful cutter in a few weeks, it depends on whether the child has had the chance to use scissors before as well as the level of motor development.

Although there is a tendency to think of curriculum areas in relation to the factual and cognitive elements in them, many subjects require that the children should develop a high level of fine motor skill in order to succeed. Writing, drawing, painting, sewing, mapwork, mathematics, CDT and musical instrumental work all require eye hand coordination. Planning the curriculum should take account of these fine motor skills. Indeed some schools actually take a skills based approach to many activities. Perhaps the best policy is to integrate both the information content and the skill content.

Taking the needs of fine motor skill learning into account does mean that teachers have to consider the most efficient method of helping children to develop their skills. A neat piece of applied work by Baddeley and Longman (1978) can help to illustrate this. They were set the task by the Post Office of finding out the most efficient schedule for training their employees to touch type. The options were that the employees could be taken off regular work and undergo an intensive course of training for two hours twice a day; or they could continue with their regular work and just have one hour a day of training. The results showed that, in terms of hours needed to become skilled typists, the one hour a day schedule was much the most efficient. This fits in with our general views on skill learning, that spaced practice is much more efficient than massed practice. In education we are concerned to develop the whole child so a little *frequent* practice in many areas may well be the optimal way of learning.

An important caveat here: do *not* apply the Baddeley and Longman research literally to children. An hour of practice is much too long for children. Young children cannot be expected to practise any skill for that length of time and show any learning or improvement. Even when highly motivated they will need to have breaks and changes in activity.

Handwriting

Unless they are very physically handicapped all children will have to learn to write. I am aware that there are more and more computers available, but at the moment I cannot envisage a world where the need to write with something like a pen or pencil on something like a piece of paper will not be necessary. Certainly at the moment all children are taught to write and I think it is worth our spending some time considering what we require of children and the materials that we provide for them in order that they can write. I am *not* here considering the content of the writing, only the skill that is involved, though, in fact, as we shall see, the two cannot entirely be divorced.

To start with, handwriting is the perfect example of a fine motor skill. One of our goals in teaching children to write is that they should gain such a fluent skill that they do not have to spend any cognitive effort thinking about how to form the letters and they can spend all their time thinking about the content of their writing. We want the activity to become entirely automatic.

Coincidentally, we want them to be able to write in such a way that anyone else can read what they have written. There is no point in being able to write very quickly and to give no thought to the act of writing if the end product is completely illegible to everyone else. This does not mean that we are wanting to make value judgments about the beauty of the handwriting. As long as it is legible, easy and speedy for the writer then that may be enough. Beyond that we may want to make it possible for the children to explore calligraphy so that they can choose to write 'beautifully', although what is considered beautiful changes with the times. Introducing children to the possibilities of attractively presented work right from the time they enter school can only lead them to develop a more legible hand later on as well as developing their aesthetic appreciation.

To get a feel of what I mean by fluent automatic writing take a clean piece of paper and a pen or pencil; close your eyes and write your name and address down.

Now what have you got before you?

It often surprises people. Indeed you may find that you have written it much better than with your eyes open because you concentrated a bit more. The point of the demonstration is that you are so skilled at writing that you do not even need visual feed back. Though of course you couldn't write with your eyes closed all the time.

Before we can begin to teach children to write we have to consider the environment in which they will learn to write and then subsequently in which they will continue to write.

Firstly they have to have tables and chairs which are the correct size for them. They have to be able to get their knees under the table and to be able to bend over in comfort. It is recommended that tables should be roughly half the child's height with a slight slope and the chair should be roughly one third the child's height. I recognize that here much of what I say will relate to the best of all possible worlds. In times of financial stringency in education schools have to balance many differing needs; however, with local financial management where schools have to discuss allocation of money they should at least consider the quality aspects of materials as well as the quantity.

Once we have the children settled in a comfortable table and chair in which to write we then have to turn our attention to the materials we provide.

Firstly the paper. Adults tend to write on paper with the longest edge placed vertically so that they have shorter lines and they can write down the page. It seems to be easier for us to write this way and produces an aesthetically pleasing result which is easy for others to read. However when young children begin to write it is better for them to have the longest axis placed horizontally. This both encourages left–right awareness and takes account of their shorter arms. Teachers have to be careful to watch what the children are doing as they write because there is as tendency to move the arm down the page rather than move the page up the desk. This means that the children end up trying to write with their wrists hanging off the edge of the table.

Once the size of the paper has been decided upon, we then have to consider the question of whether the paper should be lined or plain. In many infant schools children are only presented with plain paper and they do not experience using lines until they progress to junior schools.

The reason for this is that it was felt that the lines predetermine the size of the children's handwriting at an age when fine motor control is still developing. The feeling was that lined paper would be likely to restrict the children; indeed the Bullock Committee in their report said: ' . . . the paper on which children are to write should always be unlined and of sufficient size to be unrestricting' (*A Language for Life*, HMSO 1975, Chairman Sir Allan Bullock).

I am going to present a counter argument to this view. Think for a moment about adult behaviour. When do adults ever write extensively without lines? The most usual time is when they are writing letters and then they buy pads which provide them with a ruled underlay. In other words, adults find it easier to write neatly and legibly with the aid of lines . . . and adults are skilled handwriters.

Pasternicki (1987) has shown that legibility for children between 6 and 9 was judged to be significantly higher when they used lined paper. One of my own students found exactly the same results but also showed that the syntactic complexity of the stories was also greater with lined paper.

If we take an information processing approach to the question we can see that providing children with guidelines for where to write does make the task just that bit easier. They do not have to worry about wobbling all over the page. In the state of Victoria, Australia, where there is a state-wide policy on handwriting, all children are given books with main lines and dotted intermediate lines to help legibility (see Figure 2.3).

Now I can quite see why schools might object to having books with all lines because, particularly in the infant school, children do a lot of drawing which would be spoiled by lines. The answer to this is to produce your own custom-made underlay guidelines. These can fit neatly under the page and can be tailor-made for each child.

Figure 2.3   Robert (age 7), Verdale Primary School, Melbourne, Australia

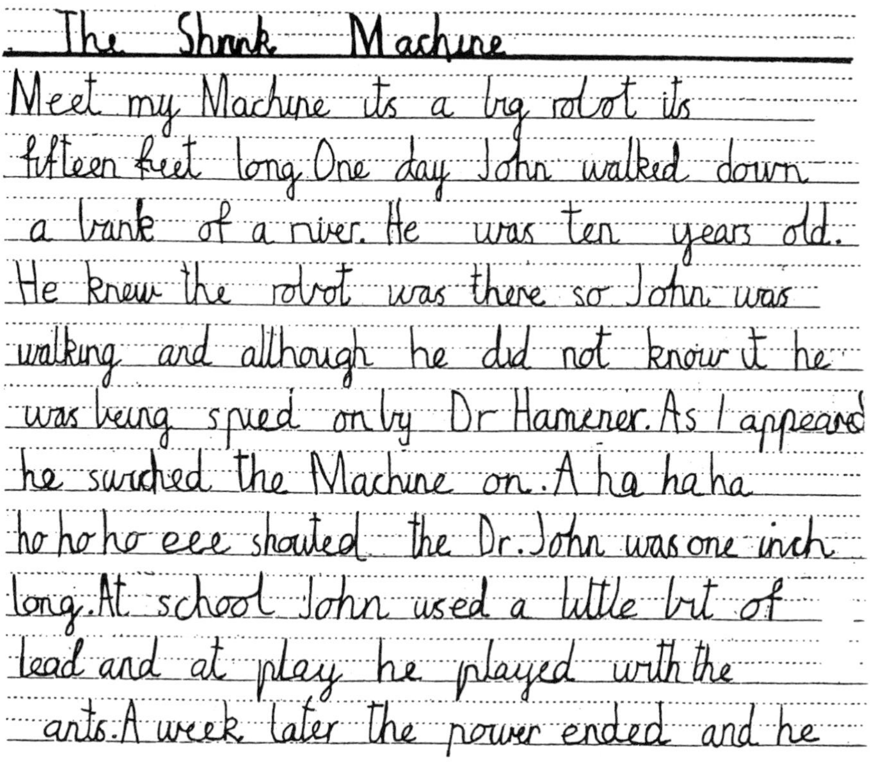

The Shrink Machine
Meet my Machine its a big robot its
fifteen feet long. One day John walked down
a bank of a river. He was ten years old.
He knew the robot was there so John was
walking and although he did not know it he
was being spied on by Dr Hamener. As I appeared
he switched the Machine on. A ha ha ha
ho ho ho eee shouted the Dr. John was one inch
long. At school John used a little bit of
lead and at play he played with the
ants. A week later the power ended and he

We tend to concentrate on writing, i.e. words, when we think about hand-writing, but the same is true for number work. Once children begin to have to set out sums for themselves, the legibility and therefore the resultant accuracy of the work is increased through the use of squared paper. Squared paper enables the child to put one digit per square and so avoid confusion about which numbers are under one another and which aren't.

Now we have considered the type of paper, we have to think about where it is on the table. Many people are under the mistaken impression that they must sit square to the table with the paper's edge parallel to the edge of the table. Just try writing naturally and you may well notice that you turn the paper to a slight angle. This enables you to write comfortably and see what you are writing — but the angle depends on whether you are right- or left-handed. The most comfortable position for a right-hander is to tilt the paper slightly to the *left* and for a left-hander to tilt the paper about 30 degrees to the *right*. In this way the hand can flow across the paper without contorting the wrist position. Obviously, by the nature of the direction of writing in English, it is easier for a right-hander to write than it is for a left-hander. The right-hander tends to pull the pencil or pen gently across the page and the hand does not cover up the work that has been produced. The left-hander tends to push the stylus across the page and the work gets covered up and smudged even as it is being produced.

The writing implement used is important for all children. It should allow a smooth flow across the page. Many schools use soft-leaded triangular pencils for their infants. These are easy to hold and flow nicely. Certainly pencils produce a smooth line, but only if they are kept sharp. Some schools do not like children using ball point pens at all in the belief that they 'ruin' handwriting. If this is the case then it must be a case of 'do as I do', because one cannot ban ball points for pupils but use them oneself.

Given that the children have been provided with the best tools for the job, then we have to consider the fine motor task of writing itself. To be able to write in a controlled way, children have to have sufficient fine motor coordination to pick up a pencil and hold it in a variation of a dynamic tripod grasp. This means that it is held by the ends of the thumb, first and middle fingers with the two remaining fingers acting as a supportive arch. The digits holding the pencil then move in a delicate controlled manner. There is some controversy about how closely a grasp should approximate to a classical grasp (Sassoon 1983) since if we were to monitor the way a whole cross-section of the population held their pens we would find a wide variation. Certainly, for writing in the Roman alphabet, a tripod grasp seems to be most successful, but this would, for example, be inappropriate for Chinese writing.

There does seem to be a developmental pattern in the ability to develop a tripod grasp. One-year-olds tend to hold crayons in their fists. By 2 to 3 they will have progressed to holding them in their fingers with the wrist pronated. Between

3 and 4 they will begin to develop the beginnings of a tripod grasp, but the whole hand will move as a unit.

When children enter school it is important that their fine motor skill is observed so that they can be helped towards a a form of the dynamic tripod grasp that is most comfortable to them. To this end, schools can provide triangular pen grips or the more modern anatomically designed ones. On the other hand, teachers can make individual ones out of Fymo type material.

Finally we have to think about the style of the writing itself. At the moment, in this country, it is more usual for children to learn print script in the infant schools and then to progress to cursive script in the juniors. In other countries children begin forming letters in such a way that they can quickly move into cursive writing without having to re-learn how to form their letters. It is very easy for British people to recognize American and French writing because of their distinctive way of forming letters. Their children learn these forms right from the start and do not have the problem of transferring from one style to another. It was thought that print writing would be easier for children because it approximated to the type face that they would see in reading books. However, since we hope that children will be exposed to a wide variety of print this seems to be of dubious benefit.

One of the unfortunate effects of learning print script is that in some schools, because of the pressure to fulfil other curriculum requirements, teachers do not introduce cursive script at all in the junior schools. This means that some children are transferring to secondary schools still having to rely on printing as a means of writing. Printing is a very slow method. As we said above, we need to enable children to write both legibly *and* quickly. Speedy, legible cursive writing is an important study skill with which all children should be equipped. If writing remains slow, then putting one's thoughts down on paper becomes tedious and something to be avoided. Some children, recognizing that others are using cursive script, attempt to teach themselves. Sometimes this can be successful, but often I find that some of my students are not actually writing in a cursive form at all. What they do is print, but form the letters so close to each other that it looks like a joined up hand. They themselves say that writing is a slow process and that taking notes is difficult. If children are left to find out a method of cursive script for themselves then they often form the letters in an inefficient manner which makes the joins clumsy and the writing illegible.

Fortunately, this state of affairs should soon be a thing of the past. The National Curriculum Council English document accepted in total the recommendations of the English Working Group under the chairmanship of Professor Cox and has laid down detailed attainment targets on handwriting. By the end of the primary years children will be expected to be able to 'produce a more fluent cursive style in independent work' (Attainment Target 5: Handwriting, Level 4).

Writing is a fine motor skill which needs a lot of practice for it to become automatic. This means that children need to be taught efficient and legible ways of forming the letters right from the start because once they have internalized poor letter formation it is very difficult for them to unlearn and relearn a new style.

Remember the message from Baddeley and Longman. Some short practice every day at cursive patterns and pure letter formation will be needed to establish the skill. There is even a case for copying and not creating because in that way the meaning element can be reduced and the children can concentrate all their efforts on the form and line.

Some children, no matter how they try, will find that they have such poor motor coordination that they can never produce written work of legible quality. These days this need not be a problem. Primary school word processing programs mean that even the most illegibly written piece of work can be well presented for publication or wall display. Computers do not mean that handwriting skills need not be practised, but they do mean that some children can have their self-esteem greatly enhanced.

Clumsy Children

Some children with very poor fine motor control may be diagnosed as being Clumsy children. Bremner *et al.* (1967) suggest that there is an incidence of about 6 to 7 per cent of children who have perceptual-motor difficulties. This means that there may be two children in any one primary school class who are experiencing difficulties with coordination, learning of physical games and fine motor skills. Many children just learn to cope within the classroom without any additional help at all. However, they may well have poor self-esteem and find it difficult to relate to other children. We cannot underestimate the importance of being 'one of the gang' when it comes to general school performance. To really succeed children need to be happy and contented. There is often a hidden curriculum which puts a premium on good motor skills so that children who experience difficulty in these areas can become depressed and even exhibit behaviour problems.

Children who do have developmental problems in this area may not have their difficulties noticed but may present with general learning difficulties and it is only when the educational psychologist takes a detailed history and examination that the particular problems and needs of the child can be identified.

The learning problems are real enough. As we have said, so much of the primary school curriculum depends not just on mastery of 'cognitive' material but also on fine motor tasks. If writing is so poor that it is illegible then it may be difficult to diagnose whether the child cannot understand the task or has not got the motor coordination to carry out the task.

Once the motor coordination problems have been recognized then the needs of the child can be catered for. Allowances can be made for limited handwriting skills and self-esteem can be enhanced by using word processing as a means of presenting important work. Detailed step by step practice programmes can be implemented to improve coordination and skill.

On the games field, individual rather than group goals can be stressed. Since all children show differing physical abilities this is a sensible approach across the class. However, we would be denying reality if we did not acknowledge the importance of physical prowess in growing children. This means that the clumsy child could definitely be placed at a disadvantage socially if the ethos of the school did not make it quite clear that all children, regardless of ability, were equally valued.

Children in Wheel Chairs

Finally let us consider the requirements of children in wheel chairs. With the integration of children with special needs into mainstream schools becoming an increasing reality, schools need to make certain, when they have wheel chair bound children in their classrooms, that access is thought through carefully. Children will need to feel as independent as possible so the fullest possible consultations need to take place between school, home and the local advisory teacher for the physically handicapped children. Ramps, wide doorways and toilet facilities are obvious features to appraise, but there needs to be more than this if the children are to feel free. Teachers need to look carefully at the storage areas in the classroom and see whether all children can reach things and to make certain that the wheel chair bound child is not excluded from fetching and gathering tasks because of inefficient planning. The school library may be a particular weak spot. Even when books are accessible, wheel chairs are often not compatible with the catalogue system.

Being in a wheel chair may at first appear to exclude children from some physical education lessons, but this must not be the case. Wall bars may not be appropriate, but ball skills and other eye hand coordination activities are just as important for physically handicapped children as for able-bodied ones. Integration means teachers must be flexible and imaginative. If children in wheel chairs are to reap the benefits of integration, as is their right, the school must ensure that sufficient resources, both in terms of building modifications and extra teaching help, are guaranteed at the outset.

Conclusion

In this chapter we have been primarily concerned with the motor performance of children in school. However, it becomes clear that motor performance cannot be considered in isolation. Even as children are taking part in PE lessons, they are learning to integrate movement with language; they combine physical skill with perceptual understanding. Unless children have independent fine motor skills they will find that many curriculum subjects cannot be pursued to the full.

Finally, even though it means wear and tear on the clothes and shoes, all children need the chance to run around and let off steam at a number of points during the day. Children cannot sit still for long periods of time, they soon begin to fidget. A good run around the playground may do far more than any number of exortations to 'sit still, concentrate and get on with your work'.

Further Reading

Alston and Taylor (1987) *Handwriting: Theory, Research and Practice*. This collection of readings provides a useful reference collection of papers on teaching handwriting. Alston and Taylor have also published *The Handwriting File* (1984) which sets out guidelines for diagnosing and remediating handwriting difficulties. Jarman (1979) *The Development of Handwriting Skills* and Sassoon (1983) *The Practical Guide to Children's Handwriting* are two further books to give you detailed information about the teaching of handwriting.

Sheridan (1973) *From Birth to Five Years: Children's developmental progress* provides a comprehensive guide to early development. Two books that would be of use in extending knowledge about children with motor difficulties are Gordon and McKinlay (1980) *Helping clumsy children* and Laszlow and Bairstow (1985) *Perceptual Motor Behaviour*.

Chapter 3

Perception

Introduction

At some stage or other, every child seems to ask the question that goes something like 'How do I know that what I see as green grass is the same as what you see as green grass?' This question is at the same time most profound and perhaps irrelevant. It is profound because it is so important that children should develop the awareness that other people have things going on inside their heads that are not directly knowable by anyone else. On the other hand, in terms of real life, it actually does not matter. We can leave it to philosophers to discuss the question of the reality of objects. What is important to us as social humans is that we should be able to share our experiences. The area of perception to which we shall address ourselves is concerned with models of the world. Since the world is only knowable through the mediation of the senses, we all have to construct our own model of the world by making use of our innate perceptual abilities and those that we develop during life. In order for me to be able to communicate with you it is necessary that the model of the world that I have constructed should roughly coincide with the model of the world that you are using. If these two models coincide, then when I talk about a dog you will understand what I am talking about. We both conceive of an object out there with four legs and fur which barks and we agree to call it 'dog'. We receive the visual information from outside ourselves and we classify it and interpret it. This is what perception is. It is the interpretation of messages that reach the brain via the senses organs. These messages are compared with previous experiences that have been stored so that a working, useful interpretation of the present stimulus can be arrived at. Try explaining that to the next group of 5-year-olds who ask you if what they see as green is the same as what you see as green.

Definitions of Perception

We need to have a more systematic discussion of what we mean by perception. All our knowledge of the world has to come to us from outside ourselves, at least initially. The world exists as a physical entity separate from ourselves. The only way that we can experience the world is through the interpretation of messages that reach the cortex of the brain via the sensory system. The world then is not directly knowable, it is only experienced through the medium of our own interpretation. There is a Sufi tale about the blind men and the elephant that goes something like this.

One day some blind men came across a King in the desert. This mighty King had an elephant amongst his camel train. The blind men had heard about elephants, but they had never seen one and they wanted to know what it was like. The King allowed them to touch the beast so that they could tell one another what they could feel. The man who felt the ear said that it was large and flat like a rough mat. The one who felt the trunk said 'No, you are wrong, it is like a hollow pipe that moves on its own. It is very powerful.' The third man said that they had both misunderstood. He felt the leg and said that it was strong and firm like a stone pillar in a mosque. Finally the last man came and felt the tusks. 'How can you say this?' he said. 'It is smooth and curved and has a sharp point that can spike you.' Each man knew a part of the whole, but none of them knew all.

The message of the tale is that nothing is absolutely objective. Each person understands from his own view point. However, we do know that people tend to construct a model, an interpretation of the world that is roughly similar to everyone else, and even more similar to those people who are closest to them.

This definition of perception implies that we have to interpret the world in an active manner. Does this imply that everything that we perceive is the result of learning to interpret or are there any interpretations that are built in? Amongst psychologists, there has been an age old split between those who are *nativists* and those who are *empiricists*. Putting it simply, the nativist view is that most of our perceptual abilities are built in. They are the result of heredity and maturation. The empiricist view, on the other hand stresses the importance of the environment and experience in forming the way we perceive the world. You can only decide for yourself your own particular philosophical persuasion. However, there seems to be a mood in the work of the perceptual developmentalists which suggests that children are born with considerable abilities for interpreting the world. Neonates are not entirely devoid of perceptual abilities (Leslie 1987). Having some abilities from the start enables the child to begin to build a veridical model of the world from the very earliest experiences.

As far as teaching primary children is concerned, the debate about new-borns, though of great fascination, is not central to our concerns. What we need is an appreciation of what perception is so that we can take account of it in our dealings with children.

It is perhaps most useful to think of children as having perceptual abilities at birth that they subsequently have to adapt to enable them to deal with the world. The *using* of the perceptual input to make sense of the environment is what concerns us. This means that I am presenting perception as an essentially active process. The perceptual system generally receives the stimulation from outside the body and then transforms it so that the person *knows* what they have perceived. Noise is interpreted as *voice* or *dog barking* or *dripping tap*: light is interpreted as *face* or *dog* or *sunshine*: smell is interpreted as *food* or *flower* or *dustbin* or *dog*. It is the interpretation of the incoming stimulation that is primarily of concern to us as teachers. Look at figure 3.1. What do you see?

Figure 3.1   Duck or Rabbit?

A duck or a rabbit? Some people see the duck first, some people see the rabbit. Of course, there is no correct answer because it is an ambiguous figure. However, as we shall see later on, ambiguous figures serve to show us how we have to use our model of the world to interpret our sensory inputs.

The Senses

We are born with a number of different sensory channels through which we receive input from outside our brains. These sensory *modalities* are: sight (visual), hearing (auditory), touch (haptic), taste, smell (haptic) and kinesthesis. None of these will be new to you except perhaps kinesthesis — the sense of movement and where the body is in space.

While in no way suggesting that the last four mentioned senses are not important, we will only mention them briefly. This is because there has been much less work done in these areas. Obviously, in Chapter 2, you could see how important it is for teachers to be aware of the need to take account of the body in space when teaching, both from a gross and a fine motor point of view. There are some remedial methods which try to educate the whole body and thus they involve a lot of cross-modal work involving all the senses (Hulme 1981). Nevertheless, we tend to use touch, taste and smell as peripheral senses rather than central ones in education. By this I mean that though we will certainly strive to educate the senses, we do not teach through smell and taste. We give children a wide variety of sensory experiences and hope that they will be able to understand what they are experiencing and subsequently comment upon them. In this way we use the senses to develop aesthetic awareness and language ability, but we do not use the touch, taste and smell channels as means of major input of information.

The two major senses in education are sight and hearing. In this chapter we will consider the development of perception through the modality of sight. The next chapter will concentrate entirely on hearing because of its central role in language.

The Visual System

Figure 3.2 is a representation of the visual system. We have two eyes that both receive information, and which both send information to both cerebral cortices. Remember, we said in Chapter 2, that the representation of the visual fields was not ipsilateral. *Both* visual fields are represented in *both* cortices.

Light rays enter the eyes via the pupils. The rays are then inverted as they pass through the lens and travel to the *retina* at the back of the eye. It is when the light reaches the retina that the information from outside begins to be registered by the system. Up to the point of the retina, the eye functions mechanically to enable the light to hit the retina at the correct spot and in a focused image. If we are in a darkened room then the iris muscles will contract to enlarge the pupil to allow more light into the eye. If we are in a very bright room then the iris relaxes and the pupil becomes smaller. The retina is a very delicate organ and needs protecting. If the light is too bright, then the retinal cells can be permanently damaged. Children, and adults, should never look directly at the sun, or directly at an eclipse.

The retina is composed of about 125 million receptor cells which are of two types, named after their shape. The *rod* cells are sensitive to the amount of light and are more plentiful, making up about 96 per cent of the receptor cells of the retina. The *cone* cells are sensitive to colour. The cones themselves are not evenly distributed across the retina. There are more of them concentrated in the *fovea*. This means that light hitting the fovea is likely to be discriminated more sharply.

Figure 3.2   Diagram of the Visual System

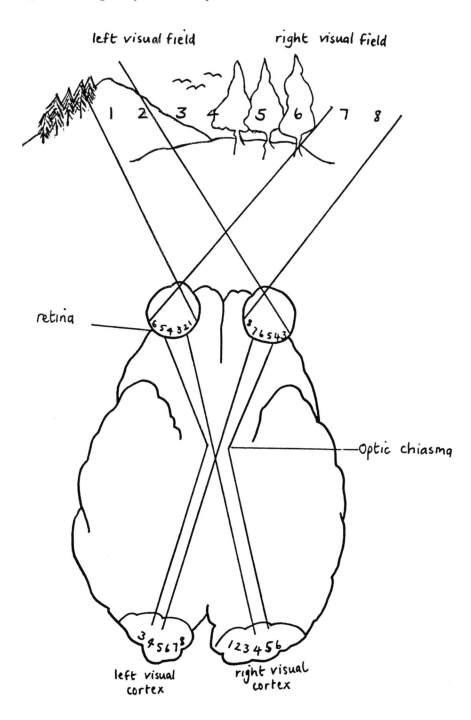

When we focus on an object, then the two eyes are both positioned so that the light from that object falls on the fovea. This is why we need sufficient ambient light to focus on objects without getting tired. If the level of light falls, then the iris will enlarge. The light from objects will be less concentrated on the fovea and so the image will be less sharp. Often, during winter afternoons, the light in the classroom fades; but because it happens so gradually, the teacher does not notice and fails to turn on the lights. The children may be trying to do close work in books and they may find it quite difficult to see the page. Their concentration will be severely taxed.

Of course, ambient light that is too bright will be equally irritating. The tendency to replace tungsten light fittings with fluorescent tube lights may save on electricity bills, but it leads to classrooms with harsh ambient light.

Colour Vision

The cone cells are the ones which are sensitive to colour. Provided they are working correctly and present in the correct combination, then we can see all the colours of the visible spectrum from red through to violet.

Babies are not born with a completely mature visual system, but within a few weeks of birth they can discriminate between the colours. Having the ability to *see* colours does not of course imply that the children know what colour is or can name colours. As far as pre-school children are concerned, the colour of an object is of lesser salience than its function or shape. This means that isolating the colour attribute and naming the colour of an object may take quite some time for a child to learn. Children who have been to nurseries and pre-school groups will have done many tasks designed to enable them to name colours consistently; and of course many parents will do the same sort of activities within the home. However, most reception class teachers do feel the need to check on this important perceptual/linguistic capacity. On the whole, they seem to be concerned about the linguistic side of the task; i.e., can the child *name* the colours. Often they assume that the child will have the ability to discriminate between the various shades. However, the child may well be colour blind. A boy who seems to be confused over colour naming should be checked for colour blindness as early as possible.

Most children are given a medical during their first term at school and this will include a test for colour vision. The most usual one is the Ishihara Colour Vision Plates. Colour blindness is an inherited characteristic. It is also sex linked, so that you will find that it is the boys who are affected. The condition can take many forms. The children do not simply see things in black and white; instead they have difficulty in distinguishing between some colours. Classically the little boy may not be able to see any difference between red and green. However, other children may have difficulty in distinguishing between green and brown. The detection rate of colour blindness in schools is about 10 per cent of the boys. This means that the actual figure of colour blindness in the population is probably somewhat higher. Ten per cent means that you can probably expect to have one or two children per year in your class affected.

Colour blindness can be an inconvenience, but it should never become an educational 'problem'. Many schools use a colour coding system for reading books, the library, their equipment stores, etc. It is up to the teachers to remember this and to have an alternative dual coding to accommodate colour blind children. It is not appropriate simply to use a colour coded system and then to tell the colour blind boy that of course he cannot use it.

Spectacles

As we said above, the function of the lens is to project a focused image of the outside world onto the retina. However, if the eye ball is not quite the correct shape then the image may be blurred. Under these circumstances people need spectacles to bring the image into sharp focus at the level of the retina rather than in front of it or behind it.

The most common problem is where the projected image falls short and though near vision is clear, the child cannot see distances. This is *myopia*. The children will be able to read books with little trouble, but will find difficulty in seeing the board, wall charts and television. They will have to walk out of their seats to check what they are looking at. They may well therefore come to be seen as being disruptive. Though some children will have glasses prescribed even before they enter school, many children begin to need spectacles from about the age of 9, i.e. during the junior years. These are the years when there are fewer school medicals so a child may well go undiagnosed. If you notice that one of your class has to get up to check what is on the board, always sits very close to the television, and seems to have screwed up eyes for distance vision then it is worth having a word with the parents so that they can arrange for an ophthalmic examination.

Children who have long sight — *hypermetropia* — will have no problem with seeing the board, but they will have the problem of focusing on print in reading books and work books. With so much close work in school, they may begin to complain of headaches. This is why near sight as well as far sight should be checked.

A third refractive problem which can be corrected by spectacles is *astigmatism*. This is where the curve of the eye is misshapen. This can mean that the child receives a distorted image which can lead to difficulty in identifying and copying letters.

Another eye problem that can affect reading is *strabismus*, a squint. Under normal circumstances, the muscles of the eye work together so that both eyes focus on the object that we are looking at. With a strabismus this does not happen so the child has difficulty in focusing on an object and will have double vision.

Stand in front of a window and hold out your hand at arm's length. Now look into the far distance. How many fingers do you see? The number will vary. A child with a squint, whose eyes cannot converge, will be experiencing just that sort of problem, but all the time. Often, what can happen is that they learn to ignore the messages from one eye and concentrate on the messages from the other one. This ignored eye becomes 'lazy'. It is not that it does not receive visual input and send it to the visual cortex, but the cortex 'chooses' to ignore the messages from this eye in favour of the other eye. To all intents and purposes, the children become one eyed. The lazy eye sometimes appears to wander around at will, particularly when the child is tired.

If the strabismus is very pronounced then the children may have one or more operations to correct the squint. However, if it is not too pronounced then they may wear spectacles with grating stuck on to force the eye to correct itself.

For long sight, short sight and squints, children will need to wear glasses to school. They may well not enjoy wearing them and you will have to exercise a great deal of sympathetic tact to make sure that they do wear them when they are supposed to. You will certainly need to have consultations with the parents so that there can be a consistent policy about when the children must wear them and when they can exercise a degree of discretion.

One of the points in relation to classroom teaching is that the children will be able to hear better when they are wearing their glasses. This is not just an odd myth. When wearers have their specs on their noses they can see faces more clearly and in particular can read lips. Though, obviously, we use our ears as the main organ for receiving speech, we do make use of visual information from the lips and so find it just that more taxing to 'hear' without glasses. Alas, as those of us who wear specs are all too aware, the lenses do tend to get very mucky very quickly. Particularly with young children you will need to give an occasional hand in wiping them clean. A pair of glasses that are so greasy and paint-smeared that they can hardly be seen out of makes very little sense.

These days the children will probably be wearing glasses with plastic lenses which are much safer than glass ones, but even so, some children may decide to take their glasses off for PE and general physical activities in the hall. This may mean that they tend to prefer to do activities near to a wall because they will feel safer there. They will also feel a wee bit vulnerable when having to jump off high boxes etc., and of course they will find it slightly more difficult to hear what you are saying. Do make certain that they organize themselves so that they know where they put their specs in order to put them back on again after the lesson.

Some children may feel much more confident in PE if they keep their glasses on, and certainly outside ball games will be less problematic if they can actually see the ball. Obviously, it is important that children should be able to see the world clearly, rather than through a blurred image; but in the area of perception, we are more concerned with the interpretation that the children make of the images they receive, rather than the status of the images themselves. You can see how that can be from colour blindness. Yes, the child has a 'mechanical' defect, and nothing wrong with his cognitive processing; but the colour blindness itself may lead to his *appearing* to have a problem with perception. The messages about the world that he receives are actually different from the messages that everyone else receives. He has an extra bit of learning and interpretation to do. If he has red/green colour blindness he has to learn that grass is green and that roses are red even though they appear to be the same colour to him.

Constancy and Illusions

Constancy is an interesting aspect of our model of the world. What we mean by constancy is that we have the ability to see objects as remaining the same even though they have undergone a variety of spatial transformations.

We do not think that an object has become smaller when it goes away from us or become larger as it comes nearer to us. Instead we interpret that changing image size as being caused by a change in distance. This is size constancy. Bower (1966) has shown that infants show size constancy by about 2 months so it is a very early perceptual ability. This is a useful ability to have when building up a model of the world. A model that presupposed that things changed size would be rather unhelpful. We do need to believe that we live in a stable world. Though this is an ability that manifests itself in very early infancy and may well be pre-determined rather than learned, it does not mean that it does not improve with age. There is evidence that children do not achieve adult levels of size constancy until about 10 years. Experiences with judging distances, drawing objects in relation to one another and size estimations throughout the primary years will all be invaluable in developing constancy ability.

Shape constancy enables us to understand that an object does not change shape just because we view it from a different perspective. You can have great fun with children by presenting them with pictures of objects taken from unusual angles. School children have no problems in understanding that things remain the same even when the actual retinal image is very different.

Figure 3.3 shows you how visual constancy works. The railway sleepers are obviously not getting smaller and smaller, but if you measured each one with a ruler, you would see that the image of each is very different. Our size constancy enables us to interpret this as the railway lines getting further into the distance.

Figure 3.3   (a) Visual Constancy — railway lines

Figure 3.3   (b) Visual Constancy — chairs

The two chairs are absolutely standard, but the retinal image that we receive from each of them is very different.

The phenomenon of constancy shows us that interpreting the world requires very complex cognitive processes. Information based on knowledge of the world supplied by the higher cognitive processes is necessary in order to interpret the messages received via the sense organs.

Figure 3.4 The Ponzo Illusion

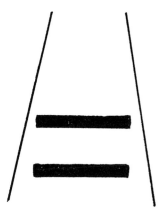

The way our model of the world interacts with our sensory input can be seen through the effects of visual illusions. Figure 3.4 is an example of the Ponzo Illusion. The two horizontal lines appear to be different sizes, yet if you measure them you will verify that they are exactly the same size. The explanation for this relates back to the railway lines. Our model of the world, built up from our experiences in the world, tells us that as things get further from us, they stay the same size, but the image on the retina gets smaller. We also know that as parallel lines get further from us they appear to converge. Thus, the stimulus presented to us in the Ponzo Illusion appears to be similar to the railway lines. Because the second horizontal line gives the *same* retinal image, the higher cognitive processes interpret this as the line being *longer* but *further away*.

A similar interaction between sensory input and knowledge of the world to create illusory effects can be seen in Figure 3.5.

The trees are always in the same order from left to right. The three big trees are always the same size as are the middle and small trees. However, in the left hand side of the figure, the trees appear to be all the same size with the little tree a long way in the distance. On the other hand, in the right hand side of the figure, the environment in which the images are placed makes the large tree appear extra large and the little one appears as a tiny shrub.

Figure 3.5   The Effect of Environment on Size Perception

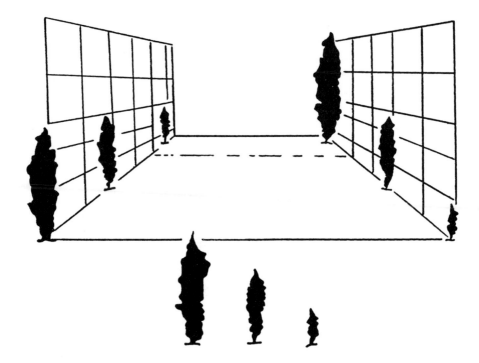

We experience illusions when we respond to stimuli that can be understood in more than one way. The ambiguous figure in 3.1 shows us this clearly. Work by Elkind (1975, 1978) shows us that perception of illusions and ambiguous figures continues to develop throughout the primary years.

Figure 3.6   An Ambiguous Figure of the Type Used by Elkind (1978)

Figure 3.6 is a simple ambiguous figure of a tree and a face. Presumably you can see both more or less simultaneously. Elkind (1978) found that 4- to 5-year-olds could typically see the tree, but tended not to see the face. By 7 to 8, they could see both, but often needed the 'second' figure pointed out to them. The 10-year-olds appeared to have adult-like perception.

In the way the figure has been drawn, the tree is said to be *figure* and the rest *ground*. The tree appears to stand out. This would explain why the younger children see the tree rather than the face. To see the face, we need to reverse figure and ground. Obviously, all the children have exactly the same visual input; the important dimension is that they have differing levels of perceptual ability.

The ability to isolate figure from ground is a useful perceptual skill. We need to be able to do this if we are to be able to read diagrams and maps correctly. Unfortunately, publishers do not always take enough account of the less developed perceptual skills of primary school children. When you are choosing books for your classroom you should look very carefully and critically at the illustrations and diagrams to make sure that the children will be able to use them. Too often we take children's abilities for granted and then become a little impatient when they appear to have problems with reading the illustrations which are meant to 'aid' comprehension.

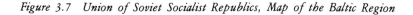

Figure 3.7   Union of Soviet Socialist Republics, Map of the Baltic Region

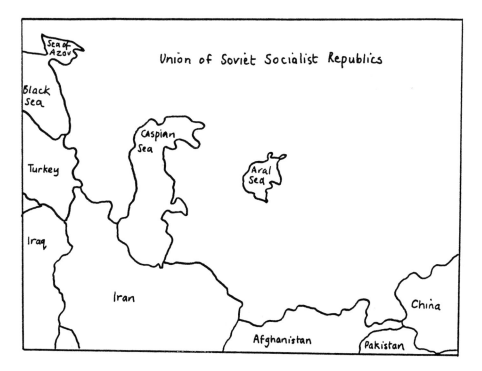

Consider the map in Figure 3.7: we know sufficient about geography to be able to tell which is land and which is sea. Under these circumstances we can consider the land to be figure and the sea to be ground. A child who is only just learning about maps and geography *and* who is still developing perceptually would find such a map confusing. I am not saying that children cannot make use of a map, but a teacher could not legitimately assume that a junior child would be able to work independently with such material. I cannot see the point of making learning more difficult for children when a little bit of foresight and thoughtfulness could smooth some of the problems away.

It is quite easy to see the need for a child to have developed the ability to distinguish figure from ground when reading diagrams and maps, but this ability is also necessary when approaching some early reading books. There are a number of books produced for children when they are just beginning to develop literacy skills where it is extremely difficult to isolate the print — as figure — from the illustrations, which in these circumstances are ground. The illustrations may well be pleasing and the idea of integrating the print and the pictures may well be sound on aesthetic grounds, but nevertheless, we have to consider the position of the child who cannot actually *see* the print. When choosing books for children we have to be able to *decentre*. This is a Piagetian term to which we will return in Chapter 7. It implies that a person is able to consider more than one dimension of a situation simultaneously. As we shall see, there is much discussion about the ability of young children to do this. However, we often find that in real life situations, although adults have the ability to decentre, they frequently take an adult perspective and do not consider the way the child would approach the situation.

A good exercise would be to go to the children's library or to your school library and to look at the books from the perspective of what we know about the developing perception of young children. Muted tones with matching print may be very visually appealing, but can the young child isolate the print from the background?

Detection of Similarities and Differences

Part of our use of sensory input to make sense of the world, is in the detection of similarities and differences. We need to be able to extract generalities and overall patterns so that we can say 'Ah yes, it's one of those.' A system that could not accept approximate similarities would be very inflexible. At the same time we also need to be able to detect very subtle differences between inputs so that we can end up with quite sophisticated distinctions between objects.

Let us consider the importance of detecting similarities. Here we are concerned with the ability to classify and categorize objects as being in some way similar to each other. Piaget spent much of his working life on this very problem. We have to be able to take a particular sensory input; then extract the features of this particular input and see if they coincide roughly with a category of object that we already have in our model of the world. If there are enough points of similarity, then we will say 'Yes, they are the same', regardless of the differences that we could detect. For practical purposes, we ignore the differences and concentrate on the similarities. At a simple level — a chair is a chair is a chair even when it is a bean bag or a hammock or a garden swing, etc. Our experience of the world has enabled us to develop a sufficiently abstract and generalized description of chairs so that we can generally find somewhere to sit down even in the most futuristic of homes.

It seems to be the case that in identifying objects we search for the *distinctive features* that define the object. Obviously we do not do this in a deliberate, conscious manner. However, as we move through the world we must be constantly registering and classifying objects and events. Once the sensory input has been classified, it becomes 'known' and we can decide whether it is important at the moment and requires responding to, or presently unimportant and therefore it can be ignored.

In identifying similarities we are necessarily also detecting differences. We make the decisions that two objects are sufficiently similar to be classed as being the same thing, but also recognize that they are sufficiently distinct to warrant being subcategorized as belonging to two related, but different, classes. The ability to perceive differences obviously relates to perceptual discrimination, but it also relates to our knowledge of the world, the way we understand the world and our interest and motivations.

To a non-birdwatcher, a bird flying around at the seaside is likely to be a seagull. However, to anyone who knows anything about birds, the size and shape of head, wings and beak, the colour of feathers, feet and beak, etc., will all serve to identify the particular species of gull. The subtle differences between the various species are lost on novices. They are not able to utilize any but the gross distinctive features. However as knowledge, experience and motivation are increased, so the distinctive features increase in number and salience.

Junior school teachers are well aware that when children begin to develop consuming passions — even if they last for a very short time — they will be able to classify and reclassify down to the tiniest detail. To a non-*cognoscente*, one dinosaur is not very different from another — it may be bigger or smaller; and its name may be even longer! However, a 5-year-old with a passionate interest in prehistoric species will be able to identify, classify and name the many different species.

The examples given of birdwatching and dinosaurs may illustrate the act of utilizing distinctive features to recognize similarities and differences; but do we, as teachers, ever make use of this? Is this side of perception of anything more than passing interest? It is at this point that we begin to see that the splitting up of human cognitive processes into neat chapter headings becomes very woolly. We consider categorization in relation to perception, but we will return to it when we consider both memory and cognitive development.

Applied Perception

Many pre-school and early years activities involve the child in pointing out which two items are the same from an array, as in Figure 3.8 (a). Other similar activities may require that the odd one out is identified, as in Figure 3.8 (b). All these types of activities require that the children have to apply their cognitive skills. These activities may be fun and rewarding in themselves, but do they serve any further educational purpose? They serve to help the child to focus on the visual aspects of the input. They also serve implicitly to suggest to the child that it is important to notice the similarities and differences because these features may be meaningful.

Figure 3.8   (a) Circle the same frog as the one on the left

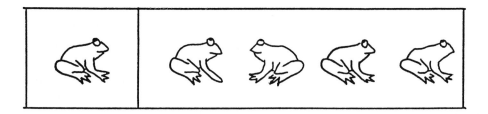

Figure 3.8   (b) Which is the odd-one-out?

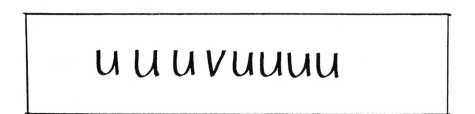

Initially, this type of activity will be based on visual images which are pictorial and nameable as in Figure 3.8 (a). However, the child will also be exposed to stimuli which are abstract and non-nameable as in 3.8 (b). Being able to handle apparently abstract symbols is a vital part of that most important of all applied cognitive activities — reading.

Reading is a complex cognitive activity which has to be learned. A number of differing cognitive skills have to be applied together in order for any of us to be able to read fluently. For you, as you read this book, for me as I write it, the activities of reading and writing are not difficult in themselves. That is not to say that it is not a struggle for me to write, or that you do not have to put some effort into understanding, but what you don't have to do is worry about the act of reading *per se* — that is apparently effortless. However, when children are beginning to learn to read, the task requires a great deal of effort. They have to learn to apply their cognitive skills in order to assign meaning to the abstract symbols on the page. We will consider reading in much greater depth later on, but for the moment we should spend some time considering the importance of perception to early reading development.

Why are exercises in spotting 'same' and 'different' so important to learning to read? Let us think about the alphabet. Each letter is different from every other letter. That much is obvious — but is it as obvious as it seems? The typeface on my word processor produces bdpq ae wm un ft in such a way that the groups are identical apart from their orientation. It is clear that orientation in reading is of major significance: 'bad' is not the same as 'bed;' 'dab' something different from 'bad'.

Up to the point when a child has to learn to read, orientation does not have quite the importance that it subsequently has to acquire. Indeed, part of the child's model of the world is the implicit knowledge that objects remain the same regardless of changes in orientation. It is not that they are unaware of the teddy lying down or standing on its head, but the orientation is not a salient feature, because it does not change the fundamental *teddiness* of the teddy. Indeed it would be a very inefficient system that could not relegate orientation to something which was of minor significance in the recognition of objects. So, there we have the young children coming along quite happily, receiving and classifying all the visual perceptual information, and then suddenly they are told 'Well yes, a chair is a chair is a chair, but a "b" is only a "b" when it's not a "d", "p" or "q".'

Gibson and Levin (1975) have shown that the ability to discriminate between letters on the basis of their orientation is an important ability when beginning to read. Children have to learn to make these discriminations automatically. They need lots and lots of practice so that they do not need to worry about which letter it is.

You will not question the need to discriminate between letters, but whereas children have to learn that orientation is so important in reading, they also have to learn that they have to tolerate all sorts of differences in the production of letters themselves. This is an a, but so is this A, and so is this *A* and so is this *a*, and this *a* and this a and this *a*. As early as 1969, Gibson suggested that in order to recognize letters we have to identify the distinctive features of the letters which will serve to discriminate them from each other. Orientation becomes one of the necessary distinctive features. As children get lots and lots of experience with letters and letter naming it could be suggested that they learn to 'write' a description of each letter with which they can compare any subsequent input. The description has to be sufficiently abstract to cope with all the possible variations in print type and size, and of course all the variations in handwriting that you can possibly imagine. Fortunately, by the time children are able to read appalling handwriting fluently, they have got beyond the stage of needing to pay much attention to the letters and can access the meaning directly.

Many children will arrive in school having had much experience with print and books and they will have learnt their alphabet quite happily. This takes a big burden off the teacher. However, all children will not have learnt this letter discrimination, and it is up to the teacher to make sure that everyone is able to discriminate and name all the letters quickly and accurately. This does not mean that you have to drill rigidly little 5-year-olds until they can bark back the answers. There are lots of exciting games that can aid matching and discriminating and the children can learn implicitly through many different activities. The important thing is that you as a teacher need to be aware, explicitly, that the children are learning letter discrimination. You also need to be aware of the child who seems to be finding it very difficult. Such a child needs to have lots of help at this early stage because, without this perceptual skill, reading may become a problematic activity a little later on.

Because of the multiplicity of typefaces and the problems of confusability, some schools feel that they can reduce the burden on the children by sticking to one print style only. In fact this really does not matter. The children have to learn to associate all the different possible 'A's together. Since they *have* to do this, it seems more efficient to expose them to any number of typefaces to avoid any lack of flexibility. Also, since we hope that they are having lots of books read to them at home, and we hope that they are having their attention drawn to all the environmental print around them, sticking to one typeface in school seems almost perverse.

I should point out that, though we have concentrated on letters in this area of perception, everything applies equally well to numbers. 6 and 9 are confusable as are 2 and 5. Confusion comes when children write 6 for 9 and then don't know which they meant. Often they will write letters and numbers back to front, but as long as they are letters like k or numbers like 3 it doesn't affect the meaning. Obviously they have to learn that they have to conform to the conventional orientation.

So far we have concentrated on perceptual matching of single letters. However in both reading and mathematics, ordering of the items is crucial. Children have to be able to discriminate between 'NO' and 'ON', between 'TEN' and 'NET', and between '12' and '21'.

Though the details of the typeface may have to be ignored, the details within the words themselves cannot be ignored. The *whole* word needs to be processed if 'THEY' is to be distinguished from 'THEN' or 'THE'.

Because of the need to be able to make these fine perceptual judgments you can begin to see that it makes sense to provide children with a context for reading words so that they can use pictorial cues and the story so far to work out what the word might be. It is much harder to read a word in isolation than in context. However, in the final analysis, the fluent reader is the one who can read individual words very quickly and accurately.

Perception in the Classroom

Let us recap on what we have learned about perception so far. I hope that you have become aware that perception is an active process of categorization and discrimination. Children are not just passive receivers. They have to learn to interpret the incoming stimuli so that they can make sense of the world around them. Teachers will make use of detailed questioning techniques to encourage children to look closely and notice fine details. Minibeast safaris encourage children to concentrate on fine detail and of course they can subsequently use their observations to draw conclusions about the meaning and usefulness of details. By the time children are in school it is the consequential nature of perception that is important. We know that they can see and hear, but we want them to use their sensory input to draw inferences about the world.

Bruner (1957) has written about the concept of perceptual readiness. In educating children we must enable them to be in a state to be able to anticipate the incoming stimuli so they will be more able to interpret them. With motor performance the child who is sufficiently skilled can anticipate the opponent's action and so organize a response earlier; so a child who is perceptually ready can interpret the stimulus more easily. However we also need to help the child not to be a perceptual maverick. Bruner also talked about perceptual *recklessness*, where the child is likely to jump to conclusions on the basis of too little input. We must encourage children to look carefully and closely. Classrooms, therefore, need to be perceptually stimulating environments. Anyone going into a British primary school today could see that this is the case. It is a pity that the same cannot be said of the average secondary school classroom.

Besides providing for perceptual stimulation, teachers have to think carefully about the organization of the classroom. Again, I'm talking about the ideal world. Teachers need to consider the position of the board in relation to the windows and the lights. They need to think about the lighting in all the areas where the children have to make independent choices. The library corner with no lighting can be a problem, and as we shall see in the next chapter we have to think about the classroom environment in relation to the perception of all aspects of sound.

A good teacher will always be concerned about the visual aspects of the classroom environment so that the particular position of a child with visual handicap in the classroom should not pose any problems. In reality, when teachers have to make provision for a visually handicapped child in their class, the environment can be enhanced for all children.

Checking on lighting in the classroom for a visually handicapped child can reveal that all the children are having to learn in less than ideal conditions. The point about visually handicapped children is that their ability to cope in less than perfect conditions is necessarily limited. Particular attention needs to be paid to colour contrast, both for displays and the overall décor. Matt surfaces reduce glare and strong colours are easier to see. Teachers may have a choice of central teaching surfaces — blackboard, white board, overhead projector. For all children, but especially the visually handicapped, board technique needs to involve the use of large clear letters and clean uncluttered backgrounds. Purple chalk is almost impossible for anyone to see on a blackboard unless it is outlined in white. Green, black and blue inks are clear on OHPs and white boards but orange and yellow do not stand out at all. White boards generally provide a clearer background on which to write, but *all* surfaces have to be cleaned regularly so that figure is contrasted with ground.

Conclusion

Children are still developing their perceptual abilities in the primary school, so teachers have to take account of this when planning the curriculum. Activities should both facilitate development, and at the same time not make unrealistic demands on the children.

Within the framework of the National Curriculum, the choice of materials is the responsibility of you as teachers and so it is important to consider the perceptual aspects of the work as well as the knowledge-based side.

Further Reading

Lindsay and Norman (1977) *Human Information Processing* provides good further reading for understanding the visual system. In addition to this, you might like to read Wilding (1982) *Perception: From Sense to Object*. Chapman and Stone (1988) *The Visually Handicapped Child in Your Classroom* is a very good book for understanding the problems faced by visually handicapped children and it provides much useful, practical advice.

Chapter 4

Hearing

Introduction

The very special sense of hearing requires a chapter all to itself. As a teacher, most of the time you will have some children in your class who have some degree of hearing loss and it is important that you understand fully the implications of this for the children concerned. Every year, in the infant classroom there will be children with mild transient losses. The hearing losses may be called mild and transient, but the effects can be very significant for the children concerned. Just occasionally, you may be asked to teach a child who has a permanent, severe hearing loss. Often such a child will need to wear powerful radio hearing aids.

It is important that you understand how the hearing system works and what can go wrong with it. You also need to know why hearing aids are *not* the auditory equivalents of a pair of spectacles. Understanding of the effects of hearing loss enables us to plan the auditory aspects of a classroom. However, all children have the right to expect that their learning will not be impaired because of acoustic problems. Good teaching practice is, after all, good teaching practice and strategies for helping all children should only need minor alterations for helping children with hearing loss.

The Auditory System

As you can see from Figure 4.1, the auditory system is divided into three sections — the *outer ear*, the *middle ear* and the *inner ear* which connects with the auditory area of the brain. The function of the system is to transpose sound waves as faithfully as possible into nerve impulses that can be coded and comprehended.

Figure 4.1   Diagram of the Auditory System

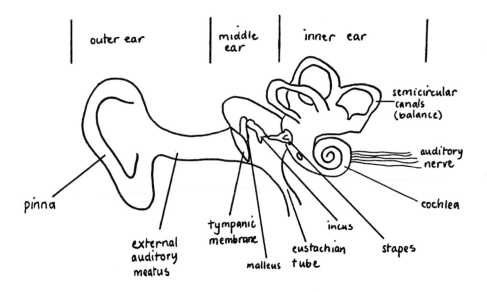

The Outer Ear

This is the part of the auditory system that we can actually see. Though it is the most prominent part, it is the least complex of the whole system. The organ that we colloquially call the ear is called anatomically the *pinna* or *auricle*. The tube which leads from the pinna to the ear drum is the ear canal, or more correctly, the *external auditory meatus*. It is this outer part of the system that children hate washing and parents love to clean. Wax is secreted by the glands in the external auditory meatus, which helps to protect the ear drum. This wax is technically called *cerumen*. It is a bitter, sticky orangey substance which is perfectly acceptable, if at times a little unaesthetic. On the other hand, Lego is definitely not acceptable! Neither are bits of apple, beads, cherry stones, etc. The ear canal is a very tempting little hole. Temporary, acute (sudden) earache in young children can be the result of a blockage in the canal, which is why a doctor will always look down the ear with an otoscope to check that there is not a foreign body lurking down there causing pain and discomfort. Remember that the ear is a very delicate instrument — *never* poke around in a child's ear yourself.

The external auditory meatus ends at the ear drum — the *tympanic membrane*. The function of the pinna is to direct the sound waves down the canal in a more concentrated way towards the tympanic membrane. At this stage, nothing has happened to the sound waves. They have neither been transformed nor analyzed. They have not yet been *heard*. Before we reached our present state of evolution, it may have been that we could 'prick' our ears in response to sound, much like other animals. Some people still have the ability to move their ears a little bit. If you can, it can be a great talking point in school.

The Middle Ear

This is the cavity between the tympanic membrane and the inner ear. It is an extension of the *nasopharynx* (throat) and is lined with a mucus membrane that is continuous with that of the nose. You can immediately see the connection between colds and earache in children — both resulting from the same infection.

The tympanic membrane is connected to the inner ear by way of a bridge of three very tiny, delicate *ossicles* — ear bones. These are, in order from the tympanic membrane; the *malleus* (hammer), the *incus* (anvil) and the *stapes* (stirrup). The malleus is attached to the tympanic membrane and the stapes has its footplate set in the *oval window* of the inner ear. These two ossicles are connected to each other by the incus.

When sound waves hit the tympanic membrane they are converted into mechanical energy. The membrane vibrates in response to the sound waves and this vibration is transmitted across the bridge of bone to the oval window and the inner ear. In a normal functioning ear the conversion of sound waves at the tympanic membrane to mechanical energy at the oval window is very faithful. No coding takes place. It is a straight one-to-one transmission.

One other structure of the middle ear that we have not yet considered is the *eustachian tube*. This leads from the middle ear to the back of the nasopharynx. Normally, in adults, the eustachian tube is in a collapsed state, but it opens when we yawn or swallow. The function of this tube is to ventilate the middle ear. The oxygen in the middle ear is constantly being absorbed into the mucus membrane. The act of swallowing allows fresh air to enter the middle ear and so replenish the oxygen and keep it sweet. This also means that the air pressure in the middle ear remains the same as the environmental pressure. This is important because the tympanic membrane is at optimal efficiency when there is equal pressure on either side. If the pressure in the middle ear is increased, then the membrane will bow outwards. If the pressure is reduced then it will curve inwards more sharply than usual. Either way the person will experience sounds as being 'fuzzy'.

You can recognize the effects of differential pressure when taking off and landing in an aeroplane, or speeding into a railway tunnel. You need to swallow consciously to stop the 'popping' sensation and then suddenly the sounds become dramatically sharper. The deadening of sound, as the pressure becomes unbalanced, is so gradual that you are not really aware that your hearing is reduced. It's only when you swallow that, with hindsight, you recognize the condition.

During early childhood the eustachian tubes are normally open. They are also more or less horizontal and so cannot drain easily. By about 8 years, the tubes will have tipped slightly and begun to function as they will in adulthood. However, until that time, the middle ear is at risk of being exposed to infections that can seriously affect hearing.

The Inner Ear

This is the true organ of hearing. Its anatomy and functioning are far too complex for detailed discussion here, but I will present enough for our purposes.

The part of the inner ear that concerns us most here is the *cochlea*. It is a shell-like structure with its basal end nearest to the middle ear and its apical end furthest from the middle ear. The sensory organ of hearing has to respond to the frequency, intensity and loudness of sounds that are changing over time, transmitted via the outer and middle ear. The cochlea is so arranged that it responds to different frequencies at different points along its length. High frequency sounds are detected at the basilar end and low frequencies at the apical end. This means that the cochlea is frequency specific along its length and so able to resolve a complex wave form, like that of human voices, into its component parts. The speed of resolution is important. The ear has to be able to detect very short low intensity sounds without their being masked out by more intense sounds. Without this, we would not be able to resolve the sounds of voices and therefore understand speech.

It is not the purpose of this book to provide you with a complete audiology course, but a diversion into some of the relevant aspects of sound in general and speech in particular would seem useful at this point.

The Parameters of Sound

Sounds can vary along a number of different parameters independently. In lay terms, they can last for a longer or shorter time; they can be loud or soft; they can be more or less intense; they can be high or low.

Duration is simple. It can be measured in time, but the ear has to be sensitive enough to detect sounds that last for very short durations measured in milliseconds. Loudness is more complicated. Loudness is the perceived strength of the sound waves as received by the tympanic membrane and transmitted to the cortex. Coupled with this is intensity, which refers to the rate of sound-energy transmission through a medium. This intensity of sound is expressed in decibels (dB) ranging from 0 dB Hearing Level (HL) to 140 dB HL. 0 dB HL is the average threshold for a sound whereby a person can just detect the sound. This will vary with each frequency. Sounds of about 140 dB HL will produce damage to the ear. The dB scale is not a linear one, so we cannot talk of 80 dB HL as being twice as loud as 40 dB HL.

The highness or lowness of a sound is referred to as its *frequency*. You may know is as *pitch* in music. Frequency is the rate of vibration of the sound source. The greater the frequency, the higher the note. We can normally hear sounds with frequencies between 20 and 20,000 Hz (vibrations per second). However, our sensitivity to sounds is not uniform throughout the range. Our ears are most sensitive to sounds in the frequency range 1,000 to 4,000 Hz. This particular frequency range is most important. Speech frequencies — the frequencies produced by the human voice — are within this middle sensitive band. Sounds above and below this range have to be more intense to be perceived. However, many important speech sounds are right at the top of this range and the ear needs to be sensitive to detect them.

A pure tone, like one produced by a tuning fork, is at a defined frequency and so it is easy to measure and describe. However, human speech is much more complex. Each speech sound has all the parameters of sound but with a number of different frequencies showing different intensities and durations all at the same time. Any one speech sound will be characterized by its intensity and duration and change over time at a number of different frequencies. These characteristic bands of energy at set frequencies are called *formants* (Figure 4.2).

It is the job of the auditory system to resolve the complex speech sounds into their component parts so that they can be identified. The formants may have a sharp rise or fall at the start of a sound. It may be that the particular combination

Figure 4.2 A spectrogram of the words heed, head, had *and* who'd, *as spoken in a British accent (speaker: Peter Ladefoged, February 16, 1973). From Fromkin and Rodman (1988).*

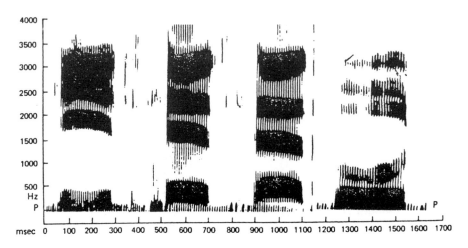

of change in frequency at this point is the crucial data on which the system bases its identification of the particular sound.

On the whole, vowel sounds are low frequency sounds, but consonants, which contain more information are often individualized by their formants in the high frequencies. Sounds like /s/ and /t/, which contain high frequency but low intensity sounds, are used in English to denote such important semantic elements as plurals, possession and past tense. This means that they require acute hearing if they are to be detected.

Hearing Tests

Because it is recognized that we need to identify the children with hearing loss as early as possible, built in to the assessments that children receive before they go to school and once they start school are a number of standard hearing screening tests. You will not be required, or indeed qualified, to carry out hearing tests, but you should acquaint yourself with how they are carried out and know what the test results mean.

There are a number of ways of classifying tests. A test may be called *behavioural* when a sound is presented to the children and they are required to do something to show that they have perceived the stimulus. A test may be called *objective* when the functioning of the system is measured, but no behavioural response is required.

Another possible classification is to call some tests *screening* tests. Screening tests are usually routinely carried out on a whole population to identify those with problems. They should be quick to carry out, but are not very complex as far as diagnosis is concerned. After a screening test there may be more sophisticated detailed tests which will be carried out if a problem has been revealed. Hearing loss can be quantified in amount of dB loss, but to aid communication the losses are grouped into bands and given descriptive terms.

Table 4.1   Terms used to describe measured dB loss

Description	Loss in dB
Mild	15–30
Moderate	31–50
Severe	51–80
Profound	81–100
Total loss or anacusis	No measurable hearing

9-month Testing

All babies should be routinely screened by their health visitor around their ninth month. This is a behavioural test where the baby sits on a parent's knee and has to respond to sounds made by objects manipulated by one of the health visitors. The baby's attention has to be captured so that a turning response has to be made to the sound, if it is heard. Noise makers are things like a small bell, tissue paper, a whisper and a spoon in a cup. You can appreciate that the level of control in such a test is fairly limited. There are now more sophisticated noise makers that can deliver a standard noise but they are not as yet routinely used. This test will serve to identify the child who has quite a marked loss, but sometimes the health visitors have to work in less than perfect conditions with phones ringing and typewriters banging in another room. Even testing in a supposedly quiet home will not solve the problem. Just go and sit in your room when there is no one else around. What do you hear? The fridge motor starts up, a dog barks down the street, a car starts up next door, the wind blows the lid off the dustbin, the telephone rings. The answer must be always to err on the side of caution and, if in doubt, babies should be referred to the local audiology clinic for a test under more controlled conditions.

Pre-school Testing

In most areas children will have a final developmental assessment by the health visitor before they start school. Besides checking on motor, social and language development a check will be made on the children's ability to hear speech, but this will be in a somewhat informal way.

Pure Tone Screening in School

During the first year in school children are given a standard hearing test across the speech frequencies using headphones and an audiometer. This is generally carried out by the school nurse so you should be able to take the chance to see the test being performed.

This is a behavioural test. The children are told that they are going to play a simple game. They wear headphones and when they hear a sound coming through one of the ears they have to place a block in a box or move a counter across a table. The point of the task is to make it more interesting for the young children and at the same time to force them to make a very overt response rather than simply mumbling a reply. The audiometer is a machine for delivering pure tones of known frequency and known dB level. Responses to five standard frequencies are checked in each ear and recorded on an audiogram.

Figure 4.3 shows the standard audiogram form. 0 dB level corresponds to the average level at which a young person can just detect a tone at a given frequency. Obviously, normal hearing varies around the 0 dB HL threshold and it is more variable at the higher frequencies. When there is a hearing loss, louder sounds than 0 dB are needed before a threshold is reached. The nurse can record the number of dB above 0 dB necessary for that particular child to hear that frequency in that ear. The number of dB above 0 dB needed for the sound to be detected is equivalent to the hearing loss. The audiogram in Figure 4.3 shows the responses obtained from a child with a bilateral loss. This shows you why patterns of performance rather than talking about average loss across all frequencies can be more informative. The loss in the low frequencies is only mild, but the loss in the high frequencies is severe, giving consequent problems for understanding speech.

Figure 4.3   Diagram of an Audiogram Showing a Bilateral-sensori Neural Loss.

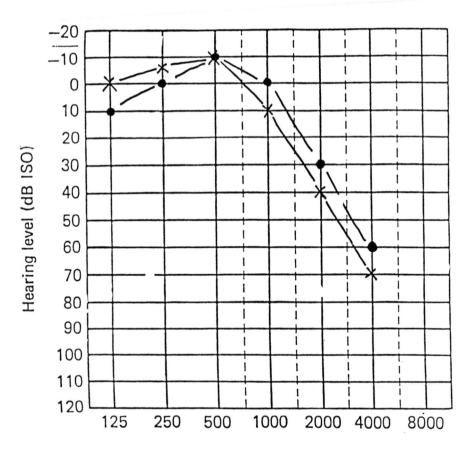

This first pure tone screening is very important since it is at school that many of the hearing losses due to middle ear infection are first discovered. Unfortunately, conditions for conducting these tests vary greatly. I have been in schools where the staff room, away from any environmental noise, has been given to the nurse. On the other hand, I have watched a hearing test taking place in an open plan school next to the hall where a music lesson was in full swing. There needs to be sensible liaison between the head teacher and the nurse so that the best conditions within any one school can be found.

Any child who is found to have a loss on this test should be immediately referred by the local school doctor to the audiology clinic through the GP. Notice the term *hearing loss*. Never talk about the children 'failing the hearing test', particularly in their presence.

Once the children with hearing loss are being treated in the audiology clinic you need to keep close communication with the parents so that you know the present state of the children and if there is any deterioration in their condition. The thing that you have to remember is that each child is unique. The effects of hearing loss on any one child will be specific to that child. A mild loss for child A may be be quite devastating, whereas child B may be able to cope apparently happily with a severe loss and a powerful aid. The important thing for you as a teacher is that you need to know sufficient about the assessment, terminology and implications of the conditions so that you can plan effectively and interact with other professionals on an informed basis.

Types of Hearing Loss

The incidence of hearing loss in children makes it necessary that teachers should have an understanding of the different types of hearing loss. We will consider these in relation to the different parts of the system that can be affected, but you should remember that many children may have a complex loss where more than one area is affected.

Outer Ear Loss

Sometimes children can be born with congenital malformations of the outer ear. These include absence of the pinna or the external auditory meatus. Absence of the meatus is much more serious, though cosmetically less noticeable, because there needs to be a canal for the sound to be conducted down to the tympanic membrane. Congenital malformations of this type may have to be treated with corrective surgery.

As we said earlier, the external auditory meatus is a grand place to poke and deposit small objects, so any sudden hearing loss or acute pain could be due to a cherry stone and should be investigated. The usual earache that children complain of is not an outer ear problem, but due to problems affecting the middle ear.

Middle Ear Loss

This type of hearing loss needs to be considered in some depth because it is probably one of the most common causes of hearing loss in childhood and one of the easiest to reverse as long as it is treated early enough. Middle ear loss is a *conductive* loss. This means that there is a malfunction of the mechanism conducting the sounds from the environment to the inner ear. The medical term for this problem is *otitis media.*

Murphy (1976) estimated that, at any one time, as many as 20 per cent of primary age children will be suffering from middle ear loss. Translated into class size numbers — if you have thirty-five children in your class, you may assume that seven of them (and not always the same seven) are having difficulty in hearing you. Obviously the figures will vary and be worse in the spring when there are so many coughs and colds, but the figures make salutory reading.

Children with middle ear loss will generally have had a history of colds and upper respiratory tract infections. Once the middle ear becomes infected, the child may complain of earache, and examination by the doctor may show that the tympanic membranes are reddish and inflamed. Generally a course of antibiotics will be prescribed with possibly a mild pain killer such as paracetamol. Do encourage parents to tell you if children have been given a course of antibiotics or any other medication. In the best of all possible worlds, any child prescribed antibiotics would be seen by the doctor after the course had finished. This is because, though the treatment will clear up the symptoms, it may not alleviate the condition itself and it could become chronic.

If the eustachian tube remains blocked, then, as the oxygen is absorbed by the lining of the middle ear, the tympanic membrane is sucked in and can no longer vibrate efficiently. The negative pressure in the middle ear draws serum from the mucus membrane and the middle ear begins to fill with fluid that cannot drain. At this point the child has two problems impeding the efficient conduction of sound — an inefficient tympanic membrane and a fluid-filled cavity affecting the function of the ossicular chain. If the hearing loss is identified at this stage, visual examination of the ear will show the fluid swishing around behind the tympanic membrane.

If the condition is not diagnosed at this stage then the serum — called an effusion — begins to thicken. The child then has that condition commonly known as *glue ear*. Glue ear results in a loss of sensitivity to sounds, initially in the low frequencies, but eventually across the full range of frequencies. Just think of the difference between waving a spoon around in the air, then stirring your tea and then stirring a tin of treacle. This will give you some idea of the effects of glue ear on the functioning of the ossicular chain.

If drug treatment appears not to lead to an improvement then you may find that the children with glue ear will be given minor surgery. The most common treatment is a *myringotomy*. The tympanic membrane is pierced under a general anaesthetic and the fluid in the middle ear is drained. If the condition is chronic, then it really is a thick glue-like substance that comes out. Some Ear Nose and Throat (ENT) specialists will insert a *grommet* into the tympanic membrane. This is a tiny, teflon tube which sits in the membrane and keeps the middle ear aerated, thus stopping the mucus membrane from secreting the serum. The grommet may well fall out after a week or two or it may stay in place for a number of months. Some children may have to return to hospital a number of times for grommets to be inserted, and though the child may only be in hospital for a day, a general anaesthetic is always serious. Teachers need to monitor the absences to make sure that 'glue ear' children do not miss anything crucial.

You will get used to children reporting that they are 'having grommets'. With a bit of luck, at least one child a year will recover the grommet as it falls out and bring it to school to show. It's a great status symbol and a bit of one upmanship on the first lost tooth!

Some children may have otitis media problems because the eustachian tubes are blocked at the end by enlarged adenoid glands. The use of antibiotics has made 'adenoidal' children far less common, but you can still spot them with their mouth breathing and hyponasal speech. Adenoids do shrink at the onset of puberty, but the ENT surgeon may decide to remove them before then if the hearing loss is marked. A child who has had an operation for removal of adenoids will be absent from school for two weeks to avoid catching any infections from other children.

For some children, the removal of the adenoids results in mild, transient, disordered speech articulation. Obviously, if you have been used to speaking with two large lumps in the back of your throat, then you will need to relearn how to make certain sounds in their absence. This should only last for a short time and the child should not be made to feel self-conscious by over-correction on the part of teachers and parents.

Inner Ear Loss

Following our previous nomenclature, this section is entitled inner ear loss because it is concerned with hearing loss due to malfunction of the inner ear. However, the more correct term is *sensori-neural loss*. The hearing loss comes about because of impairment in the functioning of the end organ or the auditory nerve itself. The sound is conducted satisfactorily to the oval window, but then there is a problem with the translation of the input into the neural code. The causes of sensori-neural loss are various and beyond our scope here, but they range from genetic factors to bacterial and viral diseases. Maternal rubella (German measles) has been identified as a major cause of sensori-neural loss. However, even the common childhood viruses such as measles, mumps and chickenpox or less common ones like infectious meningitis can lead to complications resulting in deafness. The MMR (measles, mumps and rubella) triple vaccine should prove to be a great boon here.

Regardless of the cause, once a child has been diagnosed as having sensori-neural hearing loss, there must be systematic monitoring of the condition. The losses may vary from mild to profound and also they may be progressive. This means that it may start off as a mild loss but get gradually worse. In some cases, sadly, the progression can be very rapid. You as a teacher need to know exactly what the present state is.

The consequences of this type of loss depend very much on whether the onset is before or after language has been acquired (pre- or post-lingual). One characteristic is that the loss is not uniform across the frequencies. There is generally much more difficulty in hearing high frequency sounds. Remember what we said about consonants — sounds like /s/, /f/, /v/, /t/, /d/ are all high frequency but low energy sounds. Even a mild 30 dB HL loss in the high frequencies may mean that the child has difficulty in detecting these information-loaded sounds. Loss occurring post-lingually will mean that teachers have to take great care that the children have spoken information supported by written material. Loss occurring pre-lingually will mean that the children have to have specialist help in developing communication skills. This can be through developing their language skills with very specific help in articulation, or through sign language tuition. There is much controversy about whether profoundly deaf children should be taught to use spoken language and lip reading or whether they should be given access to the sign language of their deaf community. British Sign Language is a language in its own right and the deaf community are able to use it as a means of communication just as any other language. Learning sign language does mean that profoundly deaf children do have a means of efficient communication but it does have limited use withing the majority hearing community. What can happen is that the pre-lingually, profoundly deaf child can be helped to develop language normally through signing and then acquire spoken language as a second language.

Together with hearing loss there may also be *recruitment*. This means that there is a raised threshold for hearing sounds, but that loud sounds are just as painful as they are to a normal hearing person. The children therefore have a reduced dynamic range. They may not be able to hear sounds which are below say 70 dB HL, but sounds at 90 dB HL may be perceived as being painfully loud. This gives a very limited range for hearing speech. This may help you to understand why you should not shout at people who are deaf. They need clarity above all else, not loudness. They can adjust the level of loudness with their hearing aids, and it is the child with sensori-neural loss who is likely to be wearing a hearing aid in your classroom.

Hearing Aids

The majority of hearing impaired children in your class will have mild, transient, conductive losses. These children will not need to wear a hearing aid. However, occasionally you will have children in your class who have to wear one or two aids so you need to be prepared for this.

The advance in hearing aid technology since the 1950s has been quite dramatic. However, regardless of newspaper advertisements, hearing aids do not function like spectacles. A person with a hearing loss cannot just put on a hearing aid and find, lo and behold, that they are hearing perfectly. Spectacles are technologically simple and custom-made. Hearing aids are technologically extremely complex and we are definitely not yet in the age of bespoke aids. The children will be prescribed the most suitable aid available for their particular loss but it will be one of a very small number. Minor adjustments can be made to fine tune an aid, but it will never be a new ear.

Though I can describe what an aid looks like and what its knobs do, as with all things in education, there is no substitute for first hand experience. Trying out a hearing aid is an absolute necessity for anyone dealing with the hearing impaired, and that will include you. You will need to know how to fit a new battery, how to fit the ear piece snugly and what level of amplification the volume knob is turned to.

Figure 4.4 A Post-aural Hearing Aid.

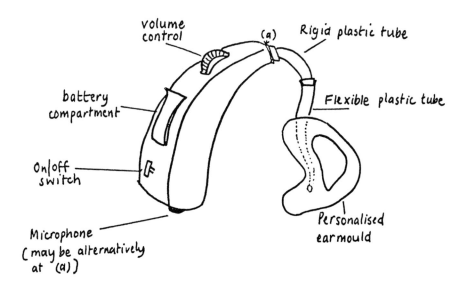

Figure 4.4 shows a behind-the-ear or post-aural aid. The majority of aids prescribed today are of this type. They are neat, compact and discreet; a boon, particularly to the adult users who do not relish being shouted at and treated like fools just because they are deaf. For children, too, they are equally useful, although the controls can be a bit fiddly. Also their very discreetness can have drawbacks. They can be forgotten. It is not a good idea to jump into a swimming pool wearing an aid — though quite robust, they are not waterproof.

Basically, regardless of the type, all hearing aids have the same function. They amplify sound. Unfortunately they are not yet intelligent so they cannot treat signals and noise differently. They amplify all sounds. This means that, in a noisy environment, the background noise may be amplified to unbearable levels such that the wearer may not be able to hear voices above the background and may prefer to switch off rather than be subjected to so much discomfort. Loud noises may be distorted by the aid, making it difficult to work out what is being said. That is yet another reason for not shouting at a person wearing an aid.

Lenses in glasses are specific to the wearer. This, as we have said, is not the case for the hearing aid. All that the wearer can hope for at the moment is an aid which has sufficient amplification of the necessary frequencies when the volume control is in about the middle of its range. This means that the aid has enough gain and power to produce amplification with as little distortion as possible. Any child needing to turn the volume up much beyond the midway point in normal sound conditions would probably be needing a more powerful aid.

Just as important as the aid itself, is the coupling of the aid to the ear. With post-aural aids, this is achieved by a piece of flexible plastic tubing which fits onto the aid and then attaches to the ear piece. The tubing needs to be clean and dry. Any perspiration or condensation in it will make the aid less efficient. It also does not have an infinite life and tends to get hard and to crack as it gets older. The tubing should therefore be replaced every year.

The ear piece itself is the one part of the aid that is custom-made. A mould is made of the child's ear and a unique ear piece is cast in plastic from the mould. For the aid to function correctly, the ear piece must be fitted exactly. If it is out of place then sound leakage will cause a high pitched feedback whine. You will soon notice it if it occurs in your class, but the child may not because it may be in the frequency range where there is maximum loss.

Radio Aids

You may be asked to wear a microphone whose output can be picked up directly by the hearing aids. These can be for post-aural aids or for body-worn aids in cases of profound loss. The aids pick up the sound waves emitted by the microphone around your neck and this means that anything you say will be transmitted directly to the child's ears. Other noises will obviously be transmitted but your voice will be the dominant signal. You have to adjust the strap so that your voice is not shadowed by your chin. You will also have to take off any jewellery that is likely to knock against the microphone as you move around. You need to discuss with the child the best possible use of the microphone. In class sessions you will need to relay other children's questions and answers because they may not be loud enough to be relayed through the microphone. You will also need to remember to turn the microphone off when you go into the staffroom at playtime. It is surprising what conversational snippets have been relayed into school playgrounds.

One final point needs to be made about the integration of hearing impaired children into mainstream schooling. As with all educational issues, you as a teacher have the right to expect that you will have the best support in order to meet the educational needs of the children. You need the necessary backup. Integration on the cheap, with no preparation, means that the children will receive an inferior education and you will experience even more stress than necessary. With the integration of a partially hearing child you should be able to call on the services of an experienced, specialist teacher of the deaf. The two of you should be able to work together as equal colleagues. The cooperation and mutual exchange of ideas between you can only benefit all the children.

Behavioural Signs of Hearing Problems

Glue ear is one of the major causes for hearing loss in young children and it is particularly prevalent during the early primary years. This means that, when you know you have organized your classroom so that children have the best chance of hearing, you must still be on the alert for those children who still seem to have problems. It maybe that you find a child's behaviour particularly troublesome, but when a diagnosis of conductive loss is made everything falls into place. If you start from a basis of being alert for possible hearing loss, you may be able to help with early diagnosis which will be of great help to the child.

Children with hearing loss will have to make greater use of visual cues so they will often peer intently at the speaker's face. However, because they miss the sounds they may well watch what other children are doing and then copy them. This will mean that they do many things in response to actions of others rather than in response to instructions. This lack of response to verbal commands may lead to them being labelled as naughty. You may find that they have to ask for you to explain things far more frequently and, at the same time, when you are addressing the class or reading a story, they will be inattentive and either drift off or be disruptive. However, when they are placed close to you or have to work in a small group, they may show much improved performance. Because of the hearing loss they will tend to sit very close to the television or a tape machine. The intermittent nature of conductive loss may lead the children to show signs of irritability and bad temper. It is not very nice not being able to hear and not knowing why. They may appear to be aggressive with other children. This may in fact be because they pull the other children towards them so that they can hear them.

You will probably notice that the behavioural signs get worse after a cold and that these children do have frequent absences for coughs and colds. Their school performance will suffer because of the illnesses, but also they may not progress at a rate you would predict. Within school they will tire easily and show poor attentional skills.

When a child has been diagnosed as having a hearing loss, all these behavioural signs will make sense. Teachers have to learn to recognize the behavioural patterns. Early diagnosis means that these behaviours do not become too ingrained. Once the hearing problem has been dealt with the children can settle down to productive learning and they should not suffer any lasting consequences.

The Hearing Classroom

In this section we will consider how you can best arrange the environment so that children can hear — all the children.

You, or more specifically your voice, is one of the most important features in the environment. Your voice must be clear and audible and interesting. What ever accent you have is immaterial, the important parameter is clarity. You should not need to shout, particularly to maintain discipline. The shout should be retained for very infrequent use or else it loses its impact. If you talk loudly, then you will be setting a noisy example for your class and they will tend to be noisy too. If you talk quietly, but clearly, then the children will be able to hear and will not need to make a noise themselves. Lowering the tone of your voice is a much better practice than raising the dB level. As a technique, it works for gaining attention and at the same time it preserves your voice.

Strictly speaking, our concern here is with the children, but as an aside, may I point out that your voice, being your source of employment and income, is a necessary resource. If you shout, particularly in the high registers, you will find that you put your vocal cords under a great deal of strain, and periodically you will lose your voice altogether. The only cure for aphonia (loss of voice) is complete silence. If you find that this applies to you, take stock. Are you abusing your voice and developing a teacher's screech? If so, do something about it now.

So, your voice must be clear, but make certain when you are speaking, that you position yourself so that your face can be clearly seen. The children need to lip read just that little bit, and to be able to read your facial expression. Nonverbal communications are very important in understanding messages. This means that there is a very simple rule. You must not talk to the class when you have your back to them. You should not write on the board and talk at the same time. Also, do not stand with your back to the window. In this position your outline will be visible but your face will be in shadow.

When you talk to the whole class, make sure that you arrange them and yourself in such a way that they can all see you. You need to be particularly vigilant about where the hearing impaired children are. When you are working with small groups, it is obviously easier to check that everyone has heard you, but again think about your position in the group. The children sitting beside you may have difficulty in seeing your face.

Teachers have to be sure that they have clear written and visual backup material for any information that is presented verbally. At the time of writing, not all educational television programmes automatically have subtitles, so if you are using TV material when you have hearing impaired children in your class, make sure that you have your own prepared material to support the programme as well as any published by the television company. If you are wearing a radio microphone, then place it near the television speaker.

You can control your voice. Controlling the architecture of the physical environment is less easy. However, given the incidence of transient, middle ear conductive hearing loss, it is a pity that more schools are not designed with greater attention paid to the acoustics and general noise levels. It is a worthwhile project simply to leave a tape recorder running in your classroom and see what gets recorded. You may be pleasantly surprised — but you also may get quite a shock. Classrooms should not be silent mausoleums, but the type of noise generated should be positive and creative and not such as to distract the children and prevent them from learning.

All chairs and tables should have rubber stops on their legs so that they cannot screech on the floor. General banging and dropping noises are likely to be distracting. They will always happen, but if the children are too cramped they will happen far too often.

What about the walls and ceiling? Are they hard and shining? No doubt great for cleaning, but hopeless for hearing. Hard, shiny surfaces mean that sound waves can bounce off them so an echo is created. You need pin board in order to display work effectively, but it serves a dual function of dampening down environmental echo. Sound insulating material can also be placed on the ceiling if necessary. Do beware of decorators bearing gifts though. One poor teacher I know had her lovely ceiling insulation painted with gloss paint over the summer holidays. Curtains at the windows, as well as enabling you to black out the room and cut out sun glare, also help in dampening down the noise and so they are much more useful than blinds and also less likely to go wrong. Carpet on at least part of the floor is essential for any primary school but incidentally provides another soft surface to aid hearing.

I appreciate that, if you are in an old classroom with high ceilings and big high windows, then this may seem all like an academic dream. All very well in theory but costly and impossible in practice. Firstly — no room is irredeemable and teachers are very resourceful at finding suitable equipment and adapting furniture for next to nothing. Secondly — if children are to learn efficiently then they have to have the best auditory environment possible. Adapting a classroom has to be made a priority and much lobbying may have to be done. Finally, in the case of any children who have hearing impairment, you have to be honest with the parents and tell them if you feel that the environment is too noisy for their children. I should point out that it is definitely not always old classrooms that present hearing problems. Many open plan, modern schools may not be suitable environments for children with major hearing loss. Murphy has recorded ambient noise levels in open plan classrooms and found that they were such that most of the time the teacher's voice was being masked out — a problem for all children, and one that architects would do well to heed.

We must also remember that children do not spend all their time in school in the classroom. The hall may present many hearing problems being so large and unlikely to have much soft furnishing. Even when the whole school are assembled, giving some chance of standing waves being absorbed, children may well have difficulty hearing and you should always check afterwards that important messages have been heard. Children wearing hearing aids may well decide to take them off for any activity lessons in the hall so, again, you have to make your instructions very clear and use body gesture and individual instruction as well as general class teaching.

Conclusion

Because so many of the skills and so much of the knowledge that we learn in school require that we can hear, teachers must take account of the auditory aspects of the classroom and the hearing capacities of their children to be effective teachers. We cannot assume that because we have said something it will have been heard, remembered and therefore learned. Children, auditory perception and memories do not work like that. Speech is transitory. You must always check and recheck because someone will always have missed something vital. Because speech is transitory you must help children to *listen* actively with attention and not just passively.

Further Reading

Besides the relevant chapter in Lindsay and Norman, you will find that Bamford and Saunders (1985): *Hearing Impairment: auditory perception and language disability* is a very detailed book and gives excellent coverage of all aspects of hearing. Webster (1986): *Deafness, development and literacy,* is a very readable book which places the whole issue of deafness in an educational context.

Chapter 5

Attention

Introduction

We must now turn to the cognitive process known as *attention*. The ideas implicit in such everyday phrases as 'Pay attention', 'Are you listening?', etc., are all subsumed under this concept. Our concern here is with the difference between *hearing* and *listening*, between being *vaguely aware* and *concentrating*. This is active processing of the input rather than passive reception. From your own experience you know that it is possible to sit on a bus and hear the babble of voices all around you and yet not to listen to a single cogent theme. Of course, by the same token, it is possible to sit alone on that same bus and to tune in to a really interesting conversation that is not meant for you. This ability to select out from the babble is of major significance.

As a teacher you will find, sometimes, that a glazed expression comes over a child's face and you know that nothing is going in. Even if you have never posed the question 'What have I just said?', you may well remember that awful sinking feeling when a teacher asked it of you. You know that you were miles away in another world only just vaguely aware of the voice. At times we all float off and stop *paying attention*.

The same effect happens in the visual modality as well. You can look out of a train window for miles and be unaware of the scenery. However, you can equally well concentrate on a particular visual input and study it intently. Just as we show a lack of attention, more importantly we have a capacity for *focused attention*. Being able to control and focus attention means that we can ignore irrelevant input and concentrate on the important aspects of the environment.

In terms of our sensory modalities, it is very difficult to stop sensory input. We can put our hands over our ears or choose to wear headphones, but generally speaking there is no way we can normally stop sounds from reaching the cochlea. We cannot stop the haptic sense, the sense of touch. If there is a food in our mouths we cannot avoid tasting it. The only sense over which we appear to have some conscious, voluntary control is sight. We can close our eyes at will. We can turn our head away and not look. Since we are therefore constantly being bombarded with sensations over which we have no control, it is very important that we learn to ignore most of the input and concentrate on the inputs which are important to us at the time. We need to be able to select our particular inputs and focus on them to the exclusion of the rest. If we were not able to do this then our behaviour would become totally random. We would simply react to everything and therefore be unable to learn anything. In education it is the details that are important. Children need to be able to focus on detail and not just gain vague general impressions.

People as Information Processing Systems

Implicit in all that we have been saying about motor behaviour and perception is the concept that people have *limited capacity*. This means that we cannot do everything at once. We have a finite amount of processing capacity available to us for performing tasks. This limited capacity means that we can only handle so much of the incoming information. We therefore have to learn to act rather than react. We process a little effectively rather than everything ineffectively. We are said to channel our attention. At the moment you are concentrating on reading this book so you have probably switched a large part of your processing capacity towards understanding the message. Some of that capacity will have to be devoted to the processing of the print itself, but because you are a skilled reader, the act of reading itself has probably become almost automatic. Because you are focused on the book, you are probably only vaguely aware of the noise of cars or of other people talking near you. Up to this point you could not feel your clothes itching or your shoes pinching and the chair was not noticeable. Now, having had your attention drawn to these things, focusing on the book becomes more difficult.

These little sensory inputs of everyday living are forever with us and we must be monitoring them all the time, but we have sufficient control over attention to concentrate on a chosen task and therefore not to be distracted. As I was originally writing the last few sentences an amazing wind blew up and my office has become suddenly very dark in the middle of the day. I do not have enough processing capacity to concentrate on writing and a storm at the same time, so I stopped writing and stared out of the window. My attention shifted away from writing as the primary task towards looking out of the window.

The fact that your author cannot write and worry about the weather at the same time is not a trivial point. We need to consider the question 'Are we able to do more than one thing at a time?' When we pose such a question we are not really considering real time. It was said of one American President that he could not walk and chew gum at the same time, but most of us can do just that.

However, in the microtime of the brain, though we appear to be doing a number of things we may be actually timesharing across tasks. When you ally this idea to the concept of our having limited capacity, you will see that this has important implications for teaching.

When you set children a task in a busy classroom situation it probably involves doing more than one thing at a time. Let us examine the example of a child writing an imaginative story. The subtasks within the task include

1 Producing the ideas.
2 Transforming these into acceptable language.
3 Producing the words: (a) doing the handwriting.
4 Producing the words: (b) generating the spellings.
5 Sitting at the table.
6 Ignoring teacher talking to the next child, etc., etc., etc.

Which task does the child see as the primary one? It is the ideas or the good story? Is it the linguistic style? Or maybe it is the handwriting or the spelling. Certainly at the start of the task, the act of creating may take up so much processing capacity that there is little left for anything else but seeming to stare into space. Once the ideas begin to flow then the focus may be getting them onto the paper, but there may be little capacity left for concentrating on spelling or handwriting. When the primary subtask is difficult the secondary tasks will be performed at less than their optimum. We discussed handwriting in Chapter 2 and you should be able to see how important it is that children become so skilled at handwriting that it does not interfere with the message of their writing.

You can check on your own limited capacity and the way you distribute it right now. Simply get up with the book and walk around the room. No problem. You can walk and read at the same time. Keep walking and now add together 192 and 47. You should have no difficulty with that. Keep walking but now try multiplying the two numbers together. That's 192×47. That is not so easy. Most people find that, if they concentrate on trying to get the right answer, they stop walking. It appears that the multiplication task takes so much processing that you have to direct the amount you normally use for monitoring walking into the mental arithmetic.

It rarely happens now, but just occasionally I see children standing at a teacher's desk holding a book and reading. For young infants coming to terms with reading, the task is so difficult that there is very little processing capacity left for standing upright. If they have to stand up and read, children tend to lean into the table or the teacher. It is just not fair. Children should sit down to read and have something on which to rest the book. This does not mean that children should never stand to read something in front of an audience. However, when they have to perform they will have practised the passage so often that the act of reading itself becomes secondary to the performance.

Focused Attention

Implicit in the idea of our being limited information processors is the concept of focused attention. In concentrating on the quality of the script for a caption to pin on a wall display, you may not notice until too late that you have written '*We went to the the zoo*'. Focusing attention means a deliberate act of turning our processing to a particular task and at the same time shutting out other interfering inputs. Without this facility we would react rather than take control of our actions. It is a vital facility in our ability to learn. This means like all human capacities that there are wide individual differences. In his biography on Rutherford, Wilson (1983) reports that this great scientist was able to concentrate on reading a book when, all around him, his school mates were having bunfights and creating pandemonium. The 'Young Fluent Readers' in Clark's (1976) research were characterized by having remarkable powers of concentration at an early age. Ball (1985) has also noted this with her readers who were taught to read by older siblings prior to school.

A Model of Attention

A diagram illustrating how people have conceptualized attention will be helpful at this point.

Figure 5.1   A Model of a Limited Attentional Processing System

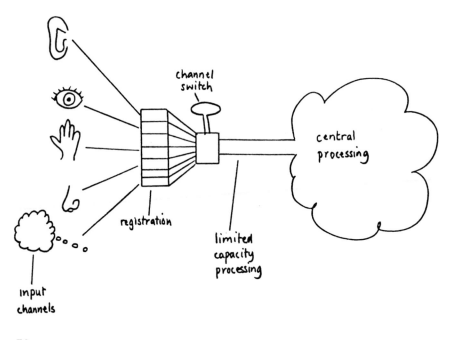

Information enters the system through the various sensory channels and is automatically registered. This is out of conscious control. It is a passive process. Once registered a particular channel can be selected for further processing. When this happens that channel will contain the attended message. The filter allows the attended message through and at the same time blocks the rest of the inputs. The switch enables the system to allow different channels to come into operation.

Selective Attention

To understand the implication of this we need to change the emphasis slightly. So far we have been considering examples of focused attention where information has been selected and the rest ignored, or where there has been a division of attention between information entering along different sensory channels — the position of walking and talking. However, when we turn to models of attention, much of the work has been based on looking at what happens when there is more than one message coming in along the *same* sensory channel. You can appreciate the problem. How do we select out that one interesting conversation from all the others on the top of the bus?

The questions are asked in pure research, but the answers have direct relevance to the classroom. Indeed the classroom can be seen as a natural laboratory where the subjects — the children — have to select out a particular message — your voice — from all the other competing messages.

Study of the processing of competing messages began with a classic description by Cherry (1956) of the 'Cocktail Party Effect'. In a very real sense, for 'Cocktail Party', we can read 'Primary Classroom'. Cherry was concerned to explain how people managed to select out and focus upon their chosen attended message, whilst filtering out the rest of the environmental noise, so that other conversations became a mere background of verbal babble. The experimental procedure used to study this was the dichotic listening task (Figure 5.2).

Figure 5.2   Dichotic Listening

I am shadowing this ear

I can't get much from this ear

I am shadowing this ear

Subjects would be wearing headphones and they would receive one message through the left ear and a different one through the right ear. Their task was to 'shadow' the message in the 'attended' ear. Shadowing means that subjects have to speak the attended message out aloud as they are receiving it. You could try to shadow a talk on the radio to get a feel of the task. The shadowing was to ensure that the subjects focused on the attended message. It does appear to be a task that requires full concentration. The question that the experimenters were interested in was how much of the *unattended* message could the subjects report. The answer initially appeared to be 'very little'. The features that could be reported on were things like whether there had been speechlike sounds and possibly the sex of the speaker. They could tell that something was being said, but they could not tell what it was. They could not even detect switches from English into French. This lead to an initial model of attention which allowed virtually nothing of the unattended message to get past the filter.

Let us test this view out in classroom terms. If this were really the case it might be logically impossible to call a class to order. They are all there on the mat after lunchtime play talking nineteen to the dozen. The teacher comes in and says 'Good afternoon, children.' If the conversations were utterly fascinating that strong filter model might predict that you would still be there at hometime.

Fortunately, children's conversations are not so absorbing, but also this model turns out to be significantly incorrect. Research was carried out into the various parameters of the unattended message that could be detected. Moray (1959) found that subjects were able to report if their own name had been spoken in the unattended ear. Messages that are highly significant to the person will be processed. Treisman (1964) suggested that the filter does not act as a total block on the unattended message, but serves to attenuate it instead. Salient messages will be processed because, even if attenuated, they will need a lower threshold of activation to be centrally processed. Added weight is given to this idea from an experiment by McKay (1973). He had subjects shadow ambiguous sentences in the attended ear whilst, concurrently, the unattended ear would contain a disambiguating word. For example, if the attended ear had a sentence containing the word 'bank', the unattended ear could either have 'river' or 'money'. Subjects who received 'river' in the unattended ear interpreted 'bank' as the edge of a river. Subjects who received 'money' interpreted it as the appropriate building. The subjects were not able to report on any of the words in the unattended ear, but there must have been some monitoring to enable the ambiguous words to be reliably disambiguated.

This weaker view of the filtering and selection stage of attention allows for a monitoring of unattended messages which can either result in their being rejected, or in their influencing the interpretation of the attended message, or in there being a switch of attention to a different channel.

This makes sense in classroom terms. Since your voice is highly salient to the children, you can gain their attention even when they are attending to other conversations. Those children who immediately attend are likely to turn towards you as well because we tend to orient our bodies towards the source of the message. This physical movement is likely to alert other children to your presence and order can be gained in a peaceful way. There will always be a few children who are so engrossed in their conversation that they carry on talking until they realize there is silence around them and become acutely embarrassed. Particularly with the younger age groups, it may be that they are not deliberately perverse in finding it difficult to come to instant attention. They may be quite genuinely at a more immature stage of attention control.

The Development of Attention Control

So far our discussion of attention has not considered the possibility of differences between children and adults. However, as you might expect, there is a development in the ability to focus and switch attention which has significant implications for teaching. Many teachers will report that they have genuine problems in dealing with some children who have extraordinary difficulty in concentrating. These anecdotes may be illuminating, but they need to be backed up by more objective observations. The ideas we shall draw on most heavily here were developed by Reynell (1977). Much of her work has been with children with special needs, indeed with severe handicapping conditions, but her work with non-handicapped children led her to develop a description of stages in the normal development of attention control. She describes six stages which roughly correspond to the first six years of life. It is the sequence which is of importance to us and not the ages in particular. There is much variability in normal development *between* individual children. There is also variability *within* any one child depending on a number of factors that we shall discuss later.

The six stages are described below. I have added behavioural titles to aid understanding.

Stage 1. Extreme Distractability

During the first year of life, babies are not able to control their own attentional direction. Focus is only momentarily held by the dominant stimulus in the environment and then quickly passes on to something else. If the environment is static and unchanging, the baby will quickly become bored and either sleep or cry.

In terms of our model of attention, you can see that at this early stage there appears to be no capacity to filter out stimuli and focus on a particular channel. The 'switch' seems to be continually flitting from one channel to the next and in a real sense the baby reacts to, rather than acts upon, the environment.

Stage 2. Inflexible Concentration

During their second year children show evidence that they can select out a particular incoming stimulus from the stream of experience and focus on it. When doing a task of their own choosing, albeit one provided by an adult, they will be able to concentrate on the activity for a length of time. This may be completing a simple inset puzzle or taking something apart and then reforming it. This may be repeated many times.

On the surface, this might appear to be quite sophisticated attention control since any interfering stimulus is cut out in order to concentrate on the task in hand. However, really what is happening is that, when the focus has been gained, it is so fragile that the children have to cut out all other information or else the concentration will be lost. At this stage, cooperation and sharing activities may be difficult. Attempts by an adult to interfere directly in the progress of the task may be found to be quite intolerable. Adult 'help' will lead to a switch in that precariously held, precious, focused attention. Reynell points out that children at this stage are unfortunately often described as 'wilful' and 'obstinate'. The perjorative overtones implicit in these terms suggest a misunderstanding of the nature of the situation. There is no wilfulness and obstinacy, but a desperate attempt by children to maintain fragile concentration in the face of fearful odds from competing environmental stimuli.

Stage 3. Single Channelled Attention

When children have reached this stage they will be able to focus on a chosen task or one provided by another person without much difficulty. Attention is still very much single channelled. This means that they need to cope with one input at a time, but the control is more reliable. Reliability leads to the children being able to afford to relax somewhat and allow a shift in focus from the task, because they can return to where they were at will. On the whole, at this stage, control of attentional focus is external and delegated to the adult. For example, where instructions are required to perform a task, the adult has to *set* attention. This means that, while the instructions are being given, the children have to *look* at and *listen to* the adult. Then *immediately* afterwards, the attention has to be transferred to the task. Sometimes it may be necessary physically to transfer attention in a gentle way. In playgroups and nurseries one can often see a child who has just been told what to do, simply sitting and staring at the teacher. At this age each child may need individual instructions.

Stage 4. Self Control

Children gradually develop the ability to control their attention set. It is almost as if they are self-consciously aware of the need to focus, so when instructions are given they stop what they are doing and look at the teacher or parent. They are still single channelled so that total attention focus is necessary to assimilate instructions. Single channelled attention also means that full attention has to be given to the task but, because at this stage there is sufficient control, they will begin to be able to cope with the competing attractions of a stimulating environment and should be able to work for a time on their own without finding the presence of other children disturbing.

Stage 5. School Readiness

In their fifth year, children begin to be able to show two-channelled attention. They can integrate directions whilst continuing to perform an activity. They no longer need to stop and look at the speaker. This means that behaviour can be modified *during* the task. They can cope with an instruction of the form 'When you have finished what you are doing, put your work away and then go and sit on the carpet.' A teacher can expect children at this stage to assimilate simple instructions and still continue the task in hand until it is finished. They will then know where to put the work and that they have to sit on the carpet. The instructions, when given in this fashion, have to be simple because of the memory factor.

Attention control is still only rudimentary and the children cannot be expected to continue on tasks for too long. Two-channelled attention means, though, that the children are ready to cope with an exciting infant classroom.

Stage 6. Mature Attention

This is the final stage described by Reynell. This is where integrated attention is well established and the children can control and focus their own attention. This will happen for longer and longer periods of time. This may be so, but we can never expect all children to concentrate on their tasks without the odd lapse whilst they talk to their neighbours or stare out of the window. Remember our original model. Though the switch will select the channel conveying the primary input, it will occasionally switch in to other competing messages. Attention control means self control here. The children should be able to recognize that attention has wandered and deliberately turn back to the task in hand.

Reynell's view, that mature attention control involves double channelled attention is important and fits in with the more sophisticated models of adult attention control. Allport *et al.* (1972) showed that the similarity between any two tasks was an important parameter when considering how much we could appear to be able to do. Adults would have no problem in shadowing and memorizing a series of pictures, but would find it very difficult to memorize words at the same time as shadowing. Children can continue to draw a picture and take in task instructions at Stage 6, but they would find it difficult to listen to something at the same time as reading to the teacher.

This description of the development of attention gives us important insights into the gradual induction of children into class teaching. When children begin school, teachers often find that parents make comments to them to the effect that their children were doing all the new classroom tasks two years ago at home. At first sight this may seem to be a perfectly valid comment. Many parents will have spent hours working with their pre-school child on the many books that include reading and maths activities of the type found in reception classes. Parents are quite rightly concerned about their children's progress.

Teachers must not dismiss these enquiries but explain the reason for this apparent duplication of activity. In attentional terms it may well be necessary for the children to do work which is cognitively a rehearsal of earlier experiences. Being in a classroom for a long time with thirty-five other children and only one adult puts great demands on the attentional capacity of any one child. A task which was easy to do whilst sitting at the kitchen table with one's own adult to help every time there is a problem, cannot be performed with the same level of efficiency in the classroom. At the beginning of the school career children need simple tasks which do not demand too much processing capacity so that there is sufficient 'spare' capacity left over to block out the distractions of the exciting arousing environment. One of the major tasks for the reception teacher is to provide a working environment where children can learn to concentrate whilst working alone, in small groups or within a class of thirty-five other children. It may be that to begin with, a reception class teacher will decide that the children have to be established into a routine where they can work independently before they begin to tackle more cognitively demanding work. You may feel the need to do some activities where the development of two-channelled attention control is the main purpose rather than learning some new curriculum material. Explaining this to parents takes tact and diplomacy, but is necessary.

Working on developing attention control — settling the children in — may save you and your colleagues much trouble later on. Although many children will have arrived in school having experienced playgroups or nursery schools, others may never have been in a group of more than six people in their short lives. These children may well experience quite strong culture shock spending every day in a classroom surrounded by thirty-six or more other people all the time.

For your own classroom control, when you are introducing something new and important, it is probably best to think that all children are at Stage 4 of development. Always make sure that they have stopped any other activity and focused their attention on you. Stop, look and listen applies to the classroom as much as to the roads.

Factors Within Children Affecting Attention

Even when all the children in your class have developed the capability to show mature attention control, their behaviour will not be up to maximum potential all the time. We have to consider the fluctuating state of the child which may well affect attention and therefore learning.

Arousal

Figure 5.3 is an idealized representation of the Yerkes–Dodson law. This states that, for any one person, there will be an optimal level of arousal for maximum performance of a particular task. The graph shows that, as the level of arousal rises, so the performance on the task improves up to a certain level. If arousal continues to increase after the optimal point, then performance on the task begins to show a decline. Arousal here means the level of cortical activity of the brain. When we are asleep there is relatively little arousal; sufficient, though, for us to be woken involuntarily by a loud noise or someone calling out our name. These stimuli may be enough to create sufficient arousal to get a rather bleary focused attention from the sleeper. You will be well aware that when you first awake you feel that your brain is not functioning at a level sufficiently high to answer deep philosophical questions. Gradually, as you continue to wake up, the cortex becomes toned up and cortical activity continues such that you begin to operate efficiently. Simple tasks like making toast and getting washed do not require very high levels of arousal to be performed efficiently.

Stimulation for raising the level of cortical arousal comes from the environment, but also from within because of interest in the task, thoughts, anxiety, etc. Arousal will fluctuate during the day and so performance on tasks will also fluctuate. If arousal is too low or too high then performance will be reduced.

Let us put this into more concrete terms and relate it more closely to attention. If children are tired then arousal level will be low. This means that their work and learning will be less than they are capable of. When they are tired they are unable to focus attention or concentrate on their tasks. On the other hand, if they get really excited, then arousal may go way over the top, but again there will be an inability to focus attention. Either way the work will have deteriorated but the predisposing reasons will be different.

Figure 5.3   An idealized inverted U curve showing the relationship between behavioural efficiency and arousal.

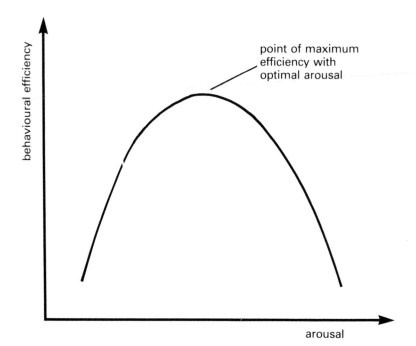

This analysis of behaviour provided by the Yerkes–Dodson function enables us to understand the problems of introducing young children to group and classroom settings. It is the case that people are, in themselves, stimulating and arousing to other people. The more people in a group, the more arousing the situation. Thus, for a young child to enter into a busy classroom is of itself arousing. Reception class teachers will tell you that some children will enter the class and rush around getting very excited, whilst others will appear to be very quiet and almost paralyzed by the experience. These are both examples of different individual responses to overarousal. Experiences in pre-school groups and preparatory visits to the school itself will all help to make the classroom familiar and therefore less arousing. Because being in a class with thirty-five others is so arousing, it is not surprising that, to begin with, some children will have difficulty in focusing attention. This underlines the argument for beginning with simple tasks.

As children progress through the school, they will begin to take classroom situations very much for granted, but any change in the environment will produce heightened arousal with the consequent minor disruption of behaviour in the class. School trips broaden children's horizons and extend their experiences, but they also serve the dual function of enabling the children to handle changes in everyday living. You may have to cope with a child who either goes wild or who is terrified on a school visit. Both behaviours are signs of overarousal and the child has to be helped to calm down. Using the model of attention, we can say that the level of arousal needs to be reduced so that the child can behave efficiently.

Children who are experiencing difficulty with the level of work in the classroom may begin to show signs of anxiety. Anxiety is associated with increased levels of arousal and so these children will be unable to perform at their optimum. Ideally, we should aim for presenting children with work which is challenging but possible. In this way they will be stimulated to learn but not overwhelmed. A child who has become so anxious that learning is interfered with needs some time to consolidate by doing easier work to regain confidence.

A parallel analysis can relate to the situation where children are continually presented with material which is too simple. There will be no positive tension in the learning environment and attention will constantly wander.

Underarousal does have a negative effect on attention. When we are tired, our arousal is low and our performance is below par. In particular it becomes very difficult to focus attention. You will be very aware that when you are tired and you are trying to force yourself to finish a passage in a book you are reading, your attention begins to wander and you cannot concentrate. Under these circumstances you could decide to do a number of things. You could decide to go to sleep and read the book when you had overcome the tiredness, or you could decide that a change of air and scenery might provide the necessary stimulus to increase arousal so that you could return to the book. You could even decide to have a cup of coffee which contains caffeine, a stimulant which will artificially increase arousal.

We cannot contemplate doling out cups of coffee to young children, but we can recognize that the act of concentrating on a task is by its very nature tiring for them so we must make sure that the task never goes on for too long. This is why you have to plan the working day with a series of changing activities. The simple change from one activity to another means that you introduce novelty and thus increase arousal and enable the children to focus attention on the new task.

One form of tiredness that is perhaps out of your control is when a child comes to school in the morning without having had enough sleep. The tiredness will mean that the child will be unable to focus attention and therefore will miss much of the message of the lessons with a consequent poor performance. Besides the affects on learning, tiredness often makes children show a fair degree of fractiousness which hampers their social relationships with other children. All this can be understood in terms of arousal and its affect on attention.

When we are at our optimum level of arousal we generally experience a feeling of wellbeing. As we get tired our cortical arousal drops. If we have had a hard day's work then we feel we have earned that tiredness and appreciate going to sleep. Children have a tendency to think that going to bed is something to be avoided at all costs. They do not appreciate the joys of sleep. As they get tired and their arousal level drops they will often show an increase in non-directed physical activity which will serve to increase their arousal level to fend off sleep. Children, who come to school not having had enough sleep, may well show this type of non-directed physical activity. This may help them to stay awake, but it does not help them to focus attention. They may be doing lots of movement, but they will not be concentrating on the task in hand. This will be of no use to them and will have a disruptive effect on the class in general. Of course, the tired child may also sit blankly staring into space, unable to focus and therefore unable to take in any information. Teachers are not in a position to give directives about bedtimes and in any case different children need different amounts of sleep; but when a child is clearly failing to reach potential because of tiredness, a quiet word with the parents may be appropriate.

Motivation

The relationship between arousal and attention can be recognized in other areas. We can use these concepts in our understanding of another internal factor, that of *motivation* or interest. It seems positively trite to say that if children are interested in a task they will work at it without the need for adult inducements. However, it is an important truism and one which is sometimes forgotten in teaching. Some of the books in reading schemes for young readers are devastating in their boredom. It is sometimes forgotten that children should be driven by the story line to turn the page and not by the inducement of ticking off yet another book in the scheme. Berlyne (1960) suggested that curiosity is a basic human motive. Day and Berlyne (1971) maintain that there are various kinds of curiosity and exploration. Curiosity may simply be at the level of perceptual curiosity, where attention is held by the novelty of the perceptual features of the input. However, there are deeper levels. There is *epistemic curiosity* which is stimulated by conceptual incongruity or ambiguity. This means that the children are driven to find out because they do not fully understand. To satisfy this curiosity, they indulge in what Berlyne and Day call *epistemic exploration*. This may take various forms of behaviour such as observation, consultation or problem solving. This curiosity will lead to focused attention on a self generated task. In these circumstances there will be no need for rewards or praise from outside, since the discovery is of itself its own reward. Children, when driven by curiosity, may concentrate for remarkably long periods of time.

This would lead us to suggest that good teaching means presenting material in such a way that the children become driven by curiosity to learn. This makes the task very hard because teachers have to adapt material to suit their particular group of children. Preparation takes up much effort in trying to match the material to the individual children.

We do not live in a perfect world and some of the time you may find that you cannot generate enough *intrinsic* motivation; i.e. motivation that is self generated. When this happens you have to use *extrinsic* motivation. This means that you have to use a system of rewards that are not of themselves part of the task. Some classes may formalize this into a star system, other classes may use extrinsic reward in a less formal way. Marking children's work and giving praise is a form of extrinsic reward. Children need to know that their work has been read and valued. If work is returned without comment children very soon begin to feel that there is no point in bothering. They must have some positive messages though, even when the work is of limited standard.

Comfort

Comfort may seem a strange term to use in a psychology book. What I mean, in this context, is the physical state of the children. If children are uncomfortable then they will find it difficult to focus attention on the task. So much processing capacity may be taken up with being aware of the state of the body that there is little left over for learning.

If the ambient temperature of the classroom is too high then the children will become drowsy. On the other hand if the room is too cold then they will not be able to work. They have to sit on their chairs for a considerable length of time so they need to sit in reasonable comfort. Stools, for example, are inappropriate because they will not be able to sit in comfort.

If children are hungry then they will experience discomfort. When the blood sugar level is low, attention will begin to wander. Many schools have a deliberate policy of allowing a playtime snack to tide the children over from breakfast until lunchtime.

Environmental Variables and Attention

There are variables within environmental stimuli which make them more or less likely to be 'attention grabbing'. What does this mean? Referring back to the model in Figure 5.2, you will remember that there is a switch which can select which incoming channel should be the one to transmit the primary message to the central processing system. There seem to be stimulus variables which are more important in gaining the 'attention' of the switch. We will consider these stimulus properties in more detail because, as they are external to the child, they are directly within your means of manipulation.

Novelty

As you will have deduced from what we said about new environments and curiosity, a novel stimulus is very attention grabbing. An environment which is forever the same becomes unnoticed. Within a known environment, the *new* will become the focus of attention and be processed. This means that you can capitalize on novelty to present material that you want the class to comprehend. You can also use novelty in both classroom arrangement and visual display. However, a word of caution: you would not want novelty to be the major factor in your technique. A constantly changing environment is not suitable for a classroom. Children need to be able to predict where things will be so that they can become independent within the classroom. It is the judicious use of novelty which is effective. You may decide that a different classroom lay-out will suit your present joint needs, but you need to work out the changes rationally and carefully. You have to be cautious about attributing any increased performance to the new arrangements. The 'Hawthorne' experience (Roethlisberger and Dickson, 1939) shows us that it may be the *change per se*. The Hawthorne effect showed increase in production by the workers was due to the *change* in the work practices and not the *new* work practices themselves, since, when they went back to the original pattern at the end of the experiment, production increased again on the *change* back. This neatly illustrates that novelty has an important effect on attention.

Contrast

When you want something to be noticed visually or auditorily then contrast is a useful property to use. This means that children's work should be mounted on contrasting paper so that it stands out and also looks more professional. A good border focuses the eye on the picture or writing and at the same time seems to enhance the appearance of the work. This means that wall displays will encourage pride in work. The purpose of using children's work for wall displays should not be simply to cover as much of the space as possible. Children need to feel that their work is of intrinsic worth and displaying their work helps them in this. They will feel that their work is of much greater value if it has been carefully mounted rather than just stuck up higgledy-piggledy with drawing pins. Obviously this takes much more time and effort but it is part of the total educational experience of the children. Children should learn to mount and present their own work for display, but they need good models.

In Chapter 3 we mentioned the need to think about the colour of writing on teaching surfaces. White and yellow chalk shows up much more clearly on a black or green board and blue and green are good on white boards and OHPs. It is the contrast that makes them stand out. But, as we said, the surfaces do need to be cleaned properly before you begin to use them.

Contrast in the auditory modality relates back to our discussion of your voice in Chapter 4. A sudden change in pitch or dB can be a very effective means of gaining attention from the class. You need to modulate your voice. Monotones send people to sleep.

Colour

Colour really is another dimension of contrast and novelty. Today we are blessed with a wonderful variety of brightly coloured felt pens and fluorescent markers. Judicious use of colour and highlighting can make learning easier and help children to make sense of a very large wall display.

You have to make your own decisions about marking work. Some people stick to the old red pen in the belief that it stands out and draws the children's attention to the mistakes. Other teachers feel that marking in a more subtle colour, particularly when there are many problems, is less likely to alienate the child.

Intensity

Finally we have the property of intensity. If all the colours on your wall display were numerous but pastel shades, they would not stand out. They would not grab the attention. Brightness in colour is a necessary attribute if the stimulus is to be noticed. The same is true of the sound stimulus.

We have to remember to temper theory with common sense. You do not need to make use of all the stimulus elements at once. The children have to be able to concentrate in the classroom!

Organizing the Classroom

An understanding of the theoretical implications of children's attentional capacities and the stimulus properties which relate to attention in general could, alone, help us to a more meaningful and useful interpretation of any classroom scene that we might observe. This in itself is probably important in enabling us to be sensitive to the children in our care. However, this highly abstract, academic area of psychology can be just as useful when turned to the very practical aspect of organizing a classroom. The theory enables us to take a rational approach to the physical as well as the cognitive features of the classroom.

A word of caution here. We have to remember that the classroom is not an antiseptic laboratory. It is possible to take theory too far and to forget that we are dealing with real children. What might be indicated from one theoretical perspective may not integrate with a different one and in any case it may not work in human terms. In the final analysis, you have to weigh up the evidence and end up with a system that you find is effective and for which you can supply objective evidence in support of your chosen organization.

Comfort

Let us return to the comfort level of the classroom — heating, ventilation, lighting, and furniture.

Most schools have some form of central heating these days; even when teachers are in temporary huts there are wall heaters. Radiators would seem to be the most sensible and safe means of heating a school. However, there does seem to have been a trend towards installing fan assisted hot air systems. This may make sense for a heating engineer, but such systems are not good from a teaching point of view. The heaters can be extremely noisy, sending out a continuous low frequency hum and then periodic bouts of greater rattles from the fan. This noise just adds to the general level of noises that can distract children and may make the teacher's voice that much harder to detect. If you are in a school with this type of heating you have to think very carefully about where you position the children in winter. Any child with a hearing problem should not be near the heaters at all. In fact the children should not be near the fans because (a) that makes them less efficient and (b) those children will be periodically cooked as well as finding your voice difficult to detect.

Allied to the heating aspect of a classroom is ventilation. Children need to be warm enough for comfort, but the rooms need to be sufficiently well aired so that they do not become drowsy. Good positioning of the windows with easy sliding modern sash windows are ideal. Far too often the opening of the windows becomes such a difficult task that they remain shut.

Windows do not just need to be easy to open and close, but they serve to give light to the room. This means that they may also give glare from the sun. You have to position the blackboard or white board in relation to the windows so that the children can read what is on the board. If the room is well endowed with windows then you may have to make certain that there are workable blinds or curtains because of sun glare, both in the summer and from the sun being low in the sky on sunny winter afternoons.

As we mentioned in Chapter 3, lighting is very important, but the efficiency of the lighting system will probably only have an insidious effect on attention. We do seem to put up with inadequate lighting both in our homes and in our workplaces, but let us consider the effects of poor lighting from an attentional perspective. Poor lighting makes it harder to read and to see what we are writing. This means that there is less capacity left over for understanding the message. It is an unnecessary irritation to have to work in an ill-lit room. Alas, the most usual form of electric lighting in schools is harsh fluorescent strip tubes. They have the advantage of only needing to be changed very occasionally but they have a number of drawbacks. They have a tendency to buzz, flicker or sometimes make quite a loud 'pinking' noise. When this happens the answer is not just to turn the light out, but to correct the fault.

You should be wary of the effect of fading light on a winter's afternoon. It is quite easy not to notice that the light has faded to the point where you are all working in the semi-gloom. Classrooms should have sufficient natural lighting for normal days, but it is always up to you to decide when to augment this. Sometimes a room can appear very gloomy even on the brightest of days and it is worth taking a critical look to find out why. It may be an original design fault about which you can do nothing other than use the lights. Sometimes trees and shrubs have grown so tall that they cut out the light so you need to have them pruned. Sometimes the positioning of cupboards, bookcases and shelving to provide interesting spaces in the room results in whole areas being cut off from natural light. You need to take a critical look at the room from a lighting point of view when deciding about organization.

The final property to consider under comfort relates to Chapter 2. We mentioned that for good handwriting you have to have the correct sized tables and chairs. If children do not fit the furniture they will wriggle and find it difficult to concentrate. You can't make the children fit the furniture. Firstly, the table and chair sizes have to match otherwise the children may not be able to get their knees under the tables or else they may be stretching to reach the surface. Then you have to make certain that the furniture is of the correct height for the children. There are standard sizes in nursery, infant, junior and secondary furniture but since we know there is such wide variation in children, they do not always fit the stock sizes. It is very difficult for junior children who have simply outgrown the tables and chairs to produce good work when they are always writing sitting sideways because they cannot get their knees under the tables.

Noise Level

When you relate attention to auditory perception you can see how vital it is to consider the sound environment of a classroom and school in general. If the children are to be able to select out your voice from all the secondary environmental noise, that noise must be kept to a minimum. If there is too much noise for your voice to be selected out then the children will pay attention to something else. If the general noise level is high, then it will be difficult for the children to concentrate on the task in hand whatever it is. When children first enter school with as yet immature attentional control, the need to keep environmental noises down to a gentle hum becomes quite important.

Unfortunately, the trend towards open plan school designs does not help noise control. With the best will in the world, one class doing a legitimately noisy task may interfere with another having a quiet reading session. Secondary schools, universities and colleges are not built with open plan designs, yet the pupils and students who have to work in them have much better attention control than primary children.

Teachers are not insensitive to the noise problems associated with open plan systems and often restructure their rooms to create areas where children can work with less distraction from others. Where one finds that an open plan system is working quietly with a minimum of distraction it is often the case that the numbers in the school are below the maximum.

Tables, Desks and Movement

In a busy, involved primary classroom, children will be moving around for a good deal of the time. Your classroom plan needs to be worked out taking account of the likelihood of 'traffic flow'. It would be wonderful to have a high speed camera to video the movement with various possible layouts so that you could decide on the most efficient system! Obviously there are certain fixed fittings like doors, windows and possibly sinks and electric points around which you have to develop your design. It would probably be a silly move to position your class library next to a busy thoroughfare or a sink. If you find you have a number of children who seem to have difficulty in concentrating, before assuming it is a 'within child' factor, it is worthwhile studying the classroom layout to see if the children are being distracted by the legitimate movements of other people. It may be that by repositioning the table you enable them all to work more successfully. Think carefully about where you reposition a child who is showing attentional problems. A seat near the teacher may seem a good idea because you can keep a careful watch, but the teacher's desk is a area of much movement and a position near it may make concentration even more difficult.

Positioning the desks and the children within a classroom is, to a great extent, within your control, so it is worth spending some time thinking about the children, your own teaching styles and what you want to accomplish together that year. In this way you can decide on an arrangement which is comfortable and efficient, where every child can see your face when you talk to the whole class and where children can write and work without disturbing each other. There can be no set format which is correct for every class and teacher so everyone has to work out their own organization.

If one of your major concerns is that children should spend time on tasks when they are sitting at their tables, then a study by Wheldall *et al.* (1981) may prove useful evidence for you.

Their brief was to investigate whether children showed more efficient work patterns if they were sitting in a classroom with one of two different desk arrangements. The desks were either arranged in rows or grouped together in tables. The measure they took was time on task — i.e. the amount of time the children actually spent doing the task set by the teacher. Their results suggest that work output was significantly higher when the children were sitting in rows. This makes sense from an attentional viewpoint. If the children are sitting in rows they have less chance of eye contact with each other so incidental conversations are less likely to arise. Such an arrangement means that no child has to turn round in the chair in order to see the teacher's face when the class is being taught as a whole group.

This 'rows v. tables' research does not necessarily mean that an arrangement of rows will be effective for every class and every teacher. The extensive work resulting from the ORACLE study is essential reading here for primary teachers. Galton *et al.* (1980) found that, of the various teaching styles that they were able to identify, the most successful were what they called the 'infrequent changers' and the 'class enquirers'. The class enquirers were the most successful in the maths curriculum area, whereas the infrequent changer style was associated with the greatest progress in reading. Though the 'rows v. tables' research, together with a class enquiring style, would suggest that the more traditional classroom is the most efficient from an attentional perspective, it is possible to be an effective class enquirer without having the children always sitting in rows.

In the perfect world each classroom would have a big carpeted area, another area for small group work and a desk for every child to work at individually.

Conclusion

I am very conscious that we do not live in a perfect world. Teachers do not have a free hand with the design of their schools or an infinite purse for buying the best and latest in classroom equipment. This does not mean that we should not start from a position of what we would ideally like to do and then modify it in the light of what is possible. Applying attention theory to the classroom can help to make the organization a little more efficient and provide a good learning environment for the children. One day you may get the chance to cooperate with an architect in designing your own new school.

Further Reading

Lindsay and Norman will again provide you with very useful material for understanding attention, but so too will a general psychology book, Lloyd, Mayes *et al.* (1984) called *Introduction to Psychology: An Integrated Approach*. Cooper, Moodley and Reynell (1977) *Helping Language Development* is the book which sets out Reynell's views on the development of attention. It also provides interesting material for considering language handicap.

Chapter 6

Memory

Introduction

In a very real sense we are our memories. We are able to contemplate our past life in solitude and also share common events with other people. Once the minute has gone, though, it can never return; it only lives on in our memories. Because we are our memories, we tend to take this cognitive ability very much for granted. Occasionally we recognize that we have problem areas and we joke about these or try to develop strategies to combat the problem. We accept myths about memory which include suggestions that children have amazing memories and that all old people forget what they had for lunch.

You will be well aware that remembering thirty-six names of children instantly can place a real strain on your own memory capacity. However you have to learn all the new names quickly at the beginning of each year because children do not like to think that their name has been forgotten. I don't know why every class of children doesn't wear labels for the first week at school. The labels lead to painless incidental learning and save any embarrassment, but in many schools it's only the tiny ones who sport name tags.

In this chapter I am going to explore the way in which children's memory develops. A knowledge of this is essential for teachers because, if children cannot remember, then they can show no evidence of having learned anything. In order to understand the development of memory in children we will first have to cover some of the material which relates to memory in general. You will appreciate that this is a massive topic so I will pick out the areas which I consider directly relate to teaching.

A Model of Human Memory

Before we consider the model, I want you to do a little memory work. Over on page 94 — **DON'T LOOK YET** — is a list of words for you to remember. To do the task properly you need a blank sheet of paper to cover up the words and a sheaf of other paper for writing down the words. When you turn over, you are to cover up the words quickly and then move the paper down so that the words are exposed one at a time. Give yourself about a second for each word and then move the paper down to expose the next word. When you get to word 28, you are at the end of the list. Close the book and try to write down as many of the words as you can in whatever order you like. When you have done that check how many you got right and then spend about four minutes studying the list before trying to write down all the items on a fresh piece of paper. Keep these two 'response sheets' with the book because you will need to refer to them later on.

As they used to say for the old 11 plus — you may turn over the page now!

Figure 6.1 is a classic representation of the structure of human memory. Remember it is a model. We do not have black boxes and clouds in our heads. Information is conceptualized as entering on the left hand side and then being processed and transformed until it becomes permanently stored on the right hand side.

Let us follow the fate of some information from the time it enters the system, through its storage until the time when it may be recalled.

Figure 6.1   A Model of Memory.

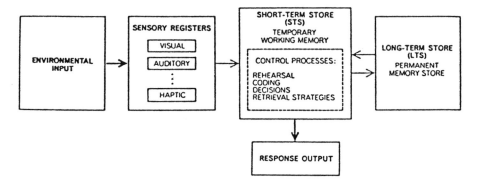

Source: Atkinson and Shiffrin (1971): *The Control of short-term memory.*

Sensory Memory

As we said in Chapter 3, information enters into our cognitive processing system via the various sensory channels. This is the same whether we are considering the aspect of cognition we choose to call perception or the aspect we call learning and memory. You have just been presented with a list of to-be-remembered words which entered your system via the visual channel. From Figure 6.1 you can see that information is initially registered in the visual sensory register. This is named the *iconic* memory. If you had been asked to read the words out aloud for another person to remember, then they would have been initially registered in the auditory sensory register — the *echoic* memory. If you were a blind person reading this in braille then the words would be initially registered in a haptic store. The point is that all information entering the system has to be registered initially and it appears that the sensory registers are modality specific.

We need to understand the parameters of these registers. Information appears to be registered in a literal manner — i.e., no coding takes place. The input is noted but the duration of the trace in this store is very short. The stimulus is subject to rapid decay.

Think about what happened when you read the list. You fixated your eye on the first word. Then you moved the paper down and fixated on the next word. If the image of the word in the iconic store perseverated then it would be as if one word was printed over the next. It would quickly be impossible to work out what you were seeing. Information would interfere. It seems to be the case that by the time you have moved your eyes to take in the next word, the iconic image has decayed in the iconic store so there is no interference when the next image is registered.

The same is true in the auditory modality. The information is registered literally and then the trace decays. If the sound was maintained in the echoic store then one could imagine that there really would be an interfering echo.

There is evidence that some children have a facility for what is called *eidetic imagery* (Haber 1969). They seem to be able to maintain a literal image of visual input for some considerable time — minutes even. This means that they can look at an incomplete visual stimulus on one page, turn over to see the rest of the stimulus — and unite the two to perceive the whole picture. As a facility it seems to be of little use and it does seem to be something which declines throughout childhood. I have never come across such a person, but wouldn't it be fascinating to follow the reading development of such a child. One could speculate about the interference effects that such a capacity would have on the development of fluent reading.

Primary Memory

Let us now follow the words as they begin to be processed in the Primary Memory System. This system has rather different parameters from the sensory registers. It seems to have a limited capacity. Experimental evidence suggests that its capacity is about 3/4 items (Baddeley and Patterson 1971). Look at your first recall list. I presume that you were able to remember more than four items. At least I hope you could. The model suggests that the Primary Store is able to hold about four items and then there is the active rehearsal loop where items are recycled to

LIST OF WORDS TO REMEMBER

1. desk
2. van
3. onion
4. pig
5. red
6. bling
7. fear
8. cat
9. parsnip
10. yellow
11. twent
12. chair
13. carrot
14. lorry
15. shock
16. car
17. dog
18. melops
19. awe
20. stool
21. green
22. table
23. derous
24. bus
25. turnip
26. horror
27. blue
28. rat

Remember to keep those two sheets. I should point out that what you have done is in no way a controlled experiment, but the insights you will have gained by doing the task may help to make the discussion about memory more meaningful to you.

---

maintain them in primary memory. This means that your immediate memory span is about seven items long. Now, I suspect that you probably managed to write down more than seven of the words in our list, but that was because the task was not very controlled. If you read out a list of seven numbers to some unsuspecting person they will probably be able to repeat them back to you in order. However, once the list gets longer the task begins to get more difficult and order information or some of the items get lost. Such a task occurs in most standardized, individual intelligence tests. The number of items in immediate recall is sometimes called the digit span. This magic number seven has been observed for a long time as being about the limit of immediate recall (Miller 1956). It is not surprising therefore that telephone numbers and car registration numbers are seven items. If they were any longer we could not expect that everyone could be given a telephone number once by directory enquiries and then be able to write it down correctly. We live in a society where numbers — personal identification numbers (PIN) are becoming all pervasive. Just watch next time a sales assistant has to write down the number on your bank card. My old one used to be only six numbers long and there was no trouble at all. Even I could remember it. My new style one is sixteen digits long and I haven't a clue what it is. The items have been arranged into four groups of four but even so shop assistants do seem to check and double check because they are obviously aware that they cannot remember the whole thing in one go.

The important point about this is that our immediate memory is limited. I have suggested that this limit is about seven items, but you may question what an *item* is. The suggestion is that we can recall about seven chunks of information. Individual digits are single chunks and, since they have no further meaning, presenting strings of numbers to children would seem a reasonably controlled way of assessing immediate memory capacity. However, it is not always the case that numbers have no meaning. If you were presented with the following list you could probably remember a lot more than seven digits:

$$106619452001$$

You could probably chunk the twelve digits into three pieces of information and immediately find the task completely unexacting. Children who had great experience in dealing with binary digits would no doubt have no difficulty in the immediate recall of:-

$$1001 \quad 111 \quad 11011 \quad 10100$$

because they would code it instantly as:-

$$9 \quad 7 \quad 27 \quad 20$$

In our information processing terms, the more we can reduce the difficulty of the task then the easier it is to remember the material because there is less strain on the system.

Another important parameter of the primary memory system relates to the rehearsal loop in Figure 6.1. New material presented for immediate recall is very labile and the only way we seem to be able to retain it is by actively rehearsing it; i.e. by seeming to say it over and over again to ourselves. Just think back to our list of words and the first reading and recall. Did you find that you were saying them over and over again to yourself? Of course if you are reading the book in a library, this rehearsal would probably be covert, although your lips may have moved in your effort to fix the list in memory.

Rehearsal seems to be the means by which material is maintained in this system and it does not seem to matter which is the modality of presentation. You received the words via the visual modality yet you transformed them into a phonological code.

Now look at that first recall paper again. You presented yourself with a serial list of twenty-eight items. In what order did you write them down? Many people reading this book will have written down something like:

turnip
horror
blue
rat
desk
van
onion . . . and then a few other items.

Did your first attempt look a bit like this?

When you presented yourself with the list you were able to rehearse the first few items: *desk desk desk van van desk van desk van onion van onion desk van onion pig pig red BLING! bling fear;* but then as the memory load got too great you had to ditch many of the middle items and could not spend as much time rehearsing them. Finally you came to the last items and closed the book. Since you had to write as many as you could immediately, the likelihood is that you off-loaded the last ones first, because they were in the primary store and then you went to the first ones, because they would have had more rehearsal and so would be more 'permanent'.

If you did show this type of recall then you have nicely demonstrated the serial position effect illustrated in Figure 6.2. The last items in a list demonstrate the *recency effect* and the first items demonstrate the *primacy effect*.

If you had been asked to recall the list in order of presentation then you would still have shown the primacy effect, but the recency effect would have been wiped out (the dotted line in Figure 6.2). Baddeley and Patterson (1971) suggest that the recency effect is evidence of the capacity of the primary memory system. Also this wiping out of the recency effect when the subject is asked to do a serial recall demonstrates that items in the primary memory system are very labile and can only be maintained by active rehearsal. The act of recalling the list prevents the last items being rehearsed so the memory trace is lost.

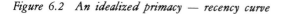

Figure 6.2 An idealized primacy — recency curve

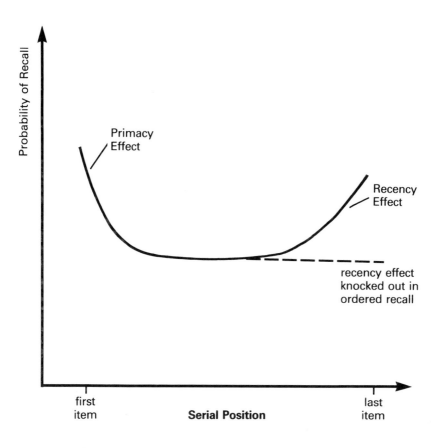

Secondary Memory

Try writing down the items on our list now without looking back. I am sure that you could remember some. We will use that third recall list later on.

Even if you could not remember any items on the list, I would suggest that you have no problem in remembering that you did do some work on remembering a list of words; i.e., you remember the event of remembering even if you cannot recall a single item that you tried to remember.

Memory for Events

Event memory seems to be a very potent human characteristic. We are able to remember episodes that happened to us throughout our lives without even having to bother consciously to remember them.

Brown and Kulik (1977) demonstrated the power of event memory when they asked Americans 'Do you recall the circumstances in which you first heard that John F Kennedy had been shot?'. People seemed to be able to recall with absolute clarity precisely what they were doing, yet clearly they had not deliberately tried to remember the event. Alas, it's a sign of age, but most of my students were not even born then so I cannot try the question out on them. The point about such flashbulb memories is that whole episodes can be recorded seemingly effortlessly. *Being* in the event is enough for it to be recorded. However, I think we should also point out that we do not seem able to recall at will the totality of our lives. We remember the broad canvas and not the individual brush strokes. Of course it may simply be that we do not choose to search for the event. You can actually surprise yourself with how much you can recall. Where was the light switch in your bedroom in the home before your present one? Where was the lock on the front door? How many windows were there?

What do you do with such questions? Many people report that they visualize themselves entering the bedroom, or walking up the path fumbling for the key or walking round the house looking out of the windows. They act out the reconstruction in their heads. Of course, short of going back to check, there is no way you can be objectively sure about the validity of your memory. This is always going to be a problem with reminiscence — thus the song from '*Gigi*' — '*Ah, yes, I remember it well*'.

This type of observation fits in with our intuitive feelings about event memory. We may remember going to school and even some teachers and some of the information that we learned, but we will be able to access very little of the minute by minute happenings. We remember the overall meaning and not the specifics.

Factual Memory

Much of the work of the primary school teacher is involved in developing skills and cognitive understanding of the world. The nature of primary education means that the children are not required to remember a lot of unrelated facts, which is fortunate because memory for facts seems to be more problematic than memory of events.

In learning facts we have to make a conscious effort to remember information. Part of this involves repeated encounters with the material. You must remember the many hours you have spent in revision for exams. You have to read and re-read the material and test yourself for recall and practise writing out the facts, etc., until you feel confident that the material is firmly fixed in your long-term store and can be accessed at will.

One thing is sure, you did not leave the material unstructured, but attempted to structure it and categorize it until it was in a form which was understandable.

We have strong evidence that material that is categorized is easier to recall than uncategorized material (Mandler 1967). Find those second and third recall sheets. I imagine that you noticed that the words fell into seven categories — vehicles, vegetables, furniture, animals, colours, words about states of mind, nonsense words. Did you recall the words under categorical headings after your second study period and after the unexpected recall? Bousfield (1953) showed that recall of randomly presented lists of sixty words was greatly enhanced when the sixty words were made up of fifteen from each of four categories. Using categories as an organizational aid helps the initial storage of material and utilizing similar cues facilitates subsequent recall.

Where the memory task seems to stand on its own without reference to any understanding we often have to resort to the use of mnemonics to fix the material. An example of this is the positions of the notes on the treble and bass clef. We teach children to expand the letters into meaningful sentences:

Good Boys Deserve Football Always
All Cows Eat Grass
Eat Good Bread Dear Father

— but what do we do about the notes in the spaces of the treble clef? They make a word: **FACE**.

No doubt you learned the order of the colours of the rainbow in the same way:

Richard Of York Gave Battle In Vain

Fortunately, most of our teaching does not require that children should have to resort to memorizing in a vacuum. Nevertheless, mnemonic aids can be useful. What they seem to do is reduce the material to manageable proportions with each little part acting as the cue for much greater amounts of material.

Representing verbal material in visual form can be an aid to memory. Paivio (1971), a Canadian psychologist, suggests that material that can be coded visually is easier to code and easier to recall. This relates both to pictorial stimuli and to words which are high in imageability. There may however be questions about whether the images themselves are stored or whether, by working at developing an image to remember, you have to work that much harder at storage.

This question of the type of processing that you need to do to be able to store the material was addressed by Craik and Lockhart (1972). They suggested that if material was subjected to a deep level of processing it would be more likely to be subsequently recalled. This was the case even when the material had not been consciously committed to memory. For example, subjects would perform better on an incidental recall task if they were asked to make judgments about the meaning of sentences than if they were asked to cancel letters in the sentences. By depth of process they were implying that processing material for meaning was a deep level process. This idea fits in with what we were saying about understanding material. Learning by rote does not allow for any elaboration of the coding so the material does not become part of a wider, complex network of integrated memories.

Working Memory

So far, then, we have considered the model of human memory as presented in Figure 6.1. The story as presented so far seems to assume that we are storing new material or recalling stored items and events. However, if we stop and think for a minute, that is not a true picture of what actually happens either in real life or in the psychology laboratory. We may be remembering a new telephone number, but it is only the *order* of the digits and the association of that order with the owner which is new. We are making use of material that is already part of our system. Occasionally we will learn a new word, or as in the list you memorized earlier, we may learn a nonsense word, but on the whole it is the meanings behind the words which we have to store and use. The conceptualization of the primary memory store was, as we said earlier, that it was a temporary store where a few items could be held for a limited time. Any longer retention required that the material should be actively rehearsed. Baddeley and Hitch (1974) suggested that a more useful way of conceptualizing this early system was as a Working Memory System. New material could be entered or old material brought up to consciousness. The system is the space for conscious manipulation of material. It has an executive function to allocate tasks; for example it may require that there be active rehearsal of material by the articulatory loop which is one of the slave subsystems of working memory; the others being a visuo-spatial scratch pad and a phonological store.

In the original paper setting out the model of memory that incorporated working memory they presented some experimental evidence in support of this central executive with its slave systems. For example they showed that subjects could perform a reasoning task whilst remembering a series of digits. However they point out that, just as in the older formulation of the model presented in Figure 6.1, the capacity of the working memory system was limited. So when the subjects had to remember a six item series, there was a marked reduction in their capacity to perform the reasoning task.

They suggest that the executive function delegates activities that may be routine to the slave systems, but when the task requirements are such that most of the processing capacity is required to fulfil the routine task, there is less capacity left for the non-routine tasks.

We also know that there is evidence for a phonological store because of what is called the phonemic similarity effect. Conrad (1964) found that people show confusions about letters that they have to remember when they are phonologically similar — *e.g. b* will be confused with *p*. This happens even when the letters have been presented visually. Hulme *et al.* (1986) showed that this also works with young children.

Teachers can immediately see the realism of a model of memory that incorporates a working memory system. Think of the situation where children are having to do mental arithmetic. Multiplying 23×9 requires bringing up the stored information of 3×9; then you have to retain this whilst retrieving 20×9; and then you have to add 27 to 180. A model which has an executive system able to take in new information, retrieve stored information and hold them both whilst performing some cognitive manipulation makes sense.

Children's Memory

I hope that you have gained the idea that much of what we recall seems to have been stored away without any conscious effort, but that some material, particularly when it is abstract and not personal, requires a lot of effort before it is permanently tucked away in an accessible place for later recall and use. Also it is easier to recall material that has been organized and categorized at input.

As adults we tend to have realistic insights into how well we perform in memory tasks. In everyday life these insights lead us to write lists, keep diaries and to recognize the need to work hard at revision for exams. Not so children. As we shall now see, the memory capacities of primary children are not the same as the capacities of adults and the difference is not just a question of quantity; there are qualitative differences between children and adults.

A study by Appel *et al.* (1972) examined this question of having insight into one's own memory performance. This is called *metacognition* or more specifically *metamemory*. They showed 4-, 7- and 11-year-old children two sets of pictures. The instructions for one set were that looking at the pictures would help performance on a subsequent task. The instructions for the other set were specifically that they should remember the pictures. However, the point of the study was that they were required to do a recall test after each set of pictures. In this way they hoped to find if the children had insights about the need to work at remembering the pictures when they were expecting a recall test. The 4-year-olds showed exactly the same behaviour towards the two sets of pictures and their performance was essentially the same on recall, regardless of the instructions. The

11-year-olds adapted their behaviour according to the instructions. They were much more likely to rehearse the picture names actively and their recall performance after instructions to recall was significantly better.

The 7-year-old group showed what could be termed transitional behaviour. They modified their behaviour after instructions to recall. They named the pictures more frequently. However, their recall performance was the same under both instructions. Appel *et al.* suggest that the 7-year-old group were beginning to be aware that they had to *do something* in order to memorize, but as yet this *doing something* was not effective enough to enhance performance.

This is not to say that young children have no awareness of their memory capacities. Kreutzer, Leonard and Flavell (1975) asked children from kindergarten (age 5) upwards whether, if they were told a friend's telephone number, it would be better to make the call straight away or to have a glass of water first. At all ages more children suggested it would be better to ring straight away. Sixty per cent of kindergarten children gave this response and the proportion grew so that 90 per cent of third (age 8) and fifth (age 10) graders gave this more sensible and insightful answer.

Children's Immediate Memory

I will begin the discussion on the changes in memory performance with the digit span. There is clear evidence that the adult memory span of seven items is not obtained until children are of secondary school age. This could appear to be a trivial observation rather like saying that children get taller as they grow older — but cognitive processes do not work like that. We do not get more intelligent because we add years. However just supposing this were true, then the knowledge that children had shorter spans than adults would still alert teachers to the need to consider the memory factors in material that they gave to children. Manipulating numbers in the head is difficult enough when your understanding of number is as yet immature — adding a large memory factor to the operation can make the task impossible. Knowledge about the limited span of infants in particular shows why children need apparatus to help them solve mathematical problems.

Nevertheless, as you will obviously be aware, the point about the memory span turns out to be non-trivial when we begin to consider other aspects of developmental memory. There is very strong evidence that young children do not spontaneously rehearse 'to-be-remembered' material. Flavell *et al.* (1966) looked at recall of lists of words whilst also assessing the amount of overt rehearsal that the children carried out. In order to measure rehearsal they had an expert lip reader watch the children. Their findings are presented in table 6.1.

Now I am prepared to agree that, as a measure of performance, lip movements are not very hi tech. It could have been the case that the children who

Table 6.1 Percentage of each age group showing lip movements

AGE GROUP	% REHEARSERS
5	10%
7	60%
10	85%

Source: Flavell, Beach and Chinsky (1966)

did not move their lips were nevertheless rehearsing. However, we have to approach the evidence sensibly without throwing out our knowledge of children in general. Since younger children do show more egocentric speech than older children, if any of the children had been rehearsing covertly it would have been more likely to be the older ones. In fact this original finding, by Flavell *et al.*, that 5-year-olds did not spontaneously rehearse, seems to be very robust.

Subsequently, Ornstein (1977) has shown that, when children do begin to rehearse at around 7 + years, their behaviour is not the same as adults. Even when they rehearse the same amount there is a difference in quality. Remember our list — we said your rehearsal performance would have been something like: *desk desk desk van van desk van desk van onion van onion desk van onion pig pig red BLING! bling fear* . . . However, Ornstein showed that children would be likely to rehearse in the following way: *desk desk desk desk van van van van van onion onion onion onion pig pig pig pig* . . . Rehearsal in this way does not allow for the possibility of developing links between items which will act as cues for recall.

One thing I should make clear is that rehearsal is an aid to recall. If subjects are stopped from rehearsing by some distraction task, then recall declines. Therefore, if children are not aware of the need to rehearse material, their immediate memory performance will be poor. The simplistic answer to this would be to show children how they can improve their memories by rehearsal. Keeney, Cannizzo and Flavell (1967) did just that. They used a group of 6- and 7-year-olds who had previously been identified as either spontaneous rehearsers or non-rehearsers. Half the rehearsers and all the non-rehearsers were then given training in rehearsal. This meant they were told to whisper the names of pictures over and over to themselves while trying to remember these pictures.

After the training all the children were given test trials in remembering sets of from two to five pictures. Figure 6.3 shows the effect of training in rehearsal very clearly. The non-rehearsers showed relatively poor performance prior to training but after training their performance was statistically no different from the other two groups. Training in rehearsal enhanced their recall.

However, they did not end the study there, and there was a sting in the tail. After ten test trials, they told the children that rehearsal was no longer a requirement, although they were free to continue using it. They then gave all the children three more test trials. Fifty-nine per cent of the initial non-rehearsers

Figure 6.3   Percentage of trials on which all pictures were remembered accurately, as a function of rehearsal training, for 6- and 7-year-old children who rehearsed spontaneously and those who did not rehearse spontaneously.

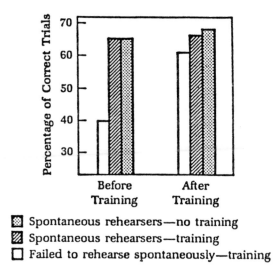

■ Spontaneous rehearsers—no training
▨ Spontaneous rehearsers—training
☐ Failed to rehearse spontaneously—training

Source: Keeney *et al.* (1967), [Graph from Kail, 1979].

reverted back to not using rehearsal but none of the spontaneous rehearsers did. What are we to make of this finding? It is clear that it is possible to teach children to use strategies which will enhance their memory performance, but we have to be wary of then leaving them to their own devices; the effects of the teaching may not be very long-lasting. It is possible that the non-rehearser group were just not ready cognitively to capitalize on the strategy.

We need to relate these findings on rehearsal to the findings on memory span and the concept of Working Memory. You will note that young children's span is roughly equivalent to the size of primary memory (Baddeley and Patterson). It is possible to suggest that the span increases as the slave system of the articulatory rehearsal loop improves in efficiency and as the executive function of the Working Memory becomes more efficient at distributing tasks.

This interpretation fits in with a finding of Kingsley and Hagen (1969). They found that when they compared the performance of 5-year-olds on a memory task, they only got the classical serial position curve from rehearsers. The non-rehearsers gave the recency effect but not the primacy effect.

It is reasonably clear to see how lack of rehearsal can account for the poorer performance of children in memory tasks; but we need to know if that is the only difference between them and adults. We know that in secondary memory, categorization and organization are important factors which influence recall performance. Moely, Olson, Hawes and Flavell (1969) found that eight years seemed to be an interesting watershed in relation to categorization. They gave children an assortment of pictures to remember. The pictures could be grouped into categories such as vehicles, animals, etc., but they were arranged in a circle pseudo-randomly with no pictures from the same category touching each other. The children knew that they were to remember the pictures and they were told that they could move the pictures if they wished.

They found that under 8 years the children rarely used the categories: the 8–9-year-olds were beginning to show categorization spontaneously; and by 10–11 years categorization was obviously a preferred, effective strategy. Again, like in the Keeney *et al.* study on rehearsal, the younger children could be trained to use categorization as an *input* strategy, but they did not use it as an *output* strategy. From 8 years onwards children become increasingly aware that category names can be effective cues for recall (Kobasigawa 1977).

The experimental work just presented leads to a general picture where we can say that between the ages of 6 and 9 children begin to use strategies for storage and retrieval of items. They are very much in a stage of transition and do not begin to reach anything like adult performance until the end of their primary years.

The results presented so far relate to experimental work rather than school based work. Teachers may say that they do not relate to classroom activities, but this is not the case. Right from the beginning of infant schooling, children have to tackle tasks such as reading and mathematics which have a very high memory factor. When reading becomes an automatic activity and children are moving up the junior schools, the memory requirements of the differing curriculum subjects begin to increase. It is necessary for teachers to reflect on the memory load and the meaningfulness of the material so that storage and learning are effective.

One further experiment will illustrate this. Figure 6.4 shows the results of a study by Chi (1978) of the recall of digits and arrays by a group of adults and a group of children whose average age was 10. You can see that the recall of digits (task 1) is in line with what you would expect, but the recall of the arrays (task 2) appears to be counter intuitive. Why?

Well, there is just one small factor that I have not yet mentioned. The arrays in question were chess pieces arranged in positions taken from real games. The children were skilled chess players but the adults were not. This meant that the arrays were meaningful to the children but just random pieces in 8 × 8 space for the adults. The amount of effort that the adults needed in order to perform the memory task was in fact much greater than for the children. The task was not actually the same task for the two groups. When the memory requirements of a task dovetail with the knowledge structure of the memorizer then the amount of processing needed to be devoted to the task is decreased.

This concept of 'meaningfulness to the subject' is a crucial one in education.

Figure 6.4   Recall of arrays by children and adults

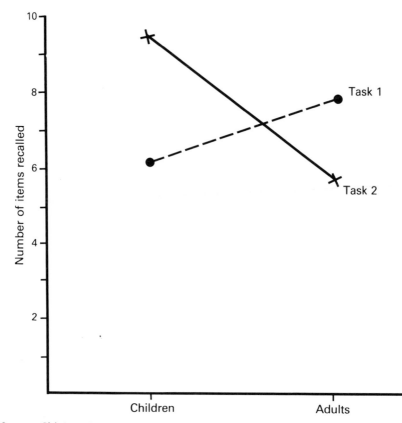

Source: Chi (1978)

If we present children with information which is so far outside their experience that they cannot see any links with their present knowledge structure, then the amount of work they have to do to incorporate the material into their long-term system is out of all proportion to the material itself. This is not to say that we do not have to broaden the children's knowledge base; however, we have to present new knowledge in such a way that they can build it onto their established systems. If there is a massive disjunction between the knowledge structures of the children and the material that the teacher is hoping they will learn, then it may be that the gap will be too wide for the children to bridge. Under such circumstances the children can show no evidence of learning anything, particularly at the younger age groups. As children progress through the school and their memory capacity improves, they may well be able to memorize much material by rote, but if it is not meaningful to them then they may well not be able to incorporate it into a dynamic system, so the knowledge will be of little use to them.

Practical Memory

Let us begin to think of how a knowledge of theoretical aspects of memory can inform classroom activities.

I have a vivid memory of a teacher saying to a group of 5-year-olds 'Don't forget to ask your Mummies for 10p for cooking'; and then she turned to me and said: 'I don't know why I bother because they'll have forgotten by the time they get their coats on.' Of course she was absolutely right. If a teacher has the experience and the insight to see that such verbal messages get forgotten, then maybe the best policy would be to change the method of sending home such messages.

We have seen that 5-year-old children, on the whole, do not spontaneously use rehearsal, but rehearsal is probably the most important strategy for remembering a verbal message. If you want to make sure that the 10 pences come in, then write a message and stick it on the door or the notice board. That is not to say that you do not encourage the children to try and remember the message; just ensure that there is one sure channel added to the one rather shaky one.

Often children have to be sent on errands around the school. Such tasks have great benefit for their sense of responsibility as well as for their memory skills. When you do send a very young child on an errand, send a pair and get them to practise the message. Tell them to say it over to themselves but also send a note if the message is vital.

In the early school years teachers have to reinforce and revise material constantly. If children are not consciously remembering, then it is up to the teacher to do lots of repetition to help them all to learn. At home they should have had many happy hours of nursery rhymes and stories. Children are really happy to listen to the same story many times and will also gaily sing the same song again and again — often to the great boredom of their parents. These experiences are vital. The problem with schooling is that the children cannot have the same intense interaction with the teacher so the control of repetition has to pass from the demands of the children into the guidance of the teacher. Because of the difference in level of intensity and intimacy, by the very nature of the relationship and the situation, each individual child's involvement in repetition is more difficult to monitor. This means that planning for revision and monitoring has to be built into the daily, weekly, termly evaluation.

Let us take a concrete example. In one of the published maths schemes for primary schools, fairly early on in the series, children gain experience with plane shapes and 3D shapes. The names they have to learn are triangle, square, circle, cube, cuboid, cone, sphere, cylinder and triangular prism. Through many varied activities they explore the properties of the shapes and they learn all about the nature of rolling and sliding in relation to inclined planes. The knowledge they gain is powerful. However, many teachers report that it takes a long time for the children to be able to remember the names of the shapes. Then, when the teachers come to revisit the knowledge, they find that the names have been forgotten. Well, we now know that this is really almost to be expected. The children could probably report in detail about the properties of a Toblerone packet, though. They may well have internalized the properties of triangular prisms but have forgotten the formal name.

What are the implications of this? I am not saying that children should not be introduced to technical terms. Indeed they love long and important sounding words. What I am saying is that we shouldn't be surprised or frustrated by the limitation of memory; particularly in relation to such disembedded information. It can be a little soul destroying to find that infants, who seemed to understand clearly one week, seem to have forgotten by the next term. That is the nature of the beast. That is why it is necessary to repeat and monitor — but the repetition should be in the full knowledge of the child's growing experience.

Let us now consider the implications for teachers of the data on digit span. Remember that we should connect this data to our model of Working Memory with the slave system of articulatory rehearsal. Is this information of any use at all? Granted that memory span is a subtest of almost all standardized individual intelligence tests, but what has this to do with teaching other than telling us how many items a child can remember immediately?

Ellis and Hennelley (1980) found that Welsh speaking children in Bangor had a shorter digit span than their English speaking peers. They suggested that this was because the vowel sounds of the digits in Welsh take longer to articulate than the digits in English. With the status of items in the primary system being very labile, the longer time taken for articulation was leading to the apparently shorter spans.

This is more than an interesting piece of abstract psychological research. It is not a trivial finding. The system is limited and one of the limitations on working memory performance is the time it takes to articulate the digits. Children whose first language is Welsh could *appear* to have more difficulty in mental arithmetic. They would not be having any greater or lesser difficulty with the cognitive understanding of the task, however. The problem with such findings, as they point out, is that without a knowledge of the functioning of human memory, unwarranted judgments could possibly be made about the children's intelligence.

As we know, children need apparatus to act as *aides-mémoire* in order to support themselves when doing early number bonding work. To begin with, when they are adding 2 to 3 they need to count from the beginning — *one, two, three* and then *four, five*. Now think about the processes involved. Firstly they obviously need to have some concept of addition; they need to have some concept of identity; they need to be able to count *one, two, three* and to remember that three is the first number in the sum; then they need to remember that two is the number they are adding on so they have to cope with counting on 2 from 3 and remember when to stop. There is quite a heavy memory factor in the task. This memory loading can be reduced by apparatus. Reducing the memory component reduces the amount of processing capacity required by the task to manageable proportions. This increases the chances that the children will succeed and the success will lead to understanding. Incidentally, as we shall see in the next chapter, since the use of apparatus enables teachers to 'externalize' the thought processes of children, it also helps them to see exactly how much of the task the children really understand.

Many children will arrive in school having accomplished the serial memory task of knowing the names of the numbers in order. This is obviously a useful accomplishment when beginning to count and to do number bonding. However, our understanding of the development of mathematical thinking has lead us to recognize that there is a major distinction between being able to recite 1-to-10 and understanding the *twoness* of two. This is where teachers need to develop good communication with parents. They may come to school and complain that their children have been counting since they were three and they have been in school for a whole term and yet they still do not seem to be doing any number work beyond ten.

Teachers have to explain to parents, with tact, that the fact that the children know the order of the numbers is a tremendous help because it enables them to tackle the mathematics more easily, but that number names and mathematics are not the same thing. Knowing quickly and accurately that '3' is 'THREE' and that it comes before 4 in the series is important. It saves all the bother of having to work it out each time. Then when the children come to an understanding about 1 + 1 + 1, they can accurately label this as 'THREE'.

As children grow older and move into the junior schools, the same can be said of multiplication tables. It is most important that children understand the process of multiplication *but* at the same time it is useful to have instant accurate recall of, say, *'four threes are twelve'*. Once the process has been well established, then the children could accurately work out the answer every time, but why not ensure that they have efficient rote memory of all the combinations up to at least twelve so that they do not have to work out from first principles each time. Having instant access to the products of multiplications enables the children to manipulate numbers more accurately and more efficiently. The most efficient way to ensure this facility is through much rehearsal. Good teachers recognize this — but make sure that the memorizing is meaningful and fun and built upon the children's level of mathematical understanding. We have to recognize that rote learning can be a chore and somewhat disembedded from real numbers, but the pay offs, in terms of efficient performance later on, are great.

Today we are in an age where practically any adult who manipulates numbers on a regular basis does so on a calculator. Does this mean that what I am saying is really irrelevant to real life mathematics? Children need to learn the basic multiplication products so that when they are adults they will be alerted when the answer on the calculator turns out to be wildly out because a wrong button has been pressed.

For example, if you are costing some laminate for a kitchen unit that is 125 cm by 82 cm and the calculator tells you that you need 6500 cm² at so much a square metre, you are immediately alerted to the fact that you must have pressed a wrong button because *'twelve eights are ninety six'*, so 125 times 82 must be greater than 9600. What happened was you pressed 52 instead of 82, a very easy mistake because the 5 is below the 8 on the calculators.

Instant access to the products of the multiplication tables can only come from over learning by much repetition. This point has been clearly made in the National Curriculum Council Consultation Report on Mathematics (1988). However, since all children are living in the late twentieth century they also need to be fully acquainted with how to use a calculator in school.

A similar story relates to reading. When children begin to read they have their linguistic knowledge, but the only strategy they have for recognizing words is to learn them by rote.

Now, I should really define 'rote'. In psychology, the term means 'learning by pure repetition, regardless of meaning and without any attempt at organization' (*Dictionary of Psychology,* Drever). The 'strategy' that children have for initial learning of words is that of remembering through multiple exposure to symbols and words. This may be via incidental learning or because parents have pointed out words to them. For example a friend's daughter suddenly said as they were driving down a road 'Look, Mummy, there's our shop going by.' It wasn't actually a mobile shop but a big juggernaut with the Sainsbury's name all over it. She wasn't reading in the technical sense, but she had remembered the sign above the shop and no doubt on all the bags and tins, etc. There are obviously individual differences between children. Some seem to be naturally curious about the meaning of signs and notice much of the environ-mental print around them. Other children remain blissfully unaware.

When they arrive in school all children receive instruction in reading. Even if they have never had much contact with books and print before, they will be exposed to print from now on. They have their linguistic competence about how sentences are formed and the only other strategy they have for remembering words is rote memory. Since we know that deliberate memorizing is problematic at this early stage and that therefore remembering new word shapes is going to place a very heavy strain on memory, it would seem a poor teaching strategy to expect children to rely entirely on memory by giving them individual words to remember. It is a much better teaching strategy to give children material with real language. Sentences are easier to read than flash cards. Sentences make sense. This means that the children can bring their linguistic intuitions to act as cues to the recall of the words. If we then add good illustrations to the language which also act as cues to the meaning of the words we are providing children with a task which is likely to be within their capabilities and therefore one where they will experience a feeling of achievement. If children have to learn 'flash card' words, the only strategy for recall is rote memory. There are no other cues which are likely to help them. They may remember that the card with the word 'Green' has got a bit of a jam stain on it. They will always then get 'Green' right but for the wrong reasons.

One necessary piece of straight memory work is the alphabet. Many children will come to school knowing all the names of the letters of the alphabet in order. They will be able to sing the sequence quite happily. Other children will be able to name visually presented letters accurately. Teachers need to check that the children can do both. Let us take letter identification first. As we shall see later on, in the development of reading, most children have to enter a phase of reading where they process the words serially on a letter by letter basis. When they achieve this stage in reading it is important that the naming of the letters is automatic. They will be hindered in the identification of the words if, as well as trying to work out the code, they have to use up precious processing capacity trying to remember which letter it is. Walsh (1988) has shown that speed and accuracy of letter naming is a very good predictor of later reading development, but only in the early stages of reading. Because you are now a skilled reader, it really doesn't matter how slow you are at naming the letters. Walsh suggests that you burnt that particular bridge once you crossed it.

Learning the letters in the correct order is a good memory feat in itself. It indicates that children have a capacity to learn and remember a series. Inability to retain a serial list may indicate that a child may have some difficulty in reading and organization of learning later on.

Another important memory aspect of the alphabet is in relation to study skills. Knowing the alphabet opens up so many possibilities for children. As they begin to be able to work independently, the alphabet will make using indexes, libraries and data bases so much easier. It makes independent dictionary work possible which again frees the children from dependence on adults and teachers for editing their own work.

Conclusion

It is really most important that teachers recognize that children's memory does not generally operate like adult memory until they are in secondary school. This means that the memory factor of a task has to be taken into consideration. Children have to be able to remember material so they may have to be helped to memorize. Teachers need to analyze tasks so that the various cognitive components are evident to them. In this way they will be making realistic demands on the children and not mistaking failure to remember for failure to understand. With understanding should come greater ability to remember the overall concepts, even if the minor details are forgotten. It may be important to remember that Paris is the capital of France, but it is also important to have an idea what another country is and what a capital city is.

Being explicitly conscious of the memory demands of tasks and the memory capacities of children will mean that matching of children to tasks can be done without waste of effort. This can be highlighted by a recent incident involving a young friend of mine. Aged 7, he had spent his infant years in a very informal school but on transfer changed to a more formal junior setting where spelling tests are part of the week's activities. By chance he made a comment to his mother about the spelling lists and the weekly tests. 'How many do you get right?' she asked. 'Oh, I get them all wrong, of course', he said. It was obviously a silly question as far as he was concerned. He did not know how to spell the words so he was obviously going to get them wrong. He clearly had no idea that, in order to get the words right, he would have to set about memorizing them. When it was pointed out to him that he could do something to learn the correct spellings everything changed. When I last heard he had been moved up to a higher spelling group. There is a salutory lesson here. We cannot take it for granted that children will realize what they have to do. Last week, my own 7-year-old told me that if he wanted to remember how to spell a new word he had to *spell it in his head*. Some children recognize what they have to do, others will have no difficulty once it has been pointed out to them and others will need specific help to enable them to memorize efficiently.

Further Reading

Baddeley (1982) *'Your Memory: A User's Guide* is one of the few psychology books ever to make the best seller list. It was written as a popular book and so makes the material very accessible; however, this does not mean that it sacrifices any academic rigour. Gregg (1988) *'Introduction to Human Memory'* is a more traditional but very thorough and readable introduction. It also includes a specific chapter on the developmental aspects of memory. Kail (1979) *'The Development of Memory in Children'* is a very comprehensive book covering all aspects of children's memories.

Chapter 7

Cognitive Development

Introduction

Any discussion about the development of cognition would be incomplete without reference to the work of Jean Piaget. It must be clear at the outset that Piaget was *not* an educationalist. However, educationalists and psychologists have studied his publications and seen relevances and applications to their own work. Also, Piaget is not without his critics, but it is probably true to say that whilst people have found areas of disagreement within the general framework they do so from a point of view of agreement in principle.

This man has probably had one of the most profound influences on the way we think about children's minds in the twentieth century. So let us begin by learning something of his life.

He was born in 1896 in Neuchâtel in Switzerland and died in 1980. For seventy-four of his eighty-four years he was publishing original research. At 10 he published his first article based on observations of an albino sparrow. Between the ages of 15 and 18 he made an extensive study of molluscs and published a series of articles that resulted in his receiving an offer of the curatorship of the mollusc collection at a Geneva Museum. This he declined in order that he might finish school! This should all serve to underline that here was a uniquely creative mind. His major interest throughout his teens was in the natural sciences, but he also became interested in philosophy under the influence of a Godfather who felt that he needed to have his outlook broadened. Nevertheless he remained loyal to the natural sciences for a time through his studies at Neuchâtel University which culminated in a Ph.D. at 21. This background must not be forgotten because it provided a particular orientation when he turned to psychology in 1917.

He first studied psychoanalysis and then went to Paris to the Sorbonne to read clinical psychology. In 1920 he went to work with Simon at the Binet Laboratory. Binet and Simon had developed the first major individual intelligence test. It was this test which was translated into English and became the Stanford-Binet Intelligence Test. An edition of this is still in use today, though with decreasing frequency.

His task at the laboratory was to standardize a French edition of some English reasoning tests — not a particularly creative or demanding occupation. However, in recording the appropriate percentage and ages of children who gave correct responses, he realized that the wrong answers were much more interesting. Correct answers will tell us that the child can do the tasks, but they give us no insight into the thinking that was behind the answers. Wrong answers, when studied in depth, can give insights into the processes involved. It was this realization that was to prove a great influence on Piaget's thinking. He set himself the task of mapping the development of thinking — and it took him the rest of his life.

He also had another profound insight into children's thinking at this stage which has greatly influenced education and thinking world wide, along with other educationalists such as Froebel and Montessori. He articulated the notion that younger children are *qualitatively* different from older children in the way they think and the way they understand the world. Children do not just get older and quicker and faster and able to do more, their thinking changes in kind. Mapping these changes was also part of his task.

A final lasting influence from the work at the Binet Laboratory was in the particular methodology that he adopted. The objective collection of data for standardization of tests left no room for trying to find out *why* the children performed as they did. The dependent variable in standardization is the number of children who give correct or incorrect responses. This is an important and valid procedure, but was not appropriate for finding the answers to the questions that Piaget was asking. Here the experience of psychoanalysis was so influential. He developed a clinical methodology of observing children in natural settings solving everyday problems. He then posed further problems for them and observed their behaviour or questioned them about why they had behaved as they did.

This then gives you a brief background into the work which resulted in a description of a stage dependent theory of how thinking develops. [Source, Ginsberg and Opper, 1969].

Piaget's Theory

Though the theory is one about the *change* in the structures of thinking, throughout there are a number of functional invariants.

If we can use our view of humans as information processing systems, then we can accept that the brain has cognitive structures for dealing with incoming information. Given the present state of the system, new material has to be incorporated into our existing model of the world. This process Piaget called *assimilation*. Here you can see the influence of the natural sciences, for this is a biological metaphor. In biology we say assimilation occurs when, for example, food is ingested. It changes and becomes part of the system.

An example of assimilation in cognition would be when children play with toys. They have ways of understanding the world and they incorporate the toys into these structures. This can be seen most clearly in imaginative play where the toys are transformed into whatever the children choose them to be. Elaborate toys which do set things are often rejected in favour of cardboard boxes which give scope for imagination.

Assimilation is changing the input to fit in with our model of the world. Its corollary is *accommodation*. This is where we have to adapt and change in order to take account of factors in the environment which do not fit in with our existing model.

It is through these two functional invariants of *adaptation* that change takes place and we develop a more veridical model of the world. This means that we are able to make more useful predictions about events and actions. The model of the world has to change and accommodate to fit the incoming information so that this same information can be better assimilated into the model.

You will find that Piaget did not use the metaphor of 'model of the world', but talked about the *schema* that we develop. A schema is a well defined sequence of either mental or physical operations which form the framework for understanding and dealing with the world. It is these schemata which have to be changed, or added to, in order to incorporate more of the incoming data.

An example will be useful here. Babies are born with reflexes which are genetically pre-determined. For example, a baby will automatically suck on some object placed in the mouth. This is biologically adaptive behaviour since it means that the baby can take nourishment from a nipple without having to learn and thus has a better chance of survival. At some stage, by chance, we can hypothesize that the baby's thumb may end up in the mouth and is sucked. Though this event does not happen intentionally, the child may remember and eventually learn to produce the sequence of actions that result in the thumb ending up in the mouth. This action can then be reproduced at will. This sequence of actions constitutes a *sensori-motor schema*. It is an organized set of motor actions which produce a predicted result. The schema is then repeated and practised. Other things that are placed in the hand are taken to the mouth. The world is assimilated into this primitive schema. Eventually, however, the result of the action may not produce the desired effect and the child will change and do something new and different. The child has accommodated and, maybe, achieved another schema, and so the repertoire has grown. As the framework of possibilities grows, so the potential for understanding and changing also grows. Eventually the sensori-motor schematas are replaced by internal representations of the actions and the child shows evidence of being able to *think*.

Obviously, the process is nowhere near as simplistic and clearcut as the above example implies, but it serves to illustrate that, throughout development, there is the process by which change and adaptation take place in order to strive for a balance. This attempt to achieve a harmony is the process of *equilibration*. In adapting to incorporate more of the data so that it can be assimilated, other inconsistencies in the system are made clear and so there has to be further change to try and achieve equilibrium.

Whilst Piaget therefore sees cognitive development as taking place as a result of a continuous process of organization and reorganization of our cognitive structures, it would be a mistake to imagine that, throughout childhood, we are on a perpetual seesaw. The results of the process are discontinuous. He conceived of our development as being differentiated into recognizable stages. The stages are named according to the characteristic mode of cognitive performance typifying them. The theory is a *stage dependent* theory. He believed that all children pass through the stages in an invariant order and in a unidirectional way. Though ages have been given to stages, there is much dispute about them and for us, as teachers, they are only useful as guidelines as long as we do not apply them to individual children. We are more interested in what the child can actually do. The age of the child only becomes important when we are considering progress. It should be clear that the description of the abilities in any one stage does not preclude us from recognizing that the children will often make use of previously acquired structures, or that they will have the occasional flash of brilliance, way above their usual level of functioning.

Implicit in the notion of a stage dependent theory is the view that the environment can have no effect. However, Piaget did not totally discount the influence of the environment. The overall pattern of the cognitive structures may be invariant, but the experiences utilized to gain the structures will vary greatly. Piaget was concerned with the underlying universal structures and not the culturally specific knowledge, though he did not deny its importance. Culturally specific knowledge would be knowing that the names of the numbers are *one*, *two*, *three*, *etc.*, or *ein*, *zwei*, *drei*. This is obviously important; however, Piaget was more concerned with how children come to an understanding of the oneness of one and that two is made up of two ones. In other words he was concerned with children's understanding of number and not with whether they knew the names of the digits.

The Stages of Development

The outline given in Table 7.1 shows the names of the stages and the typical age bands where children will appear to be functioning at those levels. Subsequent research has shown that often children can do things at a much earlier age than

Piaget would suggest, but in order for you to understand the significance of this research I will begin by taking you through the stages and giving examples of the types of problems that children can or cannot deal with. Obviously the processing in Stage 1 is not influenced by any other stage, but after that, children will be operating not just at the highest level within the stage they are in, but also using processes learned from previous stages — even when they are not necessarily appropriate.

Table 7.1   Piaget's developmental stages

Stage 1	Sensori-motor	0– 2 years
Stage 2	Preoperational	2–11 years
	(a) Pre-conceptual substage	2– 4 years
	(b) Intuitive substage	4– 7 years
	(c) Concrete operational substage	7–11 years
Stage 3	Formal Operational	11 + years

Stage 1. Sensori-motor

This stage is so named because the only way that a child has of operating on the world is through a motor response to perceptual input. Initially, the children's actions will be focused on their own bodies, but gradually they will direct actions towards objects in the environment.

During this stage memory begins to develop. Without this capacity to store events, no cognitive development can take place. Children need to be able to store information so that they can reproduce actions at will.

Piaget suggests that at this stage, the child is not able to *internalize* actions. The child can only show evidence of understanding events or relationships of objects through motor actions. In his terms, the children do not yet *think*. They do not use concepts because a concept is a *mental representation* of some aspect of an event and they only have motor responses. They are, however, beginning to store up information which will enable them to develop internal representation.

It is during this stage that children develop the notion of *object permanence*. Initially, the child conceives of objects as discrete events. When they disappear from view they no longer exist. However, by round about 8 months, the behaviour patterns will change and from this we can infer that cognition has changed.

When young babies do not have the idea of object permanence, they will not search for things even when they see them being hidden, but will simply transfer their attention to something else. This seems reasonable — if objects are discrete events in time and space, once they are no longer in view, and therefore don't exist, there is no point in searching for them. Through frequent encounters with objects, the child gradually accommodates and develops an idea of object permanence. We can infer this from the behavioural responses. If an object is hidden searching will take place.

We must remember that we should not view cognitive development and understanding of the world in isolation. This is all taking place within an integrated whole. During this first stage of development children gradually develop motor skills and therefore independence. Once they can move about at will and explore the environment, the possibilities for learning and, therefore, understanding are considerably enlarged. However, during this stage, children are pre-lingual; communication has to be through action rather than symbolically. It is not accidental that the beginnings of language usage and the beginnings of thinking, in Piaget's terms, occur at the same time.

Stage 2. Preoperational

(a) Pre-conceptual substage

During this substage language will be developing and the children are developing an increasing ability to represent one thing in terms of another — they are beginning to think symbolically. As the title of the substage suggests, children at this stage do not have true concepts. If a concept is a mental representation of some aspect of an event, it represents an abstraction. The boundaries of the concept are built up from previous experience, but are not totally idiosyncratic because we can communicate with other people. Examples of simple concepts might be colour or shape. Having concepts enables us to use categorization and to perceive relationships.

For example, when children in this substage are asked to sort a number of objects that vary along a number of dimensions so that they 'go together', they will tend to link from individual instance rather that using a stable criterion. Thus a group might be chosen as in Figure 7.1.

Figure 7.1   Early Idiosyncratic Categorization

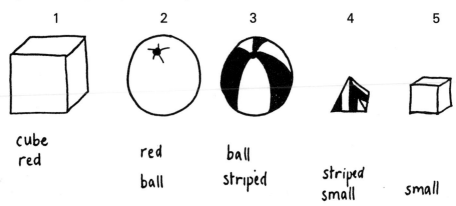

When asked why the items go together the child might reply 'Well, that's red [1] and so's that [2] and that's a ball [2] and so's that [3]. That's stripy [3] and so's that [4] and that's a small one [5] and so is that [4]. So they all go together.'

Piaget believed that the ability to form genuine, stable concepts depended on the ability to recognize that a signifier is different from what it signifies. The signifier, or symbol, represents objects and events in a generalized rather than a specific way. The ability to begin to differentiate between the two develops in this stage through play and imitation. Play — particularly symbolic fantasy play — at this stage is very important. Play facilitates assimilation. Through symbolic play objects are transformed into understandable situations.

Another characteristic of children at this stage of their development is that they are *egocentric* in their thinking. This means that they see the world from their own point of view. It does *not* mean that they show the selfish, inconsiderate behaviour of an adult who is labelled egocentric. Of course they do! Children at this stage find it very difficult to share and so, when playing with other children, fights and arguments are a characteristic of their interactions. They have to learn to cooperate. However, their egocentrism is not willful selfishness — they simply do not know any better.

The nursery class, full of children at this stage, will be a buzz of excitement. The children will be talking all the time — but not necessarily to anyone else. A characteristic of the egocentrism of this stage is that the children will talk to themselves. You will also find that they will find it difficult to appreciate that thoughts that they have had are not public. They will explain something to you assuming that you have been following a train of thought that they have had.

The basis of nursery education could be said to be Piagetian theory. Children need to be given the chance to learn to cope with other children and thus to learn that there are other views that differ from their own. They might want to play on the slide, but so will other children. Turn-taking is a necessary social skill, but it also contributes to cognitive development. The types of materials that children handle in nursery encourage concept formation. Sorting and arranging are useful activities, but choosing the right piece of Lego to complete a model is also evidence of developing categorization. My children would have conversations of the form 'I need a fourer, no, not one like that, it's got to be a flat one. Now I need a sixer', etc. ('fourer' and 'sixer' refer to the number of lumps along the longest axis). Like many children they developed their own terminology to categorize the different pieces.

(b) Intuitive substage

At this substage the children's thinking is dominated by perceptual impressions. Concepts are forming, but they are still not perfectly grasped because the children tend to *centre* — focus — on one particular aspect of an event or perceptual input and ignore other, possibly equally salient, ones. In information processing terms, taking account of two aspects of a situation probably takes up too much of their limited capacity.

Able to use symbolic representation and to carry out mental operations by this stage, children find that they can understand by doing things for themselves and drawing their own inferences — even if these inferences are sometimes not correct.

A description of thinking at this stage of development is best given in terms of some of the things that children cannot do. This will also serve to introduce you to some Piagetian tasks which he developed when charting cognitive development.

Children at this stage have difficulty with the concept of *reversibility*. Reversibility means that there is a potential for returning to the point of origin. A simple example would be if we took a ball of plasticene, rolled it into a sausage, then rolled it into a ball again. The action is reversible and we end up with exactly the same ball of plasticene that we started with.

At a slightly more advanced level reversibility means understanding that the operation

$$2 + 3 = 5$$

has potential for returning to the point of origin, i.e.

$$5 - 3 = 2$$

Something — 3 — is added to the 2 to give something new — 5. This operation can be reversed. The 3 can be taken away from the 5 and we return to our original, 2.

A child who has difficulty with reversibility will also find *conservation* problematic.

We can begin with conservation of matter. We take two balls of plasticene this time which the child agrees are the same and then we roll one of them out into a sausage as in Figure 7.2.

Figure 7.2 Conservation of Matter

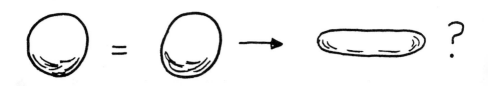

When asked to make a judgment as to whether the two pieces of plasticene are still the same, Piaget observed that children would be dominated by the perception that they looked different even though the child knew that nothing had been added or taken away. They would say that the sausage (or sometimes the ball) had more plasticene.

There are a number of other areas where conservation can be explored:

Conservation of number.

Figure 7.3   Conservation of Number

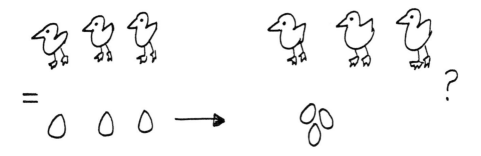

Here the child may well count up and agree that there are the same number of chickens as eggs, but when the eggs are all bunched together — in full view of the child — then perception will dominate and the judgment will change to there now being more chickens.

Conservation of volume.

Figure 7.4   Conservation of Liquid (Volume, Capacity)

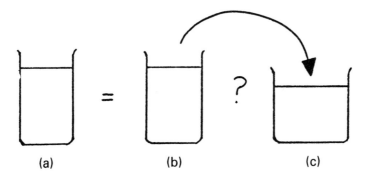

(a)   (b)   (c)

Here the child will agree that there is the same amount of liquid in (a) as in (b), but when the liquid in (b) is poured into (c) the child centres on the *level* of the liquids and judges that there is more in (a) than (c). If (c) is very tall and very thin glass then the judgment may switch to there being more in (a) 'because (a) is fatter'.

Conservation of area.

Figure 7.5   Conservation of Area

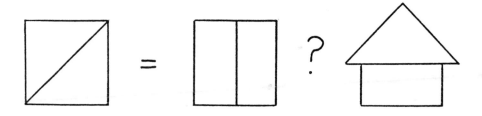

The child may agree that the cards are the same size, but when the house is made from the two different shaped halves then the judgment of equal area becomes very difficult.

I have a vivid memory, as a child, of watching a conjuror appear to create more and more water as he poured it from one jug into another. I have a horrible suspicion that this was not magic but a Piagetian in disguise. Certainly as a parent I have been able to use inability to conserve totally unscrupulously. The answer to 'He's got four pieces of toast/apple/banana and I've only got two' is to cut each one in half. Same amount — different number!

Another structure that was said to be beyond the understanding of 'intuitive' children is *seriation*. Objects in a series vary with respect to each other along a dimension. Thus the rods in Figure 7.6 are in a series.

Figure 7.6   Seriation

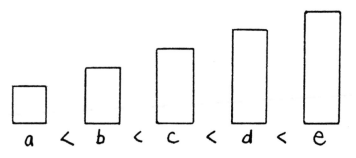

The preconceptual child would have difficulty in constructing the series at all, so if asked to form a staircase would have them in a very higgledy-piggledy order. The intuitive child would probably be able to create a non-random arrangement but would have to make a physical comparison each time a new rod was chosen. Children at this stage are said not to be able to hold a model of the order in their heads all at once.

Allied to the notion of seriation is that of *transitivity*. If we know that Jane is smaller than Susan and that Susan is smaller than Mary, then, if we can make a transitive inference, we can work out that Jane must be smaller than Mary as well. Children at this stage are said, by Piaget, to have difficulty with such inferences. Transitivity and seriation are necessary structures in the understanding of number. Again, not cultural knowledge, but understanding that 4 has a specific place between 3 and 5.

The intuitive child is beginning to show an ability to categorize, but still has an incomplete appreciation of class. A *class* is a number of things that share some property like 'all red things' or 'all cubes'. It is not enough to categorize in an isolated way. The children have to be able to see the relationship between classes and therefore understand hierarchies. In relation to children's mnemonic skills, you will remember that children at this age have difficulty in using categorization to aid storage and recall. This is understandable. If the children do not yet have a fluent understanding of categories and hierarchies they are unlikely to be able to utilize categories when they have to try to memorize items.

The classic Piagetian task for demonstrating understanding of hierarchical classes is to present children with a number of beads — 5 wooden beads composed of 3 red ones and 2 blue ones. One then asks the question 'Are there more red beads or more beads?' Children at this stage tend to say 'More red ones'. Piaget says that they get the answer wrong because they have an incomplete understanding of classification and so compare sub-class with sub-class rather than sub-class with whole class. In fact, part of the problem, as we shall see later on, is not to do with understanding of categorization, but with mis-understanding of the very peculiar question in the first place.

Perhaps a more interesting point about using true concepts comes from being able to appreciate the difference between the signifier and the thing which is signified, as we mentioned above. It is very difficult to teach a child the difference between the *number* of coins and the *value* of the coins. Given some play money and the chance to play shop, children, when told a bun costs 7p, are quite likely to hand over £2.49. This could be composed of 2 × £1 coins, 2 × 20p coins, 1 × 5p coin and 2 × 2p coins — i.e. 7 coins. It takes quite some time before they can begin to appreciate that 7p does not mean 7 pieces.

Pre-conceptual children are said to be very egocentric, but intuitive children have begun to be able to decentre in some areas of life. Socially they will be able to play together and in class they will be able to share and cooperate if encouraged to do so. Fantasy play gives way to acting out real scenes and in construction play they will tend to build accurate representations of real objects. However one task of Piaget's is used to demonstrate that appreciating another point of view can be difficult at this stage. The children view a model of mountains (Figure 7.7) from position (a) and are then given four photographs, one from each of positions (a), (b), (c) and (d). The task is to choose the view that corresponds to the view of someone in position (c). They tend to chose the view which is like the one they can see.

Figure 7.7   The 'Mountains' Task

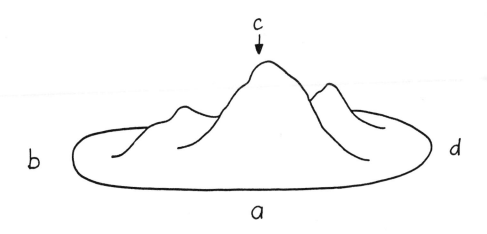

Piaget uses this as evidence that they cannot decentre. We shall see that people have questioned his discussion of decentration, but not the educational implications that we can draw from this. Children do need to have teaching which is firmly grounded within their own experience. We need to explore their own world with them in order to take them beyond it.

(c) Concrete operational substage

In terms of functioning, the child at this stage is characterized by being able to do all those things that the intuitive child could not do. But note the name of the substage — *concrete* operations. By this, Piaget means that the child has a well developed ability to think, but must have concrete and not abstract experiences in order to understand. Discussions about the relative sizes of the sun, earth and moon may appear to be understood, but unless the children are given concrete examples, their understanding will be at best partial.

In terms of egocentricity — this no longer characterizes concrete operational children. They are sociable in their play, well able to cooperate in team games, prepared even to lose (occasionally) and well able to cooperate on joint undertakings in class. Being able to decentre also means that they can take account of another perspective in cognitive acts. They can understand a map for example and are able to give other people instructions. Piagetian theory here has influenced the Cox Committee. Level 4 of Attainment Target: Speaking and Listening includes:

> Describe an event or experience to a group of peers, clearly and audibly and in detail.
> Give and receive precise instructions and follow them.
> Take part effectively in a small group discussion and respond to others in the group (Cox 8.15).

These children can form true concepts and can use categorization and classificatory systems. In their reading development they will have begun to be able to use an alphabetic strategy for decoding words into their component parts and so they can tackle any word. This enables them to become free from a reliance on context. This fits in neatly with our knowledge of the development of memory. The ability to use categorization as a means of storing material, you will remember, is developed at about this time. Reversibility, conservation, seriation and transitivity are all structures within the system.

Figure 7.8 Two-way Classification

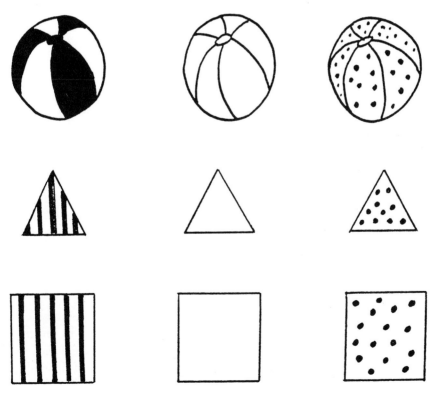

The concrete operational child is no longer perceptually dominated and can take account of more than one dimension of a problem when working out a solution. For example, if children are given a set of objects to arrange which vary along two dimensions simultaneously, they can make a perfect two-way classification as in Figure 7.8.

Because of their newly developed strategies for tackling print, children in the concrete operational stage will be becoming quite proficient readers. Though there are obviously wide variations, they tend to be very interested in stories which have an element of reality about them. Fairy stories are considered to be for 'babies'. This would be predicted from their need to have real experiences and concrete examples in solving problems.

Stage 3. Formal operational

Whilst the thinking of the concrete operational child is based on the actual, the formal operational child is able to conceive of the possible and therefore use hypothetico-deductive reasoning. At this stage they are able to be methodical in their thinking. Correct answers are not arrived at on a hit and miss basis, but worked out, making sure that every alternative has been explored. I must stress that Piaget was talking about what we are capable of, and not what we necessarily always do in our day to day lives. Everyone — even the school child — is allowed to be inconsistent and illogical occasionally.

The classic task used to demonstrate formal reasoning is illustrated in Figure 7.9.

All the flasks contain colourless liquid: (1) is dilute sulphuric acid, (2) water, (3) is oxygenated water, (4) is thiosulphate and (5) is potassium iodide. The adult demonstrates that, by combining some of the liquids together, a yellow liquid can be obtained. [Back to my conjuror: oxygenated water oxidizes potassium iodide in an acid medium such that a yellow precipitation occurs.] The children are then told that they have to find the necessary and sufficient combination of liquids to produce the colour themselves. They could do this on an entirely chance basis. They could just happen to hit on the combination of 1 + 3 + 5 give yellow. This is the sort of thing concrete operational children would do. They would have a hit or miss procedure and when they got the right combination — if they got the right combination — they would stop. However, the point of this particular set of liquids is that 1 + 3 + 5 will produce yellow, but if 4 is in there too, no colour will appear because the sodium thiosulphate causes the precipitate to disappear leaving a colourless liquid. Also, they could hit on the combination of 1 + 2 + 3 + 5 which will result in yellow, but since the 2 is water, its presence or absence has no effect — it is not necessary. A formal operational child will be able to sit down and try out every combination systematically so that the necessary and

Figure 7.9 Formal Operational Thinking Task

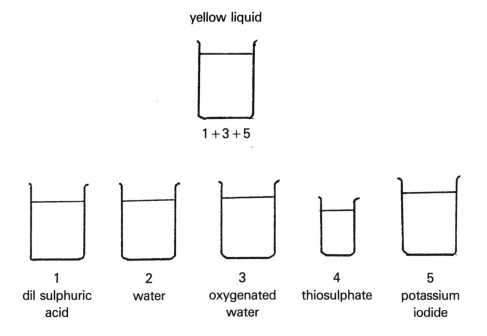

sufficient conditions are discovered as well as the neutral effect of the water and the reversible effect of the sodium thiosulphate.

Being able to appreciate the *possible* means that children who have attained formal operational reasoning can handle abstract concepts and so their discussions are capable of being logical, rational and objective. Their moral sense can develop beyond simple retribution towards being able to understand universal concepts of justice and equality. This does not mean that they will always be rational and reasonable, just that they are capable of so being.

One of the easiest ways of understanding and explaining the underlying framework of the development of cognitive structures is through realistic examples. An interesting point: as adults, capable of formal operational, abstract thought, we do find concrete illustrations aid understanding. Pictures, figures and tables in books aid comprehension. We should remember that as a teaching rule.

This point can itself be illustrated by a reasoning problem devised by Wason and Johnson-Laird (1972). They presented subjects with Figure 7.10 which represents one side of each of four cards that have a letter on one side and number on the other.

Figure 7.10   Which cards must be turned over to prove the rule?

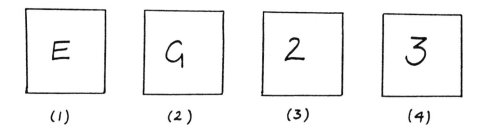

Subjects were given the information that there was a rule such that 'if a card has a vowel on one side it must have an even number on the other'. Their task was to work out which cards were the necessary and sufficient cards to turn over to see if the cards conformed to the rule.

We can state the rule in logical terms as:

If a VOWEL then an EVEN NUMBER

This logical structure of 'If p then q' is said by Piaget to typify formal operational thinking. Try and work out which cards you need to turn over — but I won't give you the answer yet. Wason and Johnson-Laird found that the task was not solved spontaneously by most of their subjects who were undergraduates and, therefore, presumably formal operational thinkers.

They then kept the basic problem but changed the situation so that it was apparently a problem to be solved by postal workers. The rule could then be posed in the form 'If the envelope is sealed it must have a 32p stamp on it.' The subjects were given a diagram similar to Figure 7.11 and asked which letters they needed to turn over to check that the letters had enough stamps on them.

Figure 7.11   Which envelopes must be turned over to prove the rule?

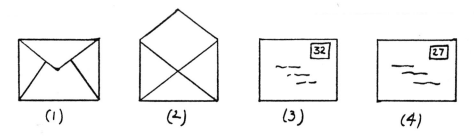

The answer to both problems is the same — 1 and 4.

You have to turn over the sealed letter to make sure that it has a 32p stamp on, 27p is not enough. You have to turn over the letter with the 27p stamp on to make sure that it is not sealed. You don't need to bother about the unsealed letter because, if it has a 32p stamp on, then the sender has just wasted 5p by not sealing it. You don't need to turn over letter 3 because the same applies — it doesn't matter if the sender did not seal it.

Return to the original problem and think about it again if you found you had the wrong answer. The point about the rule is that it says 'If VOWEL then EVEN NUMBER'. There is nothing about consonants at all. The only point about odd numbers is that they must not co-occur with vowels.

This work suggests that real life problems which may be represented in abstract terms are easier to solve than the analogous abstract problems themselves. Piaget (1972) has agreed with this point. We can see that this has a direct bearing on teaching. Drawing our examples and planning our project work from the experiences that children have, makes them more comprehensible. But this does not mean that we should not attempt to broaden their horizons — we just start from the known and move carefully to the unknown.

Real life problems are embedded within a context which leads them to be comprehended. The concept of embeddedness developed by Margaret Donaldson (1978) has lead us to rethink many of Piaget's interpretations of his findings and to refocus our views about curriculum materials.

Modifications to Piaget's Findings

Once educationalists began ro read Piaget, they found the overriding message, that children's thinking changes over time, that this thinking develops because they are actively involved in the adaptation process and that young children are very concrete in their thinking, was very compelling. It led to new ideas about how to structure the material for primary children and a belief that they should be allowed to engage actively with concrete apparatus rather than passively receive information.

However, in accepting the framework they also accepted the particular instances. This meant, particularly in mathematics, that there was a move away from formal mathematics and rote learning towards the need to understand the concepts which underlie mathematical understanding. This had both positive and negative sides to it. Being able to understand mathematical concepts requires cumulative learning. If not enough time is spent on a real understanding of why we do what we do when we add, take away, multiply and divide then children will resort to following blindly a poorly grasped algorithm rather than really understanding what they are doing. However, whilst teachers were changing the mathematical classroom in line with Piagetian thinking in the stages, but also in the ages, psychologists were showing that Piaget had considerably misjudged the ages when many structures were acquired. Appreciating the need to map mathematical learning to cognitive development was very important. Blindly following the ages of the stages in an uncritical manner was unfortunate.

Let me explain this further. The logical consequence of Piaget's view that Intuitive children were unable to conserve, understand seriation or make transitive inferences was that, until they could do these things, they were not really ready to engage in formal mathematics. However, common sense and experience told teachers that 5- and 6-year-olds could add up.

A neat experiment by McGarrigle and Donaldson (1974) on 'Conservation accidents' provides an answer to this dilemma. In the classical conservation of number task, the adult alters the arrays and asks all the questions. In their experiment, McGarrigle and Donaldson introduced 'Naughty Teddy' — a toy who would emerge from a box and alter the array by disturbing the counters. The array would be thus transformed by accident. Checking the array and asking whether there were the same number of counters in each line after 'Naughty Teddy' had been around made *real life* sense to the children. They found that many children, who, on the straight number conservation task, appeared to be in the Intuitive substage, were then able to conserve. The question was embedded in a context and therefore understanding was clearly demonstrated.

Bryant and Trabasso (1971) made a more controlled study of the ability to make transitive inferences. Originally, Piaget had three rods — A < B < C — and he questioned the children on the relationship of A and C after they had been shown the relationship between A and B and then B and C. Bryant and Trabasso felt that there were two things wrong with Piaget's interpretation. On the one hand, the children who got the answer *right* could have been correct for the wrong reasons. Since, in a series of three, A is always smaller and C is always bigger, the children could have been remembering the uniqueness of the anchor points. On the other hand the children could have been getting the answer wrong for reasons other than failure to understand transitivity. They could simply have been forgetting the comparisons that they had been shown. This would seem reasonable in the light of what we know about memory.

Bryant and Trabasso, therefore, took a five rod series — A < B < C < D < E. They argued that children who could really understand transitivity would be able to answer the crucial question about the relationship between B and D. To begin with, though, they wanted to make sure that memory failure could not interfere with reasoning so they gave all their children training in all the adjacent pairings. Only when the pairings were memorized did they ask about the B/D relationship. They found that 4-year-olds had a .90 probability of giving the correct answer, 5-year-olds had a .92 probability and 6-year-olds had a .98 probability. This means that children can make transitive inferences much earlier than Piaget would suggest and it brings into question the ages for stages as detailed in his work.

Part of the problem may lie in Piaget's original methodology. Whilst the clinical approach was important in giving insights into children's performance, as soon as more fine grained information became necessary, then a more controlled experimental procedure was appropriate. Clinical procedure means that contributory variables, that may influence the results, may not be taken into account.

Much of the work that has been carried out of recent years has been to investigate in greater detail the characteristics of children who could be said to be in Stage 2 of cognitive development. Much of this stemmed from the feeling that, though the structures that Piaget investigated may be important to the development of thinking, the characterization of children's capacities did not correlate with their performance in reality. A study reported by Hughes and Donaldson (1983) shows this exactly. The Piaget's 'Mountains' task had been used to illustrate inability to decentre. Hughes considered that, though there was concrete apparatus for the task, it did not make real sense in the children's terms. It was in essence an abstract task.

Figure 7.12 (a) shows the task. There are two intersecting walls, a policeman and a dolly. The task is to place the dolly in the scene so that it cannot be seen by the policeman. Initially this was done with discussion so that the children could show clear evidence of understanding the situation. Then the task was made more complex, as in Figure 7.12 (b). Another policeman was added and this time the dolly had to be placed so that neither policeman could spot it. Ninety per cent of the nursery children ($3\frac{1}{2}$–5 years) tested were able to do the task successfully. The task is clearly not identical to Piaget's, but in the Hughes experiment the children showed clear evidence of understanding more than one point of view. The task made real sense; but then we know that, by the time children get to infant school, they can hide successfully in a game of hide and seek.

A major criticism of Piaget's work is that, particularly in his early work, he did not appreciate the importance that language has in our understanding of problems. He obviously recognized that use of language was an important element in the shift from sensori-motor functioning, but he did not recognize that the way the children understood his questioning might relate more to their linguistic competence than to their cognitive development.

This can be clearly seen in the class inclusion task that we mentioned earlier. The wording of the question 'Are there more beads or more red beads?' represents a situation that does not make sense in human terms. It is a *bizarre* question, in Hughes' terms. The children assume that the adult is asking a sensible question and, since their attention is drawn to the *red beads*, they assume that they are being asked about red vs. blue. When McGarrigle, Grieve and Hughes (1978) studied this they used two versions of the same question in order to study understanding and the contribution of language to the problem. Instead

Figure 7.12 (a) Hiding from the policeman

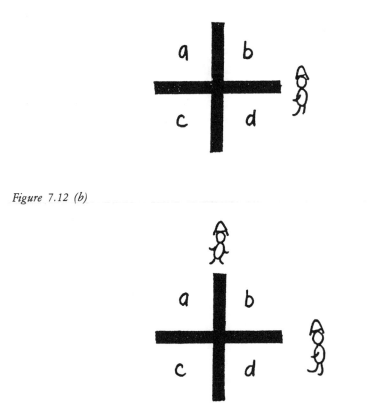

Figure 7.12 (b)

of beads they used 1 white and 3 black toy cows, which they laid down in front of the children and explained that they were all sleeping. The two versions of the question were:

1   Are there more black cows or more cows?
2   Are there more black cows or more *sleeping* cows?

Question 1 was in the standard Piagetian class inclusion form, but the addition of the adjective in question 2 served to draw the children's attention to the whole class. Twenty-five per cent of the children could answer question 1 correctly but 48 per cent could get question 2 correct.

Clearly this study shows us that cognition interacts with language competence, but there is another lesson to learn from the study. Question 2 makes *human sense*. This concept, of being able to tackle problems that make sense in this way, has been discussed by Margaret Donaldson in her very influential book *Children's Minds*. When children can hide the dolly in the McGarrigle task or when we can turn over the right envelopes in the Wason and Johnson-Laird example, we are thinking within a context. In Donaldson's terms our thinking is *embedded*. However, many of the Piagetian tasks appear to be complete in themselves; we do not have to bring our knowledge of the world to the solving of the task and thus they are *disembedded*.

This framework for understanding the development of understanding is very powerful. Embeddedness implies more than Piaget's concept of concreteness. A question, like the class inclusion one can appear to be concrete — after all the beads are there and the child can handle them — but, because it is not embedded in human sense, the question becomes difficult. In terms of the education of children we have to consider two aspects here. It may be that, as children develop, they are able to handle more and more complex problems with a number of different dimensions, but that they will find the issues basically easier if they are embedded in a context. Does that mean that we have to con-textualize everything? I think not. What it does mean is that we have to go from success with embedded material to success with disembedded examples. Children have to be helped to make this transition. To quote Donaldson:

> The process of moving beyond the bounds of human sense is unnatural in the sense that it does not happen spontaneously. The very possibility of this movement is the product of long ages of culture; and the possibility is not realised in the life of an individual child unless the resources of the culture are marshalled in a sustained effort directed to that end (*Children's Minds*, p.123).

The Work of Jerome Bruner

Whilst accepting that there are difficulties with some aspects of Piaget's theory, we can certainly use the concept of children gradually developing their under-standing of the world and building up their ability to comprehend more complex issues as they develop their capacity to categorize input. When we ally to this the Donaldson concept of embeddedness we can see that, in order to help children develop their understanding, we have first to embed material in contexts that make human sense to them. However, we have to find ways of eventually freeing children from total reliance on context. Here the contribution of Bruner to education and our understanding of children becomes highly relevant.

With great wit, Bruner is an unashamed elitist in the sense that he believes that teachers have something to give children. They know more and should help the children to learn efficiently. Every child does not have to reinvent the wheel. Teachers need to know about the development of thinking because only then can they structure the material in such a way that the children can learn. This is high-lighted with the advent of the National Curriculum. The curriculum is laid down, but unless teachers can structure the material to match the cognitive processes of the children the children will not achieve their true potential.

Whilst accepting much of Piaget's thinking, Bruner has suggested that, rather than considering stages of characteristic operational structures, we should consider the modes by which we can represent the world to ourselves. Bruner says that, initially, our only method of representation is *enactive*. This means that a problem can be represented 'by a set of actions appropriate for achieving a certain result' (Bruner 1966). Understanding comes through doing. The similarity between this and Piaget's concept of sensori-motor intelligence is obvious.

Next, he suggests, we develop an ability to use *iconic* representation. Here a problem is represented 'by a set of summary images or graphics that stand for a concept without fully defining it' (*ibid.*). When children achieve this level of representation they *add* to their earlier mode. Enactive representation is not replaced or superceded by iconic representation, but enables a fuller under-standing.

Finally we develop *symbolic* representation, where a problem is represented 'by a set of symbolic or logical propositions drawn from a symbolic system that is governed by rules or laws for forming and transforming propositions' (*ibid.*). Language is an obvious example of symbolic representation.

Once the children have developed all three modes of representation, then there will be individual differences between them as to the way they understand problems. It is quite likely that some older children may well by-pass the need for enactive and iconic mode in some areas. As the teacher presenting the material, you need to bear in mind that it will be maximally learned when all three modes of representation are made available. However, different curriculum domains will vary in the balance of emphasis that will have to be placed on the different modes.

Bruner is not alone in his emphasis on the importance of language to facilitate understanding. Vygotsky (1962) has argued that it is through language that we are able to structure our thoughts. Language has a directive function. Thus the egocentric speech of the intuitive child enables that child to monitor actions and modify planned behaviour.

Let me present one of Bruner's examples to illustrate the way a single problem can be understood at different levels. Nursery school children cannot be introduced to the mathematical equation which describes moments about the fulcrum. However, nursery school children can make a seesaw work successfully. When children move along the bar of a seesaw so that they get a good swing, they are demonstrating that they have represented the problem to themselves in an enactive manner.

This can be transferred to playing with a balance weighing apparatus, and in the infant classroom they will be engaged in weighing and measuring weights along a beam to create a balanced system. They should also be encouraged to make a pictorial representation of their findings. They will be using iconic representation.

Gradually they will be developing a capacity to talk about their discovery and write about what they have done. Eventually they will be able to represent a balanced system via a mathematical formula. All this is symbolic representation.

This discussion of the different levels by which a single problem can be represented dovetails very neatly with Donaldson's ideas. As the same problem is represented through successive modes, the problem goes from being totally embedded to being disembedded. The task for you, as a teacher, is to present material to children in such a way that they can represent it to themselves. Learning will be cumulative. Previous understanding will aid the representation of new material, but previously learned material may have to be readdressed in the light of new understandings. This means that teachers have to structure the overall path and not just the particular stepping stones. Bruner has a firm belief in children learning by discovery, but the discovery must not be left to chance. The tasks and the goals have to be set by the teachers so that understanding is always possible.

Cognitive Development and the Curriculum

When educationalists began to take the ideas of Piaget about cognitive development seriously, they did not just recognize the importance of the concept of *development* but they began to apply his work to the curriculum. There were attempts to teach the underlying structures such as reversibility and conservation. We can see with the hindsight of Bruner's and Donaldson's work that this was an inappropriate strategy. An understanding of conservation may inform understanding in a number of different curriculum areas, but of itself it would appear to be extremely disembedded.

The message that we can learn from Piaget is that children develop their thinking gradually and, particularly in the primary years, they need the chance to explore subjects through concrete experiences. When they appear systematically to misunderstand then it may be that they are not yet sufficiently cognitively developed to deal with the material. This leads us directly to a view that there has to be a match between the individual child and the curriculum material. This can only be achieved through detailed observation and record keeping.

The message from Donaldson and her colleagues is that perhaps Piaget underestimated the importance of language in cognitive development. Teachers have to be aware constantly of the possibility that problems with understanding the curriculum may arise because of the medium through which it is presented.

We can add to this Bruner's concept of the three modes of representation. By making sure that we present material so that the children can use all three modes of representation we can avoid the possibility of confusion through language.

We also need to expand on Piaget's idea of concrete experiences and utilize Donaldson's concept of embeddedness. If we begin by grounding new material within the children's own experiences, but always keep in mind that we have to help them to develop a capacity to deal with disembedded material, then we will be well on the way to achieving the match of the children with the materials.

The curriculum itself is now prescribed in England and Wales. Children in schools will be taught under the umbrella of the National Curriculum. If they are to succeed, then taking account of the cognitive capacity of the children becomes imperative. The targets which teachers must aim for are laid down. In order to help the children achieve the targets, material needs to be presented in such a way that children can represent it to themselves and thus understand it.

The programme of study for Science — Attainment Target 10 — Forces, is set out below.

> 5 to 7 In the context of the classroom and outdoor play activities, children should experience natural and manufactured forces which push, pull, make things move, stop things and change the shape of objects. Such experiences could include, for example, road safety activities.
>
> 7 to 11 Children should use measurements to compare the effects of forces in the context of, for example, bridge building. They should investigate the strengths of shapes and structures.
>
> They should experience the forces involved in floating and sinking. They should explore the forces which cause movement. This work should be set in everyday contexts such as transport (including cycling and sailing), balancing systems and hydraulic mechanisms in model making (NCC Consultation Report, Science, p.91).

The programme of study makes it clear that what we might call the principles of Newtonian physics can be taught in the primary school, but only at the children's level. The principles will be understood through using experiences that are embedded in the context of everyday life. Those children who are going to go on to be the theoretical physicists of the future need to be presented with comprehensible problems in the primary school. The situations as presented to them need to make human sense, but they also need to be helped towards tackling purely abstract problems as well. In requiring contextualized primary education we must not forget that we are educating the theoreticians of the future.

The criticism of Piaget in relation to language is important here. Bruner points out that symbolic representation is necessary for in depth understanding. Using language to externalize one's own understanding is a way of developing a capacity to deal with disembedded material. This relationship between language and thought is one that should always inform our teaching.

Conclusion

Primary schools have changed dramatically in the post-war years. Much of this change has been due to a recognition that, in order to learn, children have to understand. This approach to teaching and children is due in no small measure to the work of Piaget. However, things must never stand still. In particular, teachers need to have a detailed understanding of the ways in which children come to understand the world so that they can be effective in their teaching.

To the concept of concreteness we need to add Donaldson's concept of embeddedness. Presenting children with material embedded in a known context is the first step. Then we need to plan to help them to deal with the purely abstract. Language would seem to be the key here. Language is the subject of our next chapter.

Further Reading

You will note that I am not recommending that you should read Piaget directly. His work is not applied and also very opaque. It is much better that you should read a commentary and then concentrate on more relevant and applied books. Ginsberg and Opper (1969) *Piaget's Theory of Intellectual Development* is an excellent overview of Piaget's work. There is also a very useful appendix in Donaldson (1978) *Children's Minds*. This last book is essential reading setting out as it does Donaldson's concept of embeddedness and exploring the relationship between language and cognition. Donaldson, Grieve and Pratt (1983) *Early Childhood Development and Education* is a very comprehensive collection of papers which relates theoretical work to practical educational issues. You will probably also find that the approach taken by Liebeck (1984) in *How Children Learn Mathematics* is highly relevant to teaching and cognitive development.

Chapter 8

Language

Introduction

We all use language. It seems to us to be as natural as the air we breath. It is all part of being human. However, teachers can never take language for granted. They have to use language to teach and they have to *teach language*. Regardless of the subject that a teacher has followed throughout training, it is impossible to ignore language, so in some sense we are all teachers of language. The question then arises as to what exactly it is that a teacher needs to know about language. As we shall see, everybody, at some level, has an expert knowledge of their own language, but not everybody has had to make this knowledge *explicit*. The days have long gone since children were forced to carry out long parsing exercises using a 'grammar' that was obscure, meaningless to them, and in fact, as we know from modern linguistics, essentially wrong in any case. However, just because we recognize that it may not be necessary for all young children to undertake a course in modern linguistics, it does not mean that teachers should not. It is becoming increasingly clear that, in order for teachers to be able to facilitate the language development of their pupils, they must have an explicit and in depth knowledge of the way language works. When you go to the dentist, you do not need to be given a detailed lecture about the nature of the cavity, but you might reasonably expect the dentist to be able to discuss with you the best way to keep your teeth clean and how to go about reducing the incidence of holes in the future. You also have the right to expect that your dentist will have an expert knowledge of teeth formation, growth, cavity prevention and how to remedy any problems. The dentist will be using all this knowledge when your teeth are being drilled and because of this you get better treatment. The same with children, teachers and language. Though you may never teach linguistics explicitly, you need to understand about the nature of language so that you can understand what is happening as children develop their own linguistic competence during their time in your charge.

What is Language?

Language is a *human system* of *arbitrary symbols* that is used to *communicate* messages from one person to another. The trouble with defining language is that we have to use it to define it. Let us take each of the italicized words in turn.

Language is Unique to HUMANS

To quote from one of the most influential linguists of the twentieth century: 'When we study human language, we are approaching what some might call the "human essence", the distinctive qualities of mind that are, so far as we know, unique to man' (Noam Chomsky 1972, *Language and Mind*).

You may be questioning this point. You may have seen television programmes about chimpanzees who seem to be able to talk, about dolphins and whales that communicate with each other, about budgerigars and mynah birds who have perfect diction, and even about cats and dogs that 'understand everything that is said to them'. Why, then, am I arguing that language is unique to humans? Well, let us start with the cats and dogs. Of course animals can be trained to respond to commands. Your dog may well sit down when you say firmly 'Sit' but it will probably sit to a number of other words providing you use the same sharp tone of voice. It is not understanding the language, but responding automatically to an auditory stimulus. If you have a dog, you will be well aware that it took quite some time to train it to respond correctly. Conversely, when the dog barks and whines and stands by the back door, you interpret that as 'I want to go out'. Certainly, the animal has communicated with you, but it has not used language. It is possible for communication to take place without language at all.

What about the budgerigar? You can teach your bird to say 'Who's a pretty boy then?' and any number of other phrases which you can recognize as sounding like human speech. This does not mean that the bird is a language user. All it means is that the bird has a facility for perfect imitation. This ability is a very useful one in the natural habitat because other birds can be imitated as a means of auditory camouflage. If you tried to have a conversation with the bird, the system would break down. The animal can produce a set of noises that sound like human speech, but there is no sentient being behind the noise. It is possible to make the noise without there being any communication.

Now let us consider chimpanzees. There have been a number of attempts to teach chimpanzees language. Chimpanzees were chosen because they are primates, close, in evolutionary terms, to humans, and from all the animal learning experiments they had shown themselves to be highly capable of learning. In the 1930s the Kelloggs (1933) tried to teach Gua to speak and in the 1950s the Hayes (1951) tried to teach Viki. Both chimpanzees were brought up as if they were humans; thus, theoretically, they had the same experiences as a human child. Neither chimpanzee learned language.

One of the reasons that humans sound like humans is that we have an anatomy which enables us to produce the speech sounds that we do. Chimpanzees to not have the same facial and upper respiratory tract structure and so are physically incapable of making the same sounds. In 1966, two psychologists, Allen and Beatrice Gardner (1969), decided they would avoid the problems of vocalization and instead they would capitalize on the chimpanzees' considerable manual dexterity. To this end they began to train a young chimpanzee, Washoe, in American Sign Language. She was brought up much as a deaf child in a deaf community would be. To begin with, the study seemed to show remarkable success. She would respond to signs and also produce her own in response. In that sense, there was real communication between chimpanzee and human. After three years she had learned about eighty-five signs with various meanings. Some were 'nouns' such as *dog*, *duck* and *baby*. Others were less obviously concrete words like *hurry*, *gimme* and that very frequently occurring child's word, *more*. They suggested that they had evidence that she was able spontaneously to string words together, producing two and some three word utterances. Alas for Washoe, she was never able to get beyond that stage. She never developed a reliable system for combining words together in a rule-governed way.

There have been other attempts to develop language in chimpanzees, but a result from just one more will illustrate a point I want to make. This was a study by Terrace (1979) of sign language being taught to a chimp Nim Chimpsky (you will see the irony as Noam Chomsky was so adamant about language being unique to humans). Nim learned about 125 signs and began to produce combinations. However when the 'utterances' were analyzed it became clear that they were juxtapositions of signs and not meaningful combinations. An example can be given from one sixteen word combination. *GIVE ORANGE ME GIVE EAT ORANGE ME EAT ORANGE GIVE ME EAT ORANGE GIVE ME YOU.* Certainly, the message has been conveyed, but most of it is redundant. Young children learning language do not produce utterances like this. For the moment at least it seems to be the case that communication between human and chimpanzee will be limited. The chimpanzee does not learn the human language.

It is possible to argue that saying *human* language is unique to humans is tautological; it may that animals have their *own* languages. In fact we can go right back to Pavlov for an answer to this problem. He said that all animals had a *first signalling system*. This system would enable them to communicate about immediate environmental events that were life preserving or life threatening. Ducklings will keep up a constant *cheep-cheep* which will serve to keep a brood together and in hearing of the parents: obviously an important response for staying safe and getting fed. They will also set up a loud cacaphony if a bird of prey is spotted. Again this is a life preserving response. Many animals show these types of communication behaviours, but they cannot be considered language.

What, then, is it about language that means we cannot include bird songs or chimpanzees' calls in our definition? The system of communication that we call language is not just about signalling food or danger; it is not just about conveying messages to do with the immediate environment. Human language is so creative and flexible that we can use it to convey messages about ideas from the past and the future. We can talk about immediate concrete needs and abstract philosophical ideas. The language is infinite. It is this that makes language a system of communicating ideas that is unique to humans.

Language is a SYSTEM

The word system means that language is made up of a set of parts that are related together to form a complete whole. In truth, language is a system made up of a number of different distinct but interconnected subsystems. The subsystems are *phonology*, the *lexicon*, *syntax*, *semantics* and *pragmatics*. We shall consider these all in turn shortly, but for the moment you need to know that these subsystems form the grammar of the language. Phonology is the sound system; the lexicon is the word system; syntax is the system for combining words into well formed units, often sentences; semantics is the system of meaning; and pragmatics is language in use.

Language is a System of SYMBOLS

Though I said we would take each of the italicized words in the definition in turn, in fact it makes more sense to consider the word 'symbol' before 'arbitrary'. The symbols are the units that stand for, or represent, other things. The word 'cat' represents a small, furry animal with four legs and usually a tail that is often, though not always, a domestic pet. You will appreciate that it is much easier to give an example of a symbol representing a concrete object than it is to give a symbol representing a nebulous, complex, abstract notion.

Language is a System of ARBITRARY Symbols

It is most important that you understand the arbitrary nature of language. 'Arbitrary' means that the symbols are not based on any intrinsic characterization of the things they represent. The rules that govern the system are the rules and, because we are language users, we use them, but there is no sense in which any one rule is in some way more logical or correct than any other rule.

The word *amu* in Ewe (a West African language) has the same meaning as the word *child* in English. There is no sense in which either word bears a direct relationship to the thing they both represent. The relationship between the *form* and the *meaning* is entirely arbitrary. If we wanted to specify a particular child in Ewe we would say *Amu ye* and in English we would say *The child*. There is a rule in Ewe which leads to people having to put the definitive article *after* the noun, whereas in English there is a rule which says it must come *before* the noun.

As far as language use is concerned, we simply have to recognize this arbitrary nature of language in order to stop ourselves becoming linguistic imperialists, and then we have to accept that we have to follow the rules in order to communicate. Of course we could always behave like Humpty Dumpty:

'There's glory for you!'

'I don't know what you mean by "glory",' Alice said.

Humpty Dumpty smiled contemptuously. 'Of course you don't — till I tell you. I meant "there's a nice knock-down argument for you!"'

'But "glory" doesn't mean "a nice knock-down argument",' Alice objected.

'When I use a word,' Humpty Dumpty said in a rather scornful tone, 'it means just what I choose it to mean — neither more nor less.'

'The question is,' said Alice, 'whether you can make words mean so many different things.'

'The question is, 'said Humpty Dumpty, 'which is to be master — that's all.'

(Lewis Carroll, *Through the Looking Glass and What Alice found there*.)

Language is a System for COMMUNICATION

Since language is for communication of messages, we cannot decide to behave like Humpty Dumpty. Communication means that the messages have to be shared or made common. Thus, though the relationship between form and meaning may be arbitrary, the users of a language have to agree about the systems that they are using and the meaning of the symbols. Obviously there are many languages in the world and initially they may all appear to be very different. However, communities of people will all use a roughly similar language even though that language may be very different from the language used by another community. Occasionally there will be reports of twins developing their own language. This will be an example of a language used by a very small community. However, as the twins grow older, they begin to conform to the language environment that they find around them and gradually cease to use their secret language.

All families have some word usage which is idiosyncratic to them. A word which a child made up when first beginning to speak is retained as a talisman. Some special toys have very private names. If such a toy is to accompany a child to school at the beginning, then it is most important that the teacher is allowed to share in the knowledge so that there is not a communication breakdown. Also, such is the nature of human life that the language of toileting may sometimes be discreet to the point of obscurity. Home–school liaison should be sufficiently clear that the teacher knows the family way for asking to use the toilet. Constant re-assurance that 'You are being a good boy' can lead to very wet patches if the teacher does not realize that 'being a good boy' is a euphemism for 'Going to the toilet'.

We have ideas and thoughts in our heads that we need to communicate with others and on the whole language is the most efficient channel by which we can exchange thoughts. True, animals may have their initial signalling system, but it does not take them very far. The beauty of language is that it frees us totally from the immediate situation. We can use language to recall the past and to speculate about the future. Language frees us from the concrete and allows communication about the abstract. However, as I am all too painfully aware through writing, the relationship between the ideas and the language used to communicate those ideas is not isomorphic. There is a close relationship between language and thought, but it is by no means perfect. Thus you, as a teacher, have to enable children to develop their verbal and written language skills to facilitate the best possible communicative competence. It is possible to use language to talk about anything. Language is infinite and totally creative.

The Systems of Language

What do we mean when we say that language is creative and infinite? I can produce a sentence: 'The sky is full of bats flying home to roost.' As far as I know, I have never produced that sentence before, but I know what it means and I presume that, though the likelihood of your having heard it before is quite slim, you will have no trouble in understanding it. Not only is language infinite in the sense that it is capable of producing an infinite number of correctly formed sentences, it is also infinite in that I could produce an infinitely long sentence. But of course I'd have bored everyone to death by then. The point is that the system is totally productive. From a countable number of units we can expand to the infinite.

I should also point out that I have been talking about *language*; not *a* language or *the* language. What we have to say applies to all languages across all cultures and all dialectal forms within any one language. There is no sense that any one language has priority or is superior to any other. The language that we happen to speak relates to an accident of where we were born and what language our parents speak. We are quite capable of speaking any language; alas in Britain all too few of us are able to speak much more than our own native dialect.

The Sound System — Phonology

All languages have far more in common than they have differences between them. With the exception of sign languages, all languages are sound based. We produce sounds in a rule-governed way and these are interpreted as having meaning by other people who also know the code. If other people do not happen to know the particular language that I am speaking, they will still be able to tell the difference between when I am speaking and when I am crying or moaning.

Each language has its own distinct set of sounds. These are the *phonemes* which are the units for building up the language. We cannot just decide to combine the sounds arbitrarily. We have to follow an implicit rule system to build up the phonemes into meaningful units which are called *morphemes*. The phoneme is the smallest unit of sound in a language and the morpheme is the smallest unit of *meaningful* sound. Occasionally there are morphemes which are composed of a single phoneme. In English we have a few examples of this happening: 'I' — first person singular — is a single phoneme and a morpheme; so is 'a' — the indefinite article; so is 'owe' — to be in debt to someone. The examples I have given you are basically *words* that are made up of single sounds from the language.

Children have to learn to use the phonology of the language that is in their immediate environment. Provided that they have no phonological impairment, they could acquire any phonology, but that would not be particularly useful, so they gradually confine themselves to producing the sounds of what will be their own language. Although children are able to make themselves understood from a very early age and they appear to have much of the phonology of the language from about 2½ years, they do not attain full adult production of phonemes until they are in infant school. Many children exhibit immaturities well into their junior years. Teachers need to be aware of this. Since the immaturities are well within normal limits, they should not try to 'correct' articulation. Too much correction could inhibit a child from speaking. If articulation is so poor that intelligibility is a problem, consultations with the parents about possible speech therapy may be necessary. Never try remediation yourself without consultation.

It is vital that we do not underestimate the nature of the cognitive and fine motor skills that need to be coordinated with language skill in order to be able to produce clearly articulated utterances.

Let us consider how the sounds are produced. Basically speech is a wonderful example of nature utilizing waste products. Speech is produced on the out breath. Just try breathing in and speaking at the same time. It is possible, but your voice begins to squeak and you can go a bit red in the face.

The different phonemes result from the type, manner and place from which the sound is produced. Let us think about vowels. Try making a few. What is happening? You should find that the vowel that comes out depends on the shape of your mouth or more precisely of your lips and the way you use your tongue. Think about the 'ah' sound that you make when the doctor wants to see down your throat. When you make that particular vowel the lips are rounded and the back of the tongue is lowered. This makes it much easier to see over the tongue into the throat. The doctor would have a hard time if they asked patients to make an 'ee' sound because the front part of the tongue is raised. It is possible to classify all possible vowel sounds depending on the height of the tongue, the part of the tongue used (from front to back) and the amount of roundedness of the lips. Have a go at trying to place the vowel sounds in your particular system. It really is quite difficult to work out exactly what you are doing and yet you produce the sounds at a great speed with never a conscious thought whenever you speak.

In all fairness, I should point out that the science of phonetics is much more complex than presented here. You are not going to be phoneticians. Nevertheless, it is important that you begin to appreciate the complexity of speech production, even at this apparently simple sound system level.

Let us now contrast vowels with consonants. You have probably only considered these two classes with respect to the alphabet. The vowels are the letters A, E, I, O, U, with a question mark over the Y. The rest are consonants. You do not need much persuasion to agree that there are actually more vowel sounds than there are vowel letters. So what is a vowel and a consonant? Have a go at making the sounds and see if you can come up with an obvious difference between the two.

Let us think about how the speech sounds are made. You have a series of *articulators* which you organize into various shapes to produce the different sounds. You use your tongue placement and the shape of your lips as well as your teeth to produce different sounds. In addition to this, you can allow the vocal chords in the larynx to vibrate as the air passes through — in which case you produce a voiced sound; or you can allow the air to pass through without any vibration — in which case you produce an unvoiced sound.

The easiest way to make your knowledge explicit here, is to try making all the sounds of English, or any other language. You know how to make the sounds, but you may never have had to make this knowledge explicit. You have to do this out loud, so if you are reading this in a library or a train you might save the activity until later. Think about where you are placing your tongue whether you make the sound at the front or the back of your mouth; do you use your lips and teeth; and what about the voicing? The best way to check this is to put your fingers on your Adam's apple and experience the vibrations when you use your voice. Try making the sounds /p/ and /b/ in front of a mirror. Can you *see* any difference? The only difference between the two phonemes is that the /b/ is voiced and the /p/ is unvoiced. Now make the /th/ sound in 'the', and /d/. Can you see that you have put your tongue between your teeth for the /th/ but you place it just behind the top row teeth for the /d/? This is what we mean by a high level of fine motor skill being necessary to produce speech sounds. The distinction between /th/ and /d/ is very subtle and it is not surprising that many children are still saying 'de' for 'the' in infant school.

The sound system that we have been talking about is the system of segments that we use to form the words. In addition, within the phonological system there is the *suprasegmental* level. This is the level that informs us where to put the stress patterns in the words and sentences. In English, words tend to have one primary stress, although very long multisyllabic words may have secondary stress as well. Children have to learn where to place the stress so that the stress patterns conform to those of their native dialect. For example, the position of the stress in some multisyllabic words can alter the meaning and the syntactic status of the word. Thus *greenhouse* and *green house* have two separate meanings and with *'convert* and *con'vert* we have first a noun and then a verb.

You can see the effects that stress patterns have in sentences by saying the following sentence four times. Each time place the main stress on a different word. 'Will you eat it.'

What you should find is that you get four sentences which have four subtly different meanings.

Syntax

It is not just necessary to have a knowledge of the sound units which go to make up the words within the language. We also need to have a system which determines the order in which the words themselves can occur. There has to a be a structuring of the units so that they go together to form recognizable phrases and sentences. As we saw with chimpanzee Nim, the ordering of the words cannot be purely arbitrary. For example there is a difference in the meaning of the following two sentences:

The girl read her book to the teacher.

The teacher read her book to the girl.

Both sentences are made up of exactly the same words but the ordering affects the meaning. Both sentences are recognized as well formed sentences which have a meaning. However if you were presented with: 'Read book her the to girl teacher the', you would be able to understand each individual word but you would not recognize the string as a grammatical sentence and you would not be able to infer any meaning from the string.

The rules of syntax specify the order that the words must occur to form an acceptable sentence. This means that the syntactic system also incorporates a system for determining the syntactic category of each word. Let me explain this. The rules of syntax tell you the word order; so, for example, you will know that any string of the order:

Determiner   Adjective   Noun   Verb   Determiner   Adjective   Noun

will form an acceptable English sentence. Thus

The	*large*	*ball*	*broke*	*the*	*oval*	*window*
Det	Adj	N	V	Det	Adj	N

is an acceptable sentence, as is:

This	*big*	*girl*	*likes*	*that*	*small*	*puppy*

Since we need these rules to determine the word order, it is necessary to have a system for defining the category of each word so that it can slot into its correct place in the sentence. In other words, we need to know that *ball* is a noun and that *broke* is a verb because, without this implicit knowledge, the syntactic rules would be unusable.

If you try to generate some more sentences that are of the same structure you will quickly see how you are using your implicit knowledge about the syntactic status of words. Though this structure produces acceptable sentences, it can also lead to many strings that are recognized as not acceptable. For example:

That	*small*	*boy*	*went*	*that*	*big*	*school*

Your knowledge of the verb *went* tells you that you have to follow it by a prepositional phrase — *went to*, *went in*, *went for*. We must never forget that the sub-systems of language interact with one another. The syntactic system governs word order and word category, but this knowledge must also be stored in a matrix-like fashion in the lexical system.

The Words — the Lexicon

Up to now you have probably used the term 'vocabulary' as the collective noun for the sum total of all the words in the language. Linguists prefer to use the term *lexicon* for very good reasons. What is a word? Is *Headteacher* one word, or two? What about *foot, feet* or *buy, bought* or *school, schools*: are these one word, or two?

Obviously we would tend to say that *Headteacher* was one word, but the reasoning would tend to be 'because that is the way we write it'. In another sense it can be said to be two words. The same can be said about *foot* and *feet* — yes, they are two words, but they are very closely related, both representing 'a thing with five toes on the end'. It's just that *feet* represents more than one of these.

The lexicon must contain all the information about the sound of the individual words but it also must contain information about the relationships between the items. An example from learning French may be useful here. Once you have learned the rule for regular verbs, if you are then told that a verb is regular, you only need to be given the infinitive form to be able to generate all the other related words.

Initially, I said that the language was composed of a number of interrelated and interacting subsystems, and this can be seen most clearly in the lexicon. The sound identity of each word must be specified, but so must its syntactic identity. The lexicon needs to contain information about which syntactic category a word belongs to so that it can be slotted into the correct place in a sentence. This shows you clearly why the term 'lexical item' rather than 'word' is used. Take *school* — is this one word, or two? Clearly there is only one phonological identity here, but *school* can be either a noun or a verb. This information is needed by the language system so that well formed sentences can be produced and comprehended.

The Meaning System — Semantics

The last system we will discuss in this chapter is the *semantic* system. Clearly it is not enough to be able to produce words with the correct sound patterns in an acceptable order — we need to be able to produce meaningful language. It is actually possible to produce a sentence which is perfectly correct in all respects except semantics. Chomsky produced a famous one for us:

Colourless green ideas sleep furiously.

This sentence shows us two aspects of semantics. There is the lexical aspect — the fact that each word has a meaning; and there is meaning beyond the level of the word.

> ' . . . you should say what you mean,' the March Hare went on.
>
> 'I do,' Alice replied, 'at least — I mean what I say — that's the same thing, you know.'
>
> 'Not the same thing a bit!' said the Hatter. 'You might just as well say that "I see what I eat" is the same thing as "I eat what I see"!'

(Lewis Carroll, *Alice's Adventures in Wonderland.*)

The meaning of the sentences that we speak depends both on the meaning of the individual words and the way we combine them; but possibly, at a different level we have the meanings that we want to express. We use the language to convey these meanings and the only way that this is possible is by using semantic, syntactic, phonological rules and the lexical items in combination. We will discuss pragmatics in Chapter 9.

By now, I hope that you begin to see that language is something that we cannot take for granted — particularly in education. It is an extremely complex system that we need to study in depth. The Kingman Committee (1988) made it clear that in their view all teachers should begin to develop a knowledge of the working of the language at an explicit rather than implicit level.

Language Development

Now we have some understanding of the nature of language we need to begin to think about its development. Language development does not begin with the first words. Children are surrounded by language from the time that they are born. They may not be able to use language for communication at this early stage, but the experiences are necessary to begin the whole process of the development of language and communication.

Generally speaking we divide language acquisition into a prelinguistic stage and then the linguistic stage. In the prelinguistic stage the babies will be making sounds but these cannot be considered to be language. On the other hand they will show some evidence of communicating. Parents can hold 'conversations' with their young offspring in the sense that the adult will maybe say something and look and smile and then the baby will respond. There is a sense that the pair are having a conversation in that the baby is learning turn-taking. Besides these delightful social events, babies also have the ability to communicate needs, but not through language. The communicative function is separate from the linguistic function at this stage.

This is not to say that babies do not produce sounds! They cry and whimper and coo, but these seem to be reactions to bodily feelings of hunger or discomfort or well being. By about 6 months most babies will be 'babbling'. They will be producing many different sounds many of which they do not hear in the language around them. In this early babbling stage they seem to be trying out the effects of different movements and combinations of mouth, tongue and voice (remember that they may well not have any teeth yet). At this stage the activity does not seem to depend on any auditory feedback because there is no difference between the babbling of hearing babies and profoundly deaf babies. However, there is eventually a big difference here. The hearing babies do get auditory feedback and can also match the sounds that they produce to the sounds around them. Gradually their 'babbling' takes on the intonation patterns and phonology of the language (or languages) they are hearing around them. Deaf babies do not get this feedback and gradually they begin to stop babbling because they do not appreciate the effect of flapping their mouths around and they have no input against which to model their own behaviour. This does not mean that babbling is an essential prerequisite for language, however, because profoundly deaf children do develop language and children who have had early motor dysfunction which is later corrected, can learn to talk properly. The point is that the *usual* way that the talking side of language is acquired is a natural progression from early babbling.

Around 12 months, babies begin to use groups of sounds consistently to stand for the same thing. The 'words' may not be exact duplications of the words of their own language environment, but they show clearly, by the way they use these phonologically constant forms, that they recognize that sounds are related to meaning.

Babies at this stage will also show that they do understand language. Indeed, as is the case throughout language development, comprehension preceeds production. This does not, however, mean that children's language comprehension is very sophisticated. Parents are not talking to their babies about theoretical physics, or at least if they are, they are not expecting the baby to respond. The language that the babies comprehend is very context bound. When a parent asks a child 'Do you want some more apple?' the apple will be there in view, the rising intonation for question form will be very clear and the 'more apple' will be stressed. The baby then has many cues to aid comprehension.

The phonologically constant forms will gradually develop into a recognizable vocabulary, though with many immaturities because of the difficulty of producing so many of the words. Nevertheless, this vocabulary will be used to good effect. 'Sentences' at this stage tend to be single words. It is called the *holophrastic* stage (*holo* meaning complete or undivided). The babies produce words which stand for whole concepts. They do not have a grammar at this stage.

By about two years, the children will begin to be producing utterances made up of two words, and once this happens language can really be said to be taking off. Combinations enable them to express the relationships between ideas in a unified meaning. They can express far more than the sum total of their lexical items. After the two-word utterance stage they will begin to use three idea utterances often of the form Subject — Verb — Object: e.g. 'Me wannana' ('I want a banana'). Children will show clearly that they are using word order rules to produce their sentences. Their vocabulary is developing as well as the syntactic system and so they are able to express many more ideas, but these ideas will also be more complex. Intelligibility may not be perfect, but because the language is embedded in a shared context, the children will experience success in conveying their ideas.

We have to hold in mind the recognition that all the subsystems are developing simultaneously. This means that the children will be deriving rules to elaborate their systems. The rules are derived from their language environment, but they are not necessarily always the final rules of adult language. They will use rules that will generate as many utterances as they need for communication but, when the systems have developed and grown, they will have to adapt the rules to enable them to express even more.

Berko (1958) showed this rule use most clearly with young children producing 'correct' plurals and past tense morphemes to non-words. They would add the phoneme /z/ to make *wug* plural rather than /s/ or /iz/ which are both possible alternatives. This showed that they were implicitly using the rule which states that in English the voiced form /z/ is used to denote plurals with nouns that end in a voiced consonant.

We can also show that children overuse the rules once acquired. After all it is much more economical to so do and likely to be a successful strategy most of the time. It is only after the rule has been well developed that the exceptions to the rule are recognized. Thus, with *foot/feet*, children are likely, initially, to use the two words correctly, but not as part of a rule-governed system. Then, when they derive the rule about plurality, they overuse it and so begin to say *foots*. Eventually they become aware of exceptions, but may still feel the need to mark plurality through a plural morpheme so some children will say *feets*. In the end they all have a firm grasp of the rule and its exceptions so the *foot/feet* pair is part of a rule-governed system.

By the time children are $3\frac{1}{2}$ to 4 years they will have acquired the *basic* elements of language and will be well able to express their ideas and needs in social settings. However, because they appear so competent, it is possible to assume that they will have no difficulty with comprehension and that they only need to develop vocabulary to show adultlike performance. This is far from the case. Language development *does not stop* at 4. Language is continually developing throughout the primary years. This is not just vocabulary extension but lexical rule, syntactic and semantic development. Bowerman (1982) has characterized this process of language development as being one where the children derive generative rules which enable them to express ideas and then reorganize the systems as they collect more data and need to elaborate the systems.

When children enter school, the nature of the linguistic interchange alters. Before school the majority of interactions will be firmly embedded in a shared context. Children do not have many experiences that are not known to their parents or immediate carers. Even when they are talking about playschool, nursery, parties or playing with their friends, the context will generally be easily understood. Thus, even when there is less than perfect expression, the children will be able to communicate successfully. Also, since the parents, in the main, share the knowledge base of their children at this early age, they will talk to them in language that the children will understand and about topics that are embedded in a shared context. The adult–child ratio is so good in any case, that any failure in comprehension can be repaired fairly immediately.

Once children are in school, the nature of the discourse changes. There is not the same shared context. The possibilities for communication failure are greatly increased. Because the adult–child ratio is one to many, it is not possible to have immediate feedback to check that every child has understood. It is not a useful ploy to ask if everyone has understood because the chances are that they will all say 'Yes', and only later on, through performance on tasks, will it become clear that they did not all understand. This means that teachers have to become much more reflective on their use of language. You have to become highly skilled in using language for explanation.

The possibilities for the children misunderstanding you are considerably increased in a classroom. We know, from the post-Piagetian work we discussed in Chapter 7, that failure to comprehend what is said linguistically may create an apparent cognitive failure. This means that teachers need to be conscious of the areas of language that are still developing in the primary years. The problem is that, as yet, we have incomplete knowledge about *when* specific linguistic structures develop. This means that teachers just have to be sensitive to the possibility of communication failure because of the developing state of the children's linguistic knowledge. Where it is important that language should not make the meaning opaque, simple clear language should be used.

Having said that we have not yet mapped all the subtle developments that have to take place during the primary years, we can nevertheless illustrate some of the developments across the different subsystems.

As we said earlier, children can be expected to be still using immature articulation throughout the infant years. On the whole this immaturity does not prove a handicap to intelligibility. *De* for *the*, *fing for thing* and *lickul* for *little* are all well within normal limits at this age. Because of this, teachers should not worry or make the children self-conscious and certainly should not try to 'correct' the articulation by making the children imitate their own mature articulation. When the children are clearly using a rule-based system that is simply, as yet, immature, drawing the children's attention to this can lead to needless self-consciousness. We want the children to use language. We don't want them feeling nervous about being corrected for something that they do not even know is wrong — as indeed it is not.

There are subtle suprasegmental rules that have to be learned which may affect comprehension. Atkinson-King (1973) found that, though 5-year-olds could perceive the difference in the stress patterns between *greenhouse* and *green house*, *hotdog* and *hot dog*, they could not reliably assign the correct meaning to each term. Children cannot be expected reliably to disambiguate such terms, when the context is uncertain, until the end of the primary years.

Cruttenden (1985) has shown that understanding of stress patterns within sentences is still developing throughout the junior years. Eight- and 9-year-olds had difficulty in comprehending the difference between sentences of the form:

1   Robert gave a book to Sam and he gave one to Charles.

[*Robert gave Charles a book.*]

and

2   Robert gave a book to Sam and *he* gave one to Charles.

[*Sam gives Charles a book.*]

These subtleties of stress patterns are perfectly clear to adults, but as teachers we must be aware that utterances which rely on stress patterns for disambiguation may be very confusing to children.

At the level of lexical development, obviously children are adding to their vocabulary all the time, but then so are we. We cannot take it for granted that children will have an understanding of all the subject specific words that we use, nor can we expect them to realize when we are using everyday terms in a subject specific way. They may well be perfectly *au fait* with the term *volume* in respect to the sound level on a television, but this does not mean that they will understand the same word when it is used to describe cubical content. The term *times* in the mathematical expression 4×5 is shorthand for 'multiplied by'. Primary teachers are well aware that they have both to help the children to understand mathematical principles and at the same time to initiate the children into the particular language of mathematics. Without this linguistic knowledge, understanding of the principles may be incomplete.

Just as the lexicon has to develop, so too do the rules within the lexicon. During the primary years children will learn the rules of affixation with respect to, for example, comparatives: *small*, *smallER*, *smallEST*. An apparently simple rule but, as with so many rules, they have to learn that it only applies within constraints. They have to learn that, when the adjective has three or more syllables, affixation is not allowed. Instead we have to use *more* plus the adjective; thus *more beautiful*, *more important*, etc. Children will not have this rule reliably until the end of the primary years.

I must stress that, when we talk about children using linguistic rules, we mean that they have an implicit understanding of the rules. They show by their production and their regular errors that they are using the rules to generate language. Teachers need to have more than an implicit knowledge because they have to begin to identify what may be missing in a child's production. Certainly it is good practice to explore with the children how the rules operate and to have an exciting time finding out what happens when we violate the rules.

Though children will have a good grasp of syntax before school, there are many subtle structures that have to be acquired. Carol Chomsky (1969) made an extensive study of the development of comprehension of the complement structure. Her study shows that adult usage of the verbs *ask* and *tell* is not complete until around 10 years.

She asked children to respond to sentences of the following six forms:

1   Ask Susan [another child] what time it is.
2   Tell Susan what time it is.
3   Ask Susan her last name.
4   Tell Susan your last name.
5   Ask Susan what to feed the doll.
6   Tell Susan what to feed the doll.

At 5, the children would not differentiate between the two verbs but treat all sentences as though *tell* had been used. Thus, to Question 1, they would tell the other child the time, or more than likely respond by saying 'I don't know how to tell the time.' Understanding showed a clear developmental progression. First they would be able to differentiate between 1 and 2 and then between 3 and 4. There was an intermediary stage with Question 5 when they would begin to interpret *ask* correctly but would then say 'What are you going to feed the doll?' rather than 'What should I feed the doll?'

Warden (1976) studied the development of the use of articles with respect to given and new information. As adults we tend to introduce a new noun, or noun phrase, with the indefinite article and then subsequently we preface it with the definitive article. Thus:

Once upon a time there was **a** little girl who lived in a wood. She lived with her Grandmother. **The** little girl's name was Goldilocks.

Warden found that by 7, children would show adult usage with second mention, but even the oldest children (9 years) were still using the definitive article for new information. Five- and 7-year-olds would be using the definitive article inappropriately 38 per cent of the time.

Much of the sophistication of language development may well be facilitated by the development of reading and writing. The technicalities of complex sentences using conjunctions such as *although, since, however*, etc., can be discussed through the medium of the written form where there is concrete evidence to discuss and manipulate. There is a need to change the style of language when writing. Written language has to be explicit because there is no possibility of repairing any misunderstanding. Written language is disembedded. Children have to learn the conventions of written form which enable them to understand and communicate in this abstract medium. Because of the permanence of the written form, it is possible to reflect on the form that it takes. We are able to study the written form but we cannot, without the aid of a tape recorder, study our own spoken form. Since it is teachers who teach children to read and write, it is teachers who are the major facilitators of later language development.

Language Problems

We have said that there are a number of subsystems that function together to make up language, so it will not surprise you that children can have problems in the functioning of any or all of the subsystems. Most children will be comprehending well and producing words at 2 and using simple sentences by 3. However, some children will show *language delay*. This means that their language functioning is definitely behind that which would be expected for a child of that age. As the term implies, the language is delayed and so the children will develop along normal lines but at a possibly slower rate. Parents may well have been worried about their child and consulted a doctor who should have referred them to a speech therapist. The therapist will have to monitor the child's progress to enable a diagnosis of delay to be made and even so she (the vast majority of speech therapists are female) may still decide to give the child some therapy to enhance production and intelligibility before school. Fortunately, today, most doctors tend not to fob parents of boys off with platitudes about boys developing language later than girls, even though the speech therapy services are very stretched. Where language is concerned it is better to err on the side of caution.

When a child's language appears to be atypical and not developing along normal lines, then a diagnosis of *language disorder* may be made. The problem may be in any one or all of the subsystems of language and such children need specialist help to enable them to develop as much language functioning as possible. There will be a number of children who have an identifiable syndrome system which leads them to have cognitive deficits, and with poor language development. These children will show global lowering of functioning. However, there are some children who seem to have specific language functioning problems which are not apparently related to cognitive deficits. The cause is generally unknown. These children need to have a great deal of speech therapy and much support in school because, as they progress through the primary years, the reliance on complex language gets greater and greater.

Since most children have the basics of production and comprehension by 5, it might be supposed that any child with a language problem would have been identified before school. This is not the case. As we have said, language interactions, pre-school, take place within a known context. Parents may be able to understand their children even when production is atypical. Because the language is embedded the children may be able to respond appropriately to situations even when they do not understand the language. However, once the child is in a school setting, the language problem may begin to manifest itself. The teacher may therefore be the person who first has suspicions that all is not well, and so be instrumental in beginning the procedure to enable the child to be statemented in order to have *language* therapy. I use the term language therapy advisedly here. The speech therapist will be helping the children to develop their language systems rather than speech *per se*. Of course, speech therapists still do assist in such speech problems as articulation difficulty and fluency problems (stammering).

Initially the teacher may just have a feeling that all is not well. A particular child may not respond appropriately or there may seem to be a mismatch between verbal and nonverbal ability. Intelligibility may be very poor and the child may well have problems in communicating with other children. Teachers are not speech therapists, but there are some standardized assessments that they may carry out to confirm their suspicions. The British Picture Vocabulary Scales give a good estimate of a child's vocabulary and the Test for the Reception of Grammar shows how well the child is comprehending a whole variety of syntactic structures. Where it is clear that a child is not progressing well then teachers must, with the parents cooperation and the expert advice of the educational psychologist, seek to enlist the help of a therapist who is the expert in this area.

Once a child is receiving therapy, it is in the best interest of that child that the teacher and the therapist should work as closely as possible together so that the child does not get conflicting messages. Teachers are the experts in general learning and curriculum matters. They can advise the therapist about overall school performance, specific progress in reading and writing and the topics that are to be covered over the term. This is necessary information if therapists are to be able to contextualize their work with the children. The therapists must advise the teachers about the structures they are presently covering so that the teachers can reinforce this within the class. They can also give the teachers guidance about the language strategies that they themselves should be using to facilitate the language performance of the children. Detailed record keeping is essential so that statements of the children's needs can be realistic and therapists and teachers who have to deal with the children at later stages gain a true picture of the capabilities of the children.

As understanding of the nature of childhood language disorders becomes more sophisticated, the need for general primary teachers who are specifically trained in helping language development to work in language units alongside speech therapists increases. These teachers and the therapists then need to liaise very closely with their mainstream colleagues so that if and when integration is the best policy for the children, it becomes a smooth transition.

Conclusion

The relationship between language and cognition is very close. A very influential paper by Macnamara (1972) puts the case very clearly for a cognitive basis for language. The suggestion is that language can only begin to develop once the children have acquired some conceptual categories. They begin to build their linguistic categories on the cognitive ones.

Throughout schooling, teaching is heavily dependent upon language so, without adequate language functioning and understanding, the children cannot learn. This is not to say that learning is not possible without language; clearly it is. But, by the nature of the way we teach and the material that we have to transmit, learning in school will always require language. Children will be able to demonstrate understanding through action, but increasingly, as they progress through school, they will demonstrate their understanding through writing and talking. Detailed discussions with children about why they perform as they do enable teachers to investigate levels of comprehension. Language is one of the main media through which we externalize our thoughts. Because teaching is heavily dependent on language, it behoves teachers to have an explicit knowledge of language functions and forms in order that they make their meanings clear and enable the children to do the same.

Further Reading

Your reading on language needs to be on two levels. Firstly you need to increase your own knowledge about language. Crystal (1976) *Child language, learning and linguistics* makes a useful introduction. Fromkin and Rodman (1988) *An Introduction to Language* is an excellent interactive book with many useful exercises.

Secondly, you need to apply this linguistic knowledge to an understanding of developmental issues. Menyuk (1988) *Language Development, Knowledge and Use* is a very comprehensive and readable account of the development of all the subsystems. You might also read Harris and Coltheart (1986) *Language Processing in Children and Adults*. This is useful for understanding language but it also discusses issues to do with written language development.

Two books which will provide a good introduction to developmental language problems are Beveridge and Conti-Ramsden (1987) *Children with Language Disabilities* and Webster and McConnell (1987) *Children with Speech and Language Difficulties*.

Chapter 9

Social Aspects of Language

Introduction

In the last chapter our main concern was with the form of language and its acquisition. In this chapter we will be concentrating on the social aspects of language. Implicit in the notion that language is for communication is the concept that language is a tool of use in our social lives.

There are two main areas that will be of importance to us. We will first consider that subsystem of language, pragmatics, which we did not consider in detail in Chapter 8. Pragmatics is the term for language in use. Then we will consider the educational implications of language variety — in particular accent and dialect.

Pragmatics

It is clear from Chapter 8 that most children are fluent, competent speakers by the time they get to school. They have implicit knowledge of the rules of language which enables them to understand much of what is said to them and to communicate their ideas in reasonably well formed sentences. However, this is not the whole picture of language performance. Competent language users have to be able to use their linguistic ability in any number of social settings. We have to use the style of language which is most appropriate for the context in which we find ourselves. If we were having tea with the Queen we would not talk in the same manner as we would if we were having tea with our family.

As we said in Chapter 8, children have rather limited social interactions preschool. Their meetings are controlled by parents and carers and they generally move from known context to known context. Nevertheless they will have been exposed to some aspects of pragmatics. After a visit to friends, where there have been any number of tears, arguments and general mayhem, they will be in-structed to say, 'Thank you very much for having me.' Politeness principles will be instilled from a very early age. These include, as we shall see, saying please and thank you, modifying language, waiting to speak rather than butting in, and telling the truth as far as possible. In learning to use language in this way they will be developing pragmatic competence. They will know how to use language in different contexts so that there is effective communication and facilitation of social interaction. Saying 'I said I wanted an apple not an orange you stupid person' may be effective communication but it is hardly conducive to social harmony.

Pragmatics is a very subtle aspect of language. It is really at the interface between the triumvirate of language competence, cognitive competence and social competence. This makes it quite difficult to quantify. Often, with children, we resort to *telling* them that they have been impolite without explaining how. We say that they shouldn't 'say it like that' when there has been a breakdown in their pragmatic skill. We, ourselves, find it almost impossible to *explain why* they have been impolite. To pre-school children we often grant the licence of limited pragmatic ability. On receipt of the second identical toy at a party, we would almost expect a child to say bluntly 'I've got one of these already.' Adults would be prepared to make soothing noises to cover up embarrassment. However, we would expect a junior school age child, under the same circumstances, to be able to cover up regret and give reasonably gracious thanks.

Pragmatic competence requires that we should be able to walk a fine line, following a number of different principles of social communication which, at times, may .ontradict each other (Grice 1975). As in the above example, the child has to learn to be diplomatic. Showing concern for other people's feelings and being polite may lead to not quite telling the truth. This may happen in the class-room as well. As a teacher, you may find that a class will find it quite difficult to tell you that they have already watched that programme before or listened to that particular story. Infant children may well quite happily blurt out 'We've had this one Miss', but junior school children, with their greater pragmatic competence, may feel it more difficult to inform you. This, of course, makes it all the more embarrassing when the truth emerges. It is no use blaming the children for not telling you, because their pragmatic skills tell them that it is less than diplomatic. It does highlight the need for detailed record keeping to be shared amongst staff!

Language does not happen in isolation. Admittedly everyone talks to them-selves at times, but in the main we talk to other people. Children use egocentric speech to regulate their behaviour, but that eventually internalizes and they reserve external language for communicative purposes. Language happens as part of human interactions. (Teaching, and certainly lecturing, provides us with an example of a somewhat bizarre interaction.) This social aspect of language means that we have to recognize that as children are acquiring the phonological, syntactic and semantic subsystems of language, they are using these for a purpose. They have to learn to be able to take part in conversations which are cooperative interactions that do not happen in random fashion.

Conversational Competence

Speakers participating in conversations have to agree implicitly upon the *topic* of the discourse. Any change in topic is generally signalled so that the listener will be able to follow and respond effectively. If you were with a group of friends having a conversation about a television programme that you had just been watching on African elephants, everyone would find it a little bizarre if one of the group suddenly said 'And Uncle Fred bought a new wheel for his bike last week.' The speaker would be asked to explain such an abrupt change in topic or would simply be looked at and then ignored.

We allow children to make such interruptions into adult conversations, but with the caveat that they are told they should wait until the adults have finished. We also recognize that nursery age children, particularly, may appear to make somewhat unfathomable jumps in topic. They may have been thinking about a subject and begin speaking following on from a train of thought that has not been shared in the public domain.

An American study of conversations amongst groups of children by Dorval and Eckman (1984) is of interest here. They analyzed the degree of topic maintenance by measuring the quality of the turns taken in the free conversations. They found that 7-year-olds were well motivated to take part in the conversations but that their awareness of the need to maintain the topic was very limited. Very few of the turns were factually related to the topic and over a third were either tangentially or totally unrelated to the topic. By the 5th grade (10 years), the proportion of at least minimally related turns had increased to over 70 per cent but still the conversations were not characterized by perspective taking on the topic, as were older children's and adults. It was clear that the children had a good notion of the social aspects of taking turns and talking to each other, but their conversations were somewhat random.

We find that adult conversations are clearly not random. Even at the start of a conversation, the participants will ensure that they share sufficient common data for communication to progress. Such ploys as, 'Do you know about X? Well Y happened' may be used. Here the speaker checks that X is shared before the new information, Y, is added to it. If the listener does not know about X, then Y will be meaningless. This necessity to check on the knowledge structures of the listener before giving new information is an important aspect of teaching. The children will not be able to understand new material if they cannot build it onto old knowledge. On the other hand, it is necessary to check what the children know so that you are not repeating old material needlessly and boring the class. There is an onus on teachers to make sure that children feel that they can always question and tell the teacher when they do not understand without fear of appearing to be impolite. It is very easy to say, 'But we did this last week, you must remember', so that next time the child will not dare to ask.

It is clear from the Dorval and Eckman study that primary age children have difficulty with topic maintenance. Teachers have to provide them with the chance to have focused discussions. They should also give the children feedback so that they are able to introspect on what they are doing. This is clearly an advanced linguistic skill; one that is assessed, for example, during GCSE English, and not one that we should expect to find in polished form in the primary schools.

The need for topic maintenance or skilful signalling of change of topic does highlight another of the implicit rules of pragmatics. We have already implied that it is assumed that speakers will not tell another person that which they know that person already knows. When that happens in everyday conversation, the listener has to assess the situation and to decide whether to give the speaker some hint about the redundancy of the information without violating the politeness principle. There are cognitive implications of this. To share successfully in social use of language, speakers have to have an implicit understanding that the listeners have their own conscious life. They must understand that the listener has a model of the world and a knowledge structure which is different from the speakers but which also has many points in common. The speaker has to infer something about the present knowledge state of the listener when speaking so that new, but understandable, information is conveyed.

Studies of autistic children by Baron-Cohen *et al.* (1985) would seem to indicate that these children have a particular problem with this side of pragmatic competence. To have an ability to appreciate the independent mental life of another person requires that we should have an implicit theory of mind. Ever since it was first recognized as a syndrome by Kanner (1943), children who have been diagnosed autistic have proved an enigma. Their main characteristics seem to be that they have gross impairment in their ability to relate to other people and to communicate. They also tend to have very limited cognitive capacity. People have sought to explain the cause of the problem in the social interactions of the home and in biological abnormalities, but as yet no one knows the cause. Initially, the bizarre social and emotional behaviours were seen as the predominant symptoms, which may explain why there was an attempt to find causation within the home (Bettelheim 1967). However, as knowledge increased, the major deficit was seen as the failure to develop normal language functioning. The present studies of Baron-Cohen can be seen as crucial. In showing that these children have a problem with the development of pragmatics and, in particular, a failure to develop an understanding of the independent mental life of other people, he has clearly shown that there is a deficit at the point where language, social and cognitive skills all have to interact. This does not say anything about aetiology, but it does give pointers to the way forward for teachers who are trying to educate these children.

You will appreciate that pragmatic competence in children will necessarily develop not just because of increasing awareness of the requirements of the situation. The children have to be able to respond to the linguistic, social and cognitive aspects of the context, so their pragmatic competence will also be related to their processing capacity. Monitoring a topic, whilst at the same time taking account of the listener's needs, is a more complex task than simply making statements regardless of the listener.

Piaget suggested that the level of cognitive development of pre-school children would limit the extent to which they could take account of the listener's perspective. This was a manifestation of the egocentrism of the pre-conceptual and intuitive child. However, though children may show a failure to take account of the listener's needs, Maratsos (1973) has shown that this may be a function of the complexity of the task. When children have to explain something that is very complex and so up to the maximum of their processing capacity, they may concentrate on what they are saying (the primary task) and cease to take account of the listener (the secondary task). When they have to use language to convey something which is well within their competence, they are then able to modify their language, depending on the situation. When it is clear that the listener has not understood, even pre-school children will modify what they say or the way that they say it. They will show a sensitivity to the needs of younger children by talking to them in much simpler language than they use for adults.

Politeness

We have mentioned that pragmatic skill involves being polite to other people. This is more than using simple strategies like saying 'please' and 'thank you'. In asking someone to perform an action, we would generally not use a direct imperative of the form 'Close the window' or even 'Close the window, please'. This would be considered to be impolite. Instead we may use an indirect form of question. We would be more likely to say 'Would you mind closing the window?' We might be even more oblique and make a statement which is meant to be interpreted as a request — e.g. 'It's very cold in here.' Leonard *et al.* (1978) found that pre-school children were able to understand requests that were phrased in the form of a question, but it was not until they were 6 that children began to be able to interpret statements as requests.

Being polite in English requires that we do not use direct language. The finding by Leonard *et al.* shows that teachers have to think about the language they use for class control because it may not always be understood. When the noise level in a reception class gets too high and the teacher says 'It's getting a bit noisy in here', there is no guarantee that the children will realize that this is a request to be quiet.

In terms of their meaning, the sentences 'Would you mind closing the door' and 'Close the door' are very close. It is just that one is polite form and one is not. Using the correct style in a given situation is part of our pragmatic competence. We need to remember this, not just when dealing with children, but also when dealing with parents whose first language is not English. Whenever anyone learns a second language, the different styles for different situations are learned at a fairly advanced stage. The example that we have used of requests being phrased in the form of questions is a useful one. Parents may appear to be being very blunt and demanding when they are seeking information about their children. Teachers should recognize the difference in pragmatic usage rather than feeling threatened or aggrieved because of an apparent lack of politeness. When trying to express oneself in a language with which one is not fully confident, the primary task becomes the meaning, getting the correct words and then the syntax. The situational style is low down on the list of priorities.

Formality

Related to the concept of politeness is that of formality. The style of language used in an interaction will depend on the formality of the situation and the re-lationship between the speaker and the listener. For example, a child who has just had a disciplinary meeting with a headteacher may be told to 'Close the door on your way out'. Here we have a direct command because of the nature of the inter-view and the status differential between the head and the problem child. However, even though we have a direct command, there is also a hidden agenda. The child has to understand that this is the signal that the interview is at an end. At this point the recalcitrant is expected to leave the room.

Status differentials and degree of intimacy will determine the level of form-ality of language used in interactions. Families will be polite to each other, but they will use much less formal language than they do when talking to people they do not know. Children will be exposed to these changes in style long before they are able to modify their own language. Here again we allow a licence to small children that we deny to them as they grow older. We may find it amusing when they speak to a superior in an intimate way at $2\frac{1}{2}$, but we may well require more appropriate style from a 4-year-old. The feedback from interactions enables children gradually to be aware of the need to modify their language to suit the situation.

You can experience this very clearly in school. Even the little 5-year-olds will use different language in the playground from when they are talking to their teachers. They also show that they were able to understand the nature of the setting by taking their cues from the language style in use. This adaptation of behaviour in response to the *style* of the discourse as opposed to *the words themselves* is used by teachers all the time in maintaining discipline in the classroom. Teachers may move, imperceptibly, into using a more formal language style when they think that the children are getting out of control. This can be seen very clearly on school trips. The setting of a visit is much less formal than the classroom. Often teachers appear to be more approachable and they talk to the children in a more informal manner. This may mean that some children misinterpret the situation and begin to use an informal language style which is then considered to be overstepping the mark. The children are then considered to be *cheeky*. At this point the teacher may begin to use more formal language to create more social distance. I am not saying that teachers need to be remote and forbidding. Such a manner would be incompatible with a child-centred approach to education. However, part of the job of a teacher is to control the class so that there can be order for learning. It is through their manner that teachers maintain the social distance necessary to control the children. The language they use, and the manner in which they use it, is one of the most potent strategies they have. Teachers can be friendly towards their children but they are not the children's friends.

Signals for Turn Taking

Conversations are very skilled social interactions. As one person stops speaking, so another person begins, in a totally smooth manner. Children have to learn this skill because another of the implicit rules of conversation is that only one person speaks at a time. We know, from our discussion of attention, that people cannot process two verbal messages at the same time. This means that, for communication to take place, we have to take turns.

Children will have learned to use and respond to the signals for turn taking before they go to school. They will recognize that change of pitch and eye contact signal that the speaker is coming to the end of an utterance and they will use the same signals themselves to aid listeners. Of course performance will not always be perfect. Sometimes they may put their skills into overdrive. They will know very clearly how to interrupt.

The setting of a classroom provides particular problems for the child to exercise the pragmatic skill of turn taking. When a teacher is addressing the whole class, the nature of the interaction changes from 'normal'. Children have to realize that a question is both addressed to them as individuals, but also to the class as a whole. Within the home, when a question is directed to them they are expected to answer. In school they have to learn to wait, even when they know the answer. Putting one's hand up is a formal rule of communication that has to be learned in school. They will overlearn this rule, too, and parents will report that their little 5-year-olds suddenly start putting their hands up at home when they have a question to ask or answer!

Because of the nature of the interaction with thirty-five children and one teacher, it is necessary to develop some formalized rules in order that equality of opportunity and order reign within the classroom. These early classroom rules for answering questions, and gaining attention in order to speak, eventually manifest themselves as formal debates with written procedural rules and a person in the chair to maintain order.

Saying Enough but Not Too Much

Pragmatic skill enables us to understand the nature of the interaction so that we say enough but not too much. It was because this rule was so clearly flouted with respect to not saying enough that there was so much indignation over the statement of being 'Economical with the truth' in the *Spycatcher* hearing in Australia. Not saying enough meant that the truth did not emerge when clearly the expectation was that more would have been said.

There is a fine line between saying too much and not saying enough. This requires sophisticated knowledge of the world. If a motorist stops you on the pavement and asks 'Do you know the way to Oakthorne School?', clearly, if you do, you do not simply reply 'Yes' and walk away. This would be considered to be very impolite and would indicate a pragmatic failure. Even saying 'Oh, it's near Crowberries Park' would be inadequate. Our knowledge of the world suggests that the motorist wants to get to the school and therefore requires detailed route directions. On the other hand, if a friend said to you 'Where are you working now?', you would probably recognize that the name of the school was sufficient, or even 'Oakthorne School, the one near Crowberries Park'. The friend would be a bit taken aback if you launched into a detailed description of how to get to the school from the place where you were talking.

We know, from our pragmatic skills, which level of detail is required. When someone says 'Hello, how are you?', they generally do not expect you to tell them! However, if that someone should be a doctor in a surgery, then you would be expected to be quite expansive. As adults we take this skill for granted. Within schools we have to help children to fine tune their pragmatic competence. We want children to be able to talk fluently and directly on a topic. We do not want their contributions to be verbose and tangential and so long that no one else is able to contribute. The questioning techniques that teachers develop enable them to orchestrate children's contributions. Closed questions will elicit specific information whereas open questions will be an invitation to expand.

Telling the Truth

I mentioned the phrase 'economical with the truth' above. It has now become a euphemism for deliberate lying. An underlying assumption in all our social interactions is that people speak the truth, or, at least, they do not say that which they believe to be untrue. By and large people operate under this principle. This does not mean that we never lie. Everybody lies some time. Nevertheless, lying is not a particularly effective strategy for having good social relationships.

Children tell lies. Parents and adults try to establish truth telling as the norm from a very early age and yet their children still tell lies some of the time. There generally has to be a reason for telling a lie. It usually means that they want to impress someone or they want, deliberately, to hide the truth from them. Being able to tell a 'good', plausible, believable lie requires a sophisticated level of pragmatic skill. Since you want the listener to believe you, when you tell a lie you have to have a notion of what the listener knows about you, what the listener knows about the situation and what the listener is likely to believe. Lying definitely requires a theory of mind. An autistic child, with quite high cognitive and linguistic skill, would find it very difficult to tell an effective lie.

Infant children will exaggerate wildly and tell quite barefaced lies. They may declare that they ate 100 pancakes on Shrove Tuesday, or that they get £50 a week pocket money. They will also drop a piece of paper in front of you in the playground and blame it on someone else. They cannot tell plausible lies to adults and they are also unable to tell when one of their friends is wildly exaggerating.

By stating that being able to tell a good lie is a sign of maturing pragmatic skill, I am *not* advocating lying as morally justifiable behaviour. Social life would be impossible if we operated on the assumption that people were normally lying and not telling the truth. However, there is one positive and socially condoned reason for not telling the truth. This is when we wish to protect the listeners from something that might be hurtful to them. This can be very confusing for children. They are told by their parents that they must tell the truth and then they catch these respected persons out in what appears to be a deliberate lie. They have to learn that, where there is a conflict between telling the truth and hurting someone, society generally expects that not hurting another will take precedence over the whole truth. This lesson will have been learned by the junior years, but it can also lead to complications. Children will, by this age, be very loyal to their friends and therefore not wish to 'sneak' on someone when a problem arises. Childhood can be confusing. The children may have had years in the infant school of being told not to tell tales. They learn the lesson so well that they do not want to break rank as they get older.

Jokes

There is one social setting where all the different aspects of language, cognition and social skill come together delightfully. That is in the telling of jokes. Preschool children and infant children find *situations* funny. They may laugh at slapstick but the humour is in the situation itself and not in what is said. They may find voices funny, but not words. It is only when their semantic development is such that they can begin to understand ambiguity that verbal jokes can be appreciated as being funny. Junior school children can make up some really superb awful jokes.

Most jokes are based on an understanding that words can have more than one meaning, more than one syntactic status and that they can be segmented in unusual ways. They also require a knowledge of the world that can be reconstructed from an unusual angle:

> Knock, knock!
> Who's there?
> Felix.
> Felix who?
> Felix my lolly I'll bash him.

> Knock, knock!
> Who's there?
> Dr.
> Dr who?
> You just said it.

> Will you remember me in an hour?   Yes.
> Will you remember me in a week?   Yes.
> Will you remember me in a year?   Yes.
> Knock, knock!
> Who's there?
> You've forgotten me already.

> What's green and jumps?
> Spring cabbage.

Because this level of language development is needed to understand jokes, it does not mean that infant children do not tell jokes — far from it. They learn the scripts of jokes as part of the lore of childhood. They learn that older children tell jokes and then laugh, so they do the same. The problem is that they do not necessarily understand what makes a joke funny. They may internalize the meaning of a joke but alter the wording on retelling. Since the words are everything in jokes, this can have disastrous effects on the humour. For example:

Q: Why did the boy take a pencil to bed?

A: Because he wanted to close the curtains.

You may have to think about that.

Infant children also do not realize that part of the humour in a joke lies in the *unexpected* punch line. You may find that one child will tell you a joke, so you laugh, then immediately afterwards another child will tell you exactly the same joke. Since you laughed the first time, the reasoning is that the same joke will produce the same response.

Because they may not understand the pragmatics of jokes, you may find that infants will tell you jokes that are so rude they make your hair curl. There is obviously a pragmatic failure because it is not socially expected that children will tell rude jokes to adults, but, in this case, the pragmatic failure is probably at the level of not realizing that the joke is rude in the first place. Certainly, junior school children may become very smutty, but they generally have the pragmatic competence to tailor their jokes to fit the audience.

Accent and Dialect

This section, more than any other in this book, will involve us in trying to be objective about an area of behaviour which is fraught with an emotional agenda. Teachers have to come to terms with their own prejudices where accent and dialect are concerned. It is only through examining their own behaviour objectively that they can hope to deal fairly and sensitively with children. We have very muddled attitudes towards accents and dailects which in turn may colour our perception of people. The demands on us as teachers are that we should try to take a rational approach towards this aspect of human behaviour. At the same time we have to recognize the social implications of differences in people's language. The Cox Report makes it very clear that teachers should have a clear understanding of the nature of accent and dialect as does the Kingman Report into the Teaching of English Language.

Accent

Let us begin by defining terms. *Accent* refers to the phonological aspect of speech. The differences in the way that people pronounce their words account for the differences in their accents. Accent, therefore, only applies to the spoken word. Since everybody speaks, *ipso facto* everybody has an accent. We could more or less close this section there because there should not be any educational implications beyond that. However, it would be a little disingenuous of me to do that.

In English there are many regional accents regardless of the dialect that the people speak. Remember we are leaving aside dialect for the moment and only concentrating on pronunciation. The majority of the people in this country speak with a regional accent. This means that when they speak, listeners can guess with a reasonable degree of accuracy from where in the country they come. Thus we can identify West Country accents, Welsh accents, Lancashire accents, etc. Our ears are not particularly fine tuned, so our identification of regionality tends to be fairly sweeping. The vast majority of us cannot identify accents to within a street like Bernard Shaw's Henry Higgins.

There are some people who speak with an accent which is not related to any particular geographical location. This accent is called 'Received Pronunciation' (RP) by linguists. It is the accent which might also be called 'Oxbridge English', 'Public School English', 'BBC English' or even a 'posh accent'. Speakers of RP cannot be placed geographically but they can be placed socially. This is where the social/emotional element comes in. The higher up the social scale one is in this country, the more one is likely to speak RP and the less one is likely to speak with a regional accent. It is fact of life in British society that RP, and therefore lack of a regional accent, will mean that one is likely to be at the top of the social scale. As we go down the social scale so we find that there is a gradual increase in the regionality of the accent that is spoken. For example, teachers will, on the whole, tend to speak with less of a regional accent and with more of an RP accent than the average factory or farm workers in their locality.

There is nothing intrinsically virtuous about speaking with RP. It does not actually make us better people and most certainly there is no way that speaking with RP makes us cleverer. This is why teachers have to be very aware of the possibility of prejudice creeping into their assessments of children. It is possible to make the fallacious judgment that a child is speaking with a near approximation to RP and is therefore clever whereas another child is speaking with a lower class accent and therefore is less intellectually gifted. We may well be able to say that a child who does not pronounce the 'H' at the beginning of *head*, *heavy*, *happy* and *hill* is very possibly from a working class family, but that is a social judgment based on a knowledge of the class system in our society — it is *not* a sound educational judgment.

We can explore this a little further with relation to aesthetic judgments about accent. We make judgments about accents, calling some 'hard' and some 'soft'. We talk about 'nice' accents and 'ugly' ones. It is very important that teachers have a clear understanding that such judgments have no sound basis in aesthetics. We make these judgments because of who we, as individuals, are. We all have our own social and emotional prejudices and it is these which inform our belief that we can make aesthetic judgments about accents. Trudgill (1975) in his very useful book *Accent, Dialect and School* points out that foreigners, even when they are English speaking, are unable to make these aesthetic judgments about accents. Indeed, they often cannot even *hear* the difference between the accents. In fact, this should be very obvious to you. How many British people can hear regional French accents or even differentiate between a Canadian and a North American accent?

It is in the nature of language that there will be variations in language. It is in the nature of people that they will have irrational prejudices. It seems to be the present state of our society that we make class based and regional based judgments about people. We cannot change all that, but it must *not* be in the nature of the education system that judgments about children should be made on the basis of these irrational beliefs.

I have had students, particularly ones from the South East, who say that this is all very well but they 'cannot understand' a Northumbrian accent or a Scottish accent. My argument tends to be that, if they have sufficient intellectual capacity to become teachers, then they surely have sufficient intellectual capacity to *try* to understand the accent of the people amongst whom they will be working. Admittedly, it might take a few hours for an RP speaker or a Northumbrian speaker to understand the accent of a Devonian, but no more than that. It is intellectually dishonest, or just plain lazy, to claim that one cannot understand regional accents in this country. It may take a bit of work, initially, but where is the harm in that? Wherever we happen to live in the British Isles we rapidly attune to the local accent whether we speak it or not.

The message, then, must be that accent should not be an educational issue. It only becomes an issue if teachers misunderstand the nature of accent. If parents choose to make decisions about the accent their children will speak, that is a whole other issue. Some parents may wish to have their children speak with RP even if they themselves do not. They may thus send their children for elocution lessons, though this may be less common than it was in the past. Such decisions are the right of the parents. Teachers cannot make such decisions. This means logically that teachers cannot 'correct' a child's accent because there is no 'correct' way to speak.

Some people argue that accents may affect children's spelling development. They suggest that if children say '*ill* rather than *hill*, they are likely to write it that way and misspell it. When children are beginning to develop an ability to spell phonologically, they will spell as they speak, but this is a problem that affects all accents — RP included. All children have to learn to spell *know* with a *k*. The people who claim that dropping one's aitches is going to affect spelling would also have to claim that the RP accent is likely to lead to *bath* being spelled as *barth*. What children have to learn is how to spell regardless of their accent, and the problems encountered are much the same for all children.

Dialect

The issue of dialect is much more complex than that of accent. First we have to define the term. Dialect is the variation in the syntax and the lexicon within a given language. Logically, therefore, it is separate from accent. Indeed we can have people who all speak the same dialect but who do so with varying degrees of regional accent.

It is probably necessary at this point to discuss how language variety comes about and indeed what we mean by one language as opposed to another. Initially, it may appear that there seems to be very little similarity between English and Mandarin, but that there are more points of contact between English and German. As we saw in Chapter 8, all languages share the fact that they are made up of a series of interconnected systems and that these systems are phonology, syntax, semantics, pragmatics and the lexicon. The units and the rules for combination of units will vary between one language and the next. We cannot trace the primeval mother tongue but we can see that, though languages have much in common, they are organic and they change over time and space. Anglo-Saxon may have been very close to the language spoken at that time in Germany, but modern English is not now as close to modern German. The centuries that have intervened have enhanced the geographical and political identity of the two languages.

The political identity of a language is important. Dutch people speak Dutch. It is linguistically very close to German but the people of Holland would be very offended if we suggested that they spoke a dialect of German. We in the United Kingdom speak English and the variations that we find in the language usage are called dialects of the national language. There are undoubtedly sufficient points of contact between all the various dialects for it to be possible for us to recognize the similarities as being much more potent than the variations. I must point out, of course, that English is not the only language spoken in the United Kingdom. We have the separate languages of the different nationalities that go to make up the United Kingdom — Welsh and Gaelic, for example — as well as the many languages of the people who themselves, or whose parents, immigrated here from other countries. However, English is the predominant language and it is mainly English dialects that will be the subject matter of this section.

What is the English language?

> If that thou
> Throw on water now a stoon,
> Wel wost thou, hit wol make anoon
> A litel roundel as a cercle,
> Paraventure brood as a covercle;

And right anoon thou shalt see weel,
That wheel wol cause another wheel,
And that the thridde, and so forth, brother,
Every cercle causing other,
Wyder than himselve was . . . .

(Chaucer, *The House of Fame II*)

Well, that won't do. English today is not the language of Chaucer.

And that it was great pity, so it was,
That villainous saltpetre should be digg'd
Out if the bowels of the harmless earth,
Which many a good tall fellow had destroy'd
So cowardly . . . .

(Shakespeare, *Henry IV*, part 1)

Closer, but English today is not the language of Shakespeare.

The English that we speak today is the English of today. The language is what the speakers speak. There are actually many different dialects of English which together make up the totality of Modern English. Each dialect is defined as being grammatically distinct from every other dialect. Linguistically each dialect is of equal worth. There is no way that we can make linguistic value judgments about different dialects; we can simply point out the differences in usage between dialects.

As with accent, that could be the end of the story; but it isn't.

There is one dialect of English which is generally called Standard English. This is the language that is to be found in textbooks and which is used by those speakers who consider themselves to be, and who are generally considered to be, educated. It is the language of the schools. It is the language that is learned when English is taught as a second language. It is the codified form of the language that is to be found in the old 'grammar' books. It is simply just another dialect of English — linguistically no more and no less.

However, Standard English, because it is the dialect of the educated classes, has acquired a status all of its own. It is considered by some to be *correct*. This then leads to the assumption that other dialects are in some way *wrong*.

Educationally we have to accept that if a form of construction is used consistently by a number of people, then it is part of their dialect. That is the language that they speak and should be respected. There is no way that it is *wrong*; it is simply different from Standard. This point has been made very clearly in both the Kingman and the Cox Reports. The English Working Group points out that if children are motivated to use Standard English then they will, but we cannot force them to use it in the spoken form. In any case, let us be quite clear, much of the time we all speak in a very different way from any language of any textbook. We may be able to read about the language being composed of perfect sentences, but if you taped yourself speaking naturally over maybe fifteen minutes, you would find that you did not speak in whole rounded sentences, and you may sometimes deviate from Standard form without being aware of it.

Why then all the fuss about Standard English? Linguists and psycholinguists may have been saying for many years that all languages and all dialects are of equal worth, and they can very clearly show this to be logically correct, but this academic point of view has not necessarily been accepted emotionally or politically.

Teachers have a responsibility to enable their pupils to achieve the highest performance of which they are potentially capable. This means that they have to make Standard English accessible to all children, for without it, the language of textbooks may be less accessible. Standard English is the language of much of *written* English. As educators we have a duty to make the written word accessible to people and to enable them to write in Standard form when appropriate. If, as a nation, everyone has access to Standard English, then written communication becomes a universal dialect in its own right; rather like in China, where there is only one written form but many different languages. A speaker of Mandarin who is literate, but who cannot speak Cantonese, can communicate with a literate Cantonese speaker through the medium of print.

The English Working Group makes a very cogent case for the necessity of introducing all children to Standard English whatever their dialect so that they can use it 'where appropriate'.

When is 'where appropriate'? Clearly, when children first enter school, we are so pleased that they talk to us sensibly and write anything, that the last thing we need to do is to 'correct' their language. The time to enter into discussions about 'style' is when the children can appreciate that it is possible to say things in different ways and in different contexts. And when I say *discussion* here, I do mean having discussions with the children about what type of language is appropriate. By talking about linguistic style and trying out the effects of different constructions, the implicit understanding of style will become explicit and the children will be able to make informed decisions about usage.

Differences in style apply to speaking as well as writing, but since in speaking so much of the control of our syntactic output is below the level of conscious control, in spoken English we are really only concerned about style and clarity and not dialect. Because writing requires much drafting and redrafting we can encourage the children to use different styles, but also to recognize the need to use Standard English as a particular academic style in the written form.

Conclusion

Because of the nature of their profession, teachers have to try to free themselves, as far as possible, from the influence of irrational prejudices. This means that in the case of language they should be able to accept the varying accents and dialects that their children use and not feel the need to 'correct' usage. No one dialect is more intrinsically 'right' than any other, so no one way of speaking is better than any other. However, since we hope that all children will have an equal opportunity to achieve as much academically as possible, all children have to be given access to Standard English. Standard English (SE) is the language of education and children have a right to learn to read and write in SE where appropriate.

Recognition that SE might be a required style enables us to see that there is a link between our discussions of accent and dialect and our discussions of pragmatics. We expect children to develop pragmatic and social competence with language. Their pragmatic competence can be used to facilitate their appreciation of the need to use Standard English as a particular style in the written form. Developing the ability to use SE when writing will have the added bonus of helping comprehension of that form when reading. Reading and writing are the subjects of our last Chapter.

Further Reading

Menyuk (1988) covers the domain of pragmatics very well and so is a useful book for developing knowledge related to this Chapter as well as Chapter 8. Much of the work on pragmatics stems from a seminal lecture by Grice which is reproduced in Cole and Morgan (1975) *Syntax and Semantics, Vol 3, Speech Acts*. You will also find that Lindsay and Norman, as usual, have a very readable chapter covering this area. The *Report of the Committee of Inquiry into the Teaching of English Language* (Kingman Report) is essential reading as is Trudgill (1975) *Accent, Dialect and the School*.

Chapter 10

The Development of Literacy

Introduction

One area where the application of psychology to education seems to be fundamental is in the development of literacy. In Chapters 8 and 9 we have been concerned with the development of language and communication skills. All peoples of the world use language because it is biologically determined. The same cannot be said of reading. In the history of *Homo sapiens*, reading is a relatively recent, manufactured activity. In order to read we have to adapt and apply a number of different cognitive and linguistic skills. Because reading is an applied cognitive activity, the vast majority of children need to be given instruction in order that they will learn the skill.

The domain of the teaching of literacy seems to have been always fraught with controversy, some of which has centred on a confusion between the types of teaching method and the types of materials. Very few people would now dispute that children need to be given well written books right from the start, but provision of good materials does not necessarily lead to agreement about how those materials will be used. In this chapter I want to show how an understanding of cognitive processing can inform a teacher's approach to literacy. There is no right answer to the question 'How should *children* be taught to read?' Teachers need to be flexible and diagnostic in their teaching so that they make rational decisions about the most effective way to teach each individual child to read. A few children, such as Clark's Young Fluent Readers, (1976), arrive in school able to read without any apparent formal instruction. These children have to be seen as the exception, but we can learn something about how to teach the majority of children from the particular skills of these natural readers.

The Reading Process

A definition of reading could be that it is extracting meaning from written text. The message comes to us through the medium of print. This is a definition that we should not lose sight of. The purpose of reading is to find out what the squiggles on the page are meant to convey. For our purposes, we need to expand on this definition, whilst recognizing that different capacities will be expected at different stages in the development of literacy. Readers have to develop the skill of reading any text and therefore they need to recognize or work out what each individual word is. Most readers can *understand* the text and *identify* the words correctly. When they do this they use their understanding of the text to work out what new words are and at the same time they use their ability to identify words in order to understand the text.

The skilled reader should be able to read any word. Beyond this level we would hope that children will gain sufficient skill so that they can modify and adapt this skill to meet the different task demands of different reading situations. The way to approach the reading of a railway timetable is not the same way as to approach the reading of a novel. The way to read a novel is not the same as the way to read a textbook. You will not have felt it is necessary to read this book starting at the beginning and working your way to the end. It is possible to do this, but, when a textbook is to be used for the purposes of study, higher order skills such as skimming, depth reading and note taking are necessary.

In order to be able to apply their reading skills, children need to be helped to see, right from the start, that they can use their reading for different purposes. Teachers have to help them to achieve automaticity in word reading so that they do not have to worry about the technical side of reading, but can freely adapt their skill to the nature of the task.

By suggesting that reading involves extracting meaning and identifying words we can begin to identify that there have been two separate approaches to reading. These have been characterized as being *top-down* and *bottom-up*.

Let us take the top-down approach first. Since we have seen that children in the main are competent language users when they enter school, it is reasonable to suppose that they will bring this competence to their attempts to develop literacy. Reading is obviously a language activity. People seem to use books to 'talk'. When we are reading text, the top-down approach suggests that we predict what subsequent words are likely to be from our knowledge of language. We second guess the author. This prediction enables us to extract the meaning and to be confident about approaching unknown territory. Prediction enables us to eliminate many possible words and to centre of the probable words. The strongest advocate of this approach to reading is perhaps Frank Smith (1978).

The other way to approach reading is characterized as being bottom-up. All the various processes and subskills are analyzed in order to state precisely what a reader has to do to identify the words so that the meaning can then be accessed. A memory has to be built up of the defining attributes of each letter in terms of its lines, curves and angles. In this way each letter can be identified as being different from every other letter. Each word can be recognized in terms of the particular configuration of letters. This visual identity enables the phonological identity of the word to be accessed so that the meaning can then be identified. Ehri (1980) suggests that, as we develop literacy, we have to develop an *orthographic* identity for each word which we add to the phonological, syntactic and semantic identities. She defines the orthographic identity as 'a sequence of letters bearing systematic relationships to the phonological properties of words' (p. 313). In building up these orthographic identities we need to be able to segment words in component parts of both sounds and letters and then to marry the two sets of components.

These bottom-up processes are highly abstract but our understanding of cognitive processing tells us that something like this must be happening, because without this a word would not be recognized. The most rational approach to literacy for a teacher would seem to be to take account of both approaches when developing a policy for teaching children.

The Routes to Reading

Figure 10.1 is taken from Ellis (1984) *Reading, Writing and Dyslexia: A Cognitive Analysis.*

Let us first follow the path of a spoken word along the left hand side of the diagram. Once a word is spoken it enters our cognitive system. The sounds are analyzed acoustically so that a particular sequence is recognized as a known word. Once the phonological identity is accessed then the meaning can be available. When we speak a word, we begin from the meaning, access the phonological identity, assemble the phonemes in the correct order and then a smooth sequence of sound is produced — the word.

You will notice that the right hand side of the diagram is more complex. There is more than one route to reading. The word enters the visual analysis system and then the result of this analysis will determine the subsequent events. If the result of the visual analysis is that this is a familiar input, then the word can be identified by the activation of its particular word recognition unit — its orthographic identity. Once this has been activated the meaning can be accessed directly. If you are reading aloud then the phonological identity also has to be available. This can either be accessed via the semantic system or via the route which leads directly from the word recognition system to the phonemic word production system. Since accessing meaning is the usual purpose of reading, when reading aloud the semantic route will be used. However, those of you well

Figure 10.1   A model for both the direct and the phonically mediated recognition, comprehension and naming of written words.

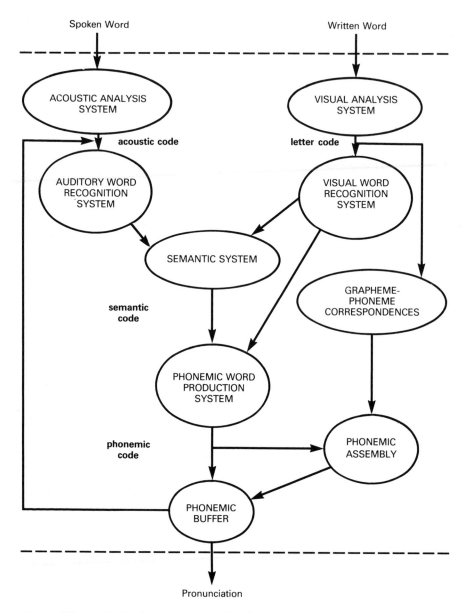

Source: Ellis (1984) *Reading, Writing and Dyslexia: A Cognitive Analysis*

practised at reading stories aloud to children will know that, at times, you seem to read a whole page perfectly whilst your attention has apparently been directed elsewhere. At times it seems possible to read aloud and yet to bypass the semantic system altogether.

If the word is an unfamiliar one, then a different set of processes comes into operation. As it is unfamiliar, there can be no visual recognition unit for it, so the outcome of the visual analysis has then to be translated into a phonemic code in order that a candidate pronunciation can be assembled. This can be converted into an acoustic code and checked via the auditory word recognition system. Most of the time this will be successful; however, if a word happens to have a very irregular spelling, then a number of possible pronunciations may have to be tried. In reality, since we tend to be reading words in context, the candidate pronunciation together with the context is likely to produce the word rapidly. We make use of both the bottom-up and the top-down process.

Sometimes the word will not just be unfamiliar in its visual form, but will actually be a word that is unknown. There will be neither a phonological nor a semantic representation. Under these circumstances the phonology and the context will have to be used to develop a first time representation. In the final analysis a dictionary may have to be used.

There are times when we will come across a word which has been spelled incorrectly and so it does not have a visual recognition unit. Teachers probably experience this more than any other people. However, very often these 'non-words' are so close to the real word that they are not spotted. The minor diference goes undetected and the intended recognition unit is activated allowing direct access to the semantic system. Proof-reading is a very special skill. Did you notice the word *difference* spelled with only one *f* above? If we want to read quickly and to extract the meaning, we do not apparently need to check on the fine detail.

As an aside here, I should point out that, since proof-reading is a particular skill, we should teach it to children. We do expect that they will eventually be accurate in their writing, but we do not want them to be inhibited by the need for accuracy when they are making initial drafts of written work. It is much better that they should be allowed free rein when initially creating and then given specific training in critical inspection for content, style and spelling accuracy so that final drafts are well presented.

There is one further route to reading that we must consider. This is the route that has to be used when we are asked to read non-words. By definition non-words have no visual or semantic representation yet we can read them. We can also distinguish between a non-word such as *derous* (from Chapter 6) which is seen as a plausible English word and *zluvskch* which is not permitted in English orthography. Our ability to read non-words is interesting since it clearly demonstrates that we must have the grapheme-to-phoneme route suggested in Ellis' model. Asking children to read aloud non-words can be a diagnostic method of assessing the extent to which they can use the sound based route to reading.

Let me recap on what we have learned from the Ellis model. It seems that as adults we can either process words visually to give direct access to the meaning, or we can use phonic mediation. We have stored identities for the words that we can read directly. These are Ehri's Orthographic Identities. They are fully analyzed units built up through an in depth analysis of the words. Just as we have implicit knowledge of the rule structure of language so we have knowledge of the orthographic (the spelling) structure of the language. We use this to build up visual identities but also to work out other unfamiliar and possibly unknown words by analogy to the stored representations. Activating the orthographic identity will lead to the phonological, syntactic and semantic identities also being available. However, we also have the indirect route to reading available which enables us to work out the plausible phonological identity from the graphemic information and thus we are enabled to work out the complete identity of the word.

Any skilled adult reader can read any and almost every word out of context, but in fact they rarely have to do so. When we read single words they are generally in a context and we may well be searching for them. For example, if you are in a railway station and you need to buy a ticket, make a phone call or go to the toilet, then you will scan the environment for a sign for *ticket office*, *telephone* or *toilet*. The ability to read such environmental print is important, but you will notice that society aids the reading of such signs by adding pictures which enhance the meaning. Most of the print that we read is in the context of other words — in some form of continuous prose. In these circumstances we are able to add top-down processing to bottom-up processing

What we are aiming for as teachers, is for as many adults as possible to become so skilled at reading that it is for them an automatic activity. We do not want the *act of reading* to interfere with the *message*. This is our goal, but when children begin to learn to read, the act of reading itself is very difficult.

Children Learning to Read

It is quite difficult for adults to have a feeling for how it must be for a child when the act of reading itself takes up so much processing capacity that there is very little left for monitoring anything else. When first beginning to read, even standing up at the same time can be too much. That is why teachers should have the foresight to give children chairs when hearing them read, and not expect them to stand at the teacher's table.

We cannot take you back to being 5 years old, but if you read out the passage below you will get an inkling of the difficulty. All the words have been printed backwards but you are to try and ignore that and read it as it should be.

It begins 'My father . . . . '

Ym rehtaf dias taht I dluoc evah a god rof ym yadhtrib. Nehw eht yad emac, I saw yrev deticxe dna I did ton tae ym doof. Ew tnew ot a ecalp erehw yeht dekool retfa sgod taht dah neeb nekasrof yb rieht srenwo. Yeht erew lla sepahs dna sezis, tub eht eno I dekil tseb saw a nat god htiw a tops revo reh thgir eye. Lla eht elpoep dias I dluohs llac reh Tops, tub I dellac reh Lufituaeb Hanid — Lufit rof trohs. Ehs saw ym tseb dneirf.

Obviously you could read the paragraph, but did you notice how intonation patterns tended to drop out? Did you find that you would manage a few words quite smoothly and then have to use deliberate bottom-up processing to identify a word? Did you find that words like *was* and *spot* fooled you because they make acceptable words when printed in reverse? Reading such passages shows us the interactive nature of top-down and bottom-up processes, but should also serve to show just how difficult reading can be.

Reading Pre-school

In our modern society, children are bathed in print. They see hoardings, print in shops, advertisements on the television, road signs, brand names on food and of course newspapers and books. Books come deliberately last on the list. All the other examples are part of the environment; they cannot be avoided, but books need to be provided as a conscious act.

Environmental print can be ignored by children in the sense that they can take it for granted and not ask about it. Some children, however, will ask about the signs and begin to understand that abstract symbols can stand for meanings. Parents will often draw their children's attention to the signs and their meanings and in so doing they will be fostering the idea that signs can stand for meaning.

Sharing books is a situation with a much greater potential. The act of sitting down and sharing a book with children is very powerful. Whilst they are listening to a story they are absorbing many messages. They learn that reading a book is a valued act, that it is fun and enjoyable. They learn that stories come from books and that the print apparently has meaning. They learn that book language is subtly different from the way we talk to each other. Watching the pages being turned from right to left and turning them themselves, they learn how to handle books. Sitting quietly and listening to a story does wonders for the development of attention.

All these activities can be called top-down processes, but by listening to stories and sharing books with adults, children can also begin to use bottom-up information. They can learn about directionality of print; the left-to-right aspects of words in English and the top-to-bottom aspects of page layout. They can learn about the spaces between words on the page and so realize what a word looks like.

They can learn that the number of words read corresponds to the number of words printed on the page. They can learn that words are made up of letters and that these letters are the ones that they learn when they learn the letters of the alphabet.

All this lays the foundations of learning to read and all of it can happen long before the children get to school. Indeed, in the best of all possible worlds, all children will have been exposed to these experiences before school, if not at home, then in the nurseries. However, since at the moment this cannot be guaranteed, teachers have to make certain that all children are given the chance to have these intimate encounters with books as soon as they start school. There is not much point in starting to instruct a child to read if that child does not know what a book is or what reading is all about. Remember, learning is more efficient if it is contextualized.

Whilst checking that all children are exposed to positive experiences, teachers should, of course, not overlook the fact that some children starting school will already be fluent readers or well on the way to literacy. There may not be many, but there are a sufficient number for us to be always vigilant. Clark's (1976) study of her Young Fluent Readers in Scotland is a salient one for all infant teachers. These thirty-two children arrived in school having developed sufficient reading fluency such that they did not need to be taught to read. Clark characterizes them as coming from sensible homes, not ones where the parents had forced the children into highly precocious achievement. The children were the pacemakers. However, the homes were ones where reading was a valued activity. The parents provided good role models and they gave the children plenty of their own time for sharing books. All the children had high measured intelligence, but this alone could not account for their achievement. They also had very good auditory skills, though this may have been related to their language environment. Certainly the children were anecdotally reported as having very good, sustained attentional capacity at an early age.

Clarke reported that, in some instances, the schools were reluctant to acknowledge the outstanding achievements of these children. It is sometimes difficult, emotionally, for teachers to accept the challenge of children who have learned to read without their help. They feel threatened by such achievement. This is perhaps understandable but of no use to the children. A better approach would be to be delighted that they can read and to capitalize on the progress, to nurture it and sustain it. It can be very fulfilling, professionally, to provide sufficient stimulating material for a child of 5 with a 5-year-old's interests but the reading ability of a 10-year-old.

Most children are not young fluent readers; they need to be taught to read. Clark noted that the children had good auditory skills but the study did not investigate this area further. Bradley and Bryant (1983) however, in a longitudinal study of 400 children, showed that one aspect of auditory skills might be significant in the development of reading. They found that, regardless of IQ or social class, children whose pre-school ability to detect rhyme and alliteration was good were significantly more likely to be good readers and spellers at 8 years. Stuart and Coltheart (1988) have also shown that pre-school phonological awareness correlates significantly with reading skill. This suggests that, certainly in the nursery schools, teachers should involve the children in many activities that draw their attention to the sound basis of words in order to prepare them for later reading development. Singing, general rhyming games, clapping syllables and becoming aware of letter names and letter sounds can all be useful early achievements.

Early Reading

Current research (Marsh *et al*. 1981, Seymour and Elder 1986, Frith 1985, Ehri and Wilce 1980, Stuart and Coltheart 1988) is beginning to enable us to build up a picture of the strategies that children may develop for processing print. The picture that emerges fits very closely with the adult model suggested by Ellis. Any one individual child will have to be treated as unique within the classroom, but nevertheless, we need to consider the processes that children are likely to have to develop on their way to becoming fluent readers. If we know what children are likely to be doing, then we can begin to tailor our teaching strategies towards developing the children's abilities.

When children first begin to read, though they may understand the purpose of reading, the majority of them seem to have little else in the way of strategies for tackling the text. Frith (1985) suggests that they read the words *logographically*. This means that words are remembered as single visual units on the basis of rather crude partial analysis. Thus Seymour and Elder (1986) found one child who read *smaller* as 'yellow'. The reason given when asked was that ' . . . it has two sticks' (the 'll').

The strategy that children use for storing words at this early stage is rote memory (Marsh *et al*. 1981). This means that they try to memorize words visually but they have no means of working out what new words are. Since we know that memory at this early stage is rather limited, they need a lot of practice with a small, but gradually growing, vocabulary. In this way they can build up a corpus of words that they can recognize and feel confident about as they are reading their books. The errors they make give us insights into the strategies they are using. When they are unsure of a word they tend to substitute one they think they should know, even if it is wrong. Seymour and Elder found that their children appeared to be able to access the semantic system directly because some of the errors made within their sight vocabulary were semantic rather than visual. Thus *room* was read as '*house*'. My own son read '*tin*' for *can* and '*Rabbit*' for *Socks*

(Socks was the dog in the reading scheme). He also developed a strategy for recognizing colour words, but would pick out one of the seven that he thought he knew entirely at random.

Memorizing words visually is a bottom-up process and, as we know, at this stage it is quite difficult. Fortunately, if children are given words in sentences with pictorial clues then they will be able to utilize their top-down skills as well and achieve some success. As we said in Chapter 6, trying to teach children to read by requiring them to learn single words on 'flash' cards places a great burden on their memories and at the same time inhibits them from using any other strategy.

An early study by Weber (1979) of the errors in reading made by first grade children in America shows how children do attempt to use both top-down and bottom-up strategies when they have text to read. As Piaget has shown, analysis of errors will always enable us to have insights into children's problem solving. Weber found that the majority of errors were semantically and syntactically plausible substitutions. When the children came across a word they did not know they substituted one that made sense and carried on to the end of the sentence. The pull for meaning was strong, and as yet they had not realized that they had to read what was actually on the page. They were cavalier with the text, showing what Bruner (1957) had called 'perceptual recklessness'.

These early substitutions can be considered positive, but eventually the children have to develop strategies which will enable them to go beyond rote memory and top-down context based processes to higher order, accurate identification of any word. This means that teachers have to be providing children with a number of different activities which will all eventually be of use in reading. Obviously they will be reading them stories and supplying them with a wide variety of books. They will also be giving them books that have creatively repetitive texts in order to build up sight vocabulary. This may be done through the children's own language, through reading scheme books or through graded commercially available books for children — or through all three approaches. At the same time they should be extending the phonological awareness of the children in relation to the words and developing letter name and letter sound knowledge so that, when the children are ready, they will be able to utilize this knowledge to develop the grapheme-to-phoneme route to reading. We might imagine that if children had to describe what they were doing when reading at this early stage they would say:

> 'I understand that reading is getting meaning from the page and talking like a book, so when I read it must make sense. I recognize some words because I have seen them lots of times and I can read them anywhere. If I come across a word on its own that I don't know, I can't read it. If I come across a word I don't know in a story then I'll have a guess at it. This guess will be on the basis of the words I think I'm supposed to know, but it will have to make the story sound reasonable.'

Getting Going

Once children have mastered a substantial, immediate recognition vocabulary they can experience a good deal of success in reading. This should be across the curriculum and not just during the obvious 'reading' sessions. They will be reading during maths and science and music and topic work.

As the sight vocabulary grows, unless the children begin to alter their strategies, the success can bring its own problems. Reliance on rote memory and incomplete visual analysis can become unreliable. An increasing vocabulary means that it becomes more difficult to distinguish between the words, so the children have to develop another system for identifying them if they are not to develop learned helplessness.

If they have been given activities to encourage phonological awareness of the segments of words and identification of letters, then they will be able to apply this knowledge to the decoding of words on the basis of letter-sound correspondences. They begin to use *alphabetic* strategies (Frith 1985). Developing a capacity to use an alphabetic code to read words is a big breakthrough *en route* to literacy. It means that any word can be attempted with a fair degree of success. The children do not have to rely on context, memory and other people. Instead they can begin to work things out for themselves. Using a code eventually simplifies the task, but developing a realization of the benefits of such a use and implicitly understanding the principles behind it is a very complex cognitive act. Children tend to move into using the segmentation strategies in reading towards the end of their infant school years. Interestingly, this correlates with when we would expect them to be becoming concrete operational in their thinking. This may not be just a coincidence. Using a coding system, which is what this stage of reading requires, is based on an ability to use categorization and to understand hierarchies.

If we were to approach this stage of reading in a simplistic way we could say that the children have to be able to hear the sounds within words and to map these onto the letters. Thus *cat* is composed of the sounds /c/ /a/ /t/ which map onto the letters C A T.

When such a simple example is given, decoding seems to be such an obvious strategy to use. Indeed, children were, and some still are, taught to read right from the start by a phonic system of sound-to-letter because it was seen as being so simple. However, since we can understand that decoding itself is a complex cognitive act, it may well be that it is an inappropriate strategy for many children as an initial method of instruction. Added to this, I think it is appropriate to point out that, in English, there are 577 different letter–sound correspondence rules (Gough and Hillinger 1980). Thus, it is not just a question of children learning to link sounds to the twenty-six letters of the alphabet when they learn to use rules. This would suggest that it might be more rational to let the children get a feeling for what reading is all about, to experience some degree of success and to develop their cognitive skills before we gradually introduce them to phonics.

Marsh *et al.* suggest that once children have developed a visual vocabulary they initially begin to use a left-to-right sequential decoding strategy. They begin by utilizing the initial letter to guess at the word and then gradually develop their decoding skills. Certainly, the point when children recognize the need to decode is very potent. Biemiller (1970) followed through Weber's work on early reading errors and found that the awareness of the need for a new strategy could be detected in the pattern of errors. It was found that the children began to enter a phase where their reading appeared, on the surface, to be far less fluent. Instead of making substitutions, the children began to stop at words they did not know and silently peruse them. This was called the *non-response* stage. The argument was that the children had to come to a realization that they had to read the text as it was printed and not just produce a roughly appropriate sentence. Biemiller suggested that the earlier the children entered this stage the better for reading development.

At the point when children do enter the non-response stage (Biemiller says that it is when at least 50 per cent of the errors are silent perusals) they may need direct help in using a letter–sound strategy to enable them to tackle the print to their own satisfaction. Some children will have come to this realization almost at the point of beginning to read; many children will be able to work out the decoding with just a little help, providing they have had some alphabet instruction. Some children will need to have very explicit help. They may find the transition from reliance on visual memory into decoding very difficult. These children will need to have a fund of exciting books with a simple vocabulary so that they can maintain their enjoyment in reading whilst trying to master the decoding system which will enable them to become more independent readers.

The application of segmentation skills, both visual and phonological, to a decoding strategy means that the grapheme-to-phoneme route to reading in the Ellis model is being developed.

What would the children say about their reading skills at this stage?

> 'Reading is getting the meaning from the print. I know a lot of words
> by heart and I can recognize them easily. When I come across a word I
> don't know, I can't just say anything so I try and work out what it
> sounds like from the letters. Sometimes I can only get a bit of it right,
> but it is often enough because I can work out the rest from the story
> and the pictures.

Developing Fluency

Using an alphabetic strategy has obvious advantages over rote memory, but there are some drawbacks. Firstly, it is not a very efficient strategy for the many words that we read frequently. A straightforward direct visual recognition strategy would seem much more economical for such words. Secondly, there are many words in English which cannot be identified by a simple decoding system. *Enough*, *Women* and Nati*on* will serve as examples. As Bernard Shaw pointed out, if we took those three words as our starting point, then *ghoti* would spell *fish*.

Even as they start using decoding strategies, children have to realize that letter-by-letter processing has to be modified. The digraph *ea* which is very common in English orthography has to be processed as a single sound and not as two. Of course, as with so much of English, there are always exceptions that have to be learned, such as *reality*.

Left-to-right processing would seem an appropriate starting point, but it has to be modified even when the spelling of words is regular. The silent *e* on the end of many words lengthens the preceding vowel so that the end of the word has to be taken into account before the whole word can be identified.

Thus, even as they are beginning to use a decoding strategy, the children are having to make use of graphemic clusters — regular groups of letters — in order to work out the identity. As they make these in depth analyses, the children are able to develop orthographic images of words which they store. These enable a direct access route to reading which is fast and accurate. Frith suggests that children begin to reanalyze even the words that they originally learned so that a true description of the words is stored rather than an underspecified one. Orthographic identities with direct access to the semantic system enable us to distinguish between the many *homophones* of English. These are words which are spelled differently but which sound the same such as *be/bee*, *in/inn*, *key/quay*, *their/there*, *told/tolled* and *saw/sore*. Different spellings may appear to be a problem, but they do help to disambiguate words.

Children at this stage would probably characterize their reading by saying:

> 'I can read anything I like, though I don't always understand it. I don't actually think about reading, I just do it automatically. If I come across a word I don't know then I work it out from the groups of letters and if that doesn't seem to fit I sound out all the letters and guess at it from the meaning of the rest of the sentence.'

Once children have the facility to read any text they then have the two routes to reading that Ellis suggests for adult reading. All the children have to do is to develop speed and accuracy so that reading becomes automatic and does not interfere with comprehension. We do, however, have to recognize that whilst most people will develop both routes, the degree to which they rely on one route or the other will depend on individual differences. Baron and Strawson (1976) and Baron and Treiman (1980) suggest that some readers prefer to use, and are more efficient at using, phonological strategies. They called these readers 'Phonecians'. They identified other people as preferring to use holistic visual approaches. They called these 'Chinese' readers. As long as children develop reading proficiency, their preferred style may not be anything other than of esoteric interest but, when children show signs of struggling to develop literacy, we need to have as full a picture of their cognitive strategies as possible so that we can help them to overcome any difficulties.

Teaching Strategies

It will be clear from what we have said in relation to memory, as well as reading development, that I feel that presenting children with isolated decontextualized words is an inappropriate teaching method. Since children come to school with well developed linguistic skills we need to capitalize on this by presenting them with little books that have exciting stories which are made up with vivid pictures and lots of repetition. In the past teachers have used a strategy of requiring children to learn all the words in a book on cards *before* they would let them have the book. Logic tells us that this must be an inefficient method. It places great strain on the children's underdeveloped memory capacities, it divorces the task from the context and, for those who do not progress as quickly as the rest, it leaves them with feelings of failure because they do not have a book.

Reading will pervade all the curriculum activities and teachers may well feel that they want to consolidate the children's early accomplishments with books in order that their word reading should become fast and accurate. This can be done through many exciting word games and written activities rather than through the ubiquitous flash cards. At the same time they should be extending the phonological awareness of the children in relation to the words and developing letter name and letter sound knowledge so that when the children are ready they will be able to utilize this knowledge to develop the grapheme-to-phoneme route to reading.

How will teachers know when the children are using different strategies? This is a particularly important question since teachers will be monitoring children's progress against the guidelines of the National Curriculum. Most schools have a policy of helping reading development through individual teaching. The children read to an adult in school and at home. This means that the strategies they use are open to inspection if we listen actively. The best way to systematize this is to tape all the children once a term or twice a year and then analyze the errors that they make. This is called *miscue analysis*. The patterns of errors that emerge will show whether the children are using early visual strategies and heavy reliance on context or whether they have progressed to using alphabetic strategies. Beyond initial decoding, miscue analysis during the junior years will show when the children have progressed to using higher order orthographic strategies. Building up a profile of taped performance can be a powerful tool in ensuring that children are making progress. It can also alert us very early on to the possibility of reading problems.

Once children have developed fluency in the skill of reading then the teacher's job is to feed them with a wide variety of printed texts so that they are constantly refining their skills. The emphasis has to pass from assisting the development of the technical aspects of reading to ensuring that the written material is appropriate for the ages and abilities of the class. Checking on the readability levels of materials is important (Mobley 1984). As a general rule of thumb, when children are expected to read textbooks independently to gain information, then the readability should be below their level of reading competence. This will mean that they can use the book without assistance from the teacher. When books are being used interactively with the group and the teacher then they can have a more advanced readability level, but not beyond the age of the children. Primary teachers go to great pains to make sure that they have a range of material for projects which will suit the varying needs of the different abilities of the children in the class. There is no point in wanting to foster independent study habits if we provide children with material which is too difficult for them to work at on their own.

Writing and Spelling

So far we have only considered the reading side of literacy. We must not forget that, at the same time as they are learning to read, children are learning to write. The National Curriculum places as much emphasis on the written as on the reading side of literacy.

A Model for Spelling

Ellis (1984) has also produced a model to account for skilled adult spelling. Figure 10.2 shows his model of addressed and assembled spelling.

Assembled spelling is when the word meaning is accessed and subsequently phonological information is used to assemble the appropriate sequence of graphemes to produce the individual letters in the correct order.

Addressed spelling is when the form of the word is retrieved from the *graphemic word production system*. The orthographic identity of the word is accessed and the spelling is available as a composite unit rather than as a series of segments.

Let us follow the various paths through the model as we did for reading. Once a word has been chosen, two initial routes are possible. If there is an easily available graphemic representation of the word this can be accessed and the spelling held in the buffer whilst the word is produced. On the other hand, rather than using this direct route, once the word has been accessed its phonological representation may be activated. This is represented in the *phonemic word pro-*

Figure 10.2   A Model for both addressed and assembled spelling.

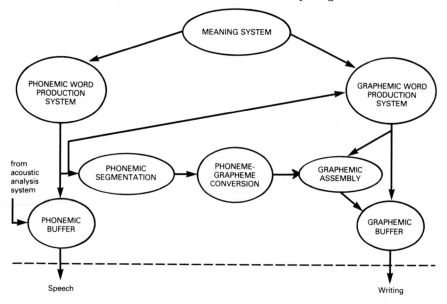

Source: Ellis (1984) *'Reading, Writing and Dyslexia: A Cognitive Analysis.'*

duction system box in Figure 10.2 and it corresponds to the same box in Figure 10.1. Once the phonological identity of the word is available, the path to orthographic realization can take two routes. The information about its sound structure can lead to more direct spelling from the graphemic system by analogy with words that sound familiar. This seems to be a combination of both addressed and assembled spelling.

If the word is spelled by a totally assembled strategy, then once the phonological representation is accessed, this is segmented into its component parts. These are then translated into their graphemic equivalents and assembled in series. Because of the nature of English orthography, the addressed route to spelling is likely to lead to greater accuracy, but only as long as the correct representation is learned in the first place. Certainly addressed spellings will enable the writer to choose the correct spelling for a word when there is one, or more than one, other homophonic representation. However, since we may often need to write words we have never written before, we need to use the assembled route as well.

The Development of Spelling

Work on the development of spelling is rather less extensive than on the development of reading, but Frith (1985) has developed a model which combines her theories of both reading and spelling development. You can see how she relates the two in Figure 10.3.

Figure 10.3   The Six-step Model of Skills in Reading and Writing Acquisition.

Step	Reading	Writing
IA	LOGOGRAPHIC$_1$	(symbolic)
IB	logographic$_2$	logographic$_2$
IIA	logographic$_3$	ALPHABETIC$_1$
IIB	alphabetic$_3$	alphabetic$_2$
IIIA	ORTHOGRAPHIC$_1$	alphabetic$_3$
IIIB	orthographic$_2$	orthographic$_3$

Source: Frith (1985) *Beneath the Surface of Developmental Dyslexia.*

Her suggestion is that children tend to make use of similar strategies as they develop their reading and spelling abilities, but that the two processes do not develop in step. She suggests that utilization of alphabetic knowledge begins first in spelling and that this then has a positive influence on the reading strategy. As children are writing, their attention must inevitably be drawn to the segmentational nature of the written word. They write with letters! A segmentation strategy is therefore a useful one in writing before it seems to be needed in reading. However, since the two processes are being developed within the same brain as it were, they do not happen in isolation from each other. It is Frith's contention that, throughout the learning process, there is a shift between reading and spelling as to which activity is setting the pace.

When children are using alphabetic strategies to spell, their written output will be clearly understood by readers, but it will not necessarily be orthographically correct. For example, you should have no trouble in deciding which words the following are meant to represent:

amung fourty cartans wershiped anoth emedgetlly

They are, respectively:

among forty cartons worshipped enough immediately

It is a very positive step when children realize the alphabetic nature of spelling and begin to produce plausible spellings. However, though using the phonological representation to generate spellings will help, it will not be sufficient to produce adult-like correct spellings except in the case of regular words.

As you can see in Figure 10.3, Frith suggests that once children have become proficient in alphabetic reading and spelling they begin to make use of higher order orthographic strategies in reading. These then influence the spelling so that larger groups of letters can be processed as units to produce orthographically correct output for words whose spelling is exceptional or non-phonological.

It used to be a common assumption in education that if children could spell a word, then they should be able to read it. Bryant and Bradley (1980) have shown that this is not necessarily the case. An individual may be at the point of using different strategies for the two different activities and therefore one would expect a mismatch between performance in reading and spelling the same material.

Teaching Spelling Strategies

Any definition of a literate person includes an assumption that that person should be an accurate speller. This means that children have to be taught to spell correctly. They have to learn to spell through the activity of spelling but, as with reading, this is best taught in a contextualized way. They should be writing with a purpose. Once they have produced material, they need to be given feedback on various aspects of their performance, including spelling. However, the correction of errors will depend on the level of development that the children have reached. When children first begin to write, we should be so delighted that they can express their own thoughts on paper that we do not have to worry whether any of the words are correct or not. If some are then it's a bonus. Real words can be given especial praise, but beginning writers can be inhibited if they feel that they are not supposed to make mistakes.

The works of Piaget and Bruner show us that children need to be actively involved in learning. They need lots of practice at writing in order to crack the alphabetic code. This writing has to be for a number of different, but all legitimate, purposes. Simple copying or only writing what the teacher has checked will tend to discourage children from active learning. Policies about encouraging writing need to be explained very carefully to parents. They may tend to look at the form the writing has taken rather than at the quality of the expression.

The need to encourage writing for a purpose without placing undue stress on accuracy in the early years is highlighted by the National Curriculum Council recommendations for English. The suggested attainment target in spelling for level 2 (attainable by 80 per cent of 7-year-olds) is:

> Produce meaningful and recognisable (*though not necessarily always correct*) [my italics] spellings of a range of common words.
> Know that spelling has patterns, and begin to apply that knowledge in order to attempt the spelling of a wider range of words.
> Spell correctly words in regular use in their own writing which observe common patterns.
> (N.C.C. English Document, Attainment Target 4: Spelling, level 2.)

It is clear that there is an expectation that the children will have begun to spell using sound—letter correspondences, but also the document makes it clear that the children need to have undertaken a wide variety of self generated writing to gain the necessary experience to achieve this level of expertise.

Having a clear grasp of the relationship between letter and sound will enable the children to spell with phonetic accuracy, but this is not enough in English since it has such an irregular system. They need to become aware of frequently occurring graphemic clusters such as -ough, -tion, -ous and -ess. It is useful for teachers to draw children's attention to the patterns of words so that gradually they can begin to develop the addressed route to spelling and become orthographic spellers. Frequently occurring words and those with regular patterns need to be accurately produced, but children must have the confidence to recognize that they need to check through work for accuracy. If these words become represented in an inaccurate form then learning the correct spelling will become very difficult. All classrooms need a range of dictionaries to which children can turn. They also need good role models. You as a teacher have to have the confidence to use a dictionary in class. Margaret Peter's (1985) policy for spelling dovetails very well with confident use of dictionaries. Her slogan is **LOOK, COVER, WRITE, CHECK**. Children need to look up the word, then make a conscious effort to commit it to memory before writing it down and then they need to check that they have reproduced it correctly. This deliberate internalizing of the spelling and active production is a much better strategy than simply copying the word.

Children with Problems in Literacy Acquisition

One of the main aims of the education system is to enable as many children as possible to achieve literacy. We have to recognize that for some children and adults with profound cognitive handicaps this is not an appropriate aim. Nevertheless, for the vast majority, achieving literacy has to be a major teaching priority. Most children may take some time and need plenty of explicit teaching, but they will achieve fluency both in reading and writing such that the processes will become automatic. However, there are some children for whom reading and writing becomes an intolerable hurdle.

The educational and psychological literature is peppered with discussion about the nature of the problem for children with difficulty in achieving literacy, the problem of the nature of the children and the problem of the naming of the problem. Some educational authorities will say that children are *dyslexic*. This is when they have a major discrepancy between their reading and spelling abilities and their measured intelligence such that the literacy problems are handicapping their educational progress. Other authorities will recognize the problem but say that the children have specific reading difficulties or specific reading retardation. Some authorities will provide special remedial help for all children who are showing literacy problems but they will be reluctant to label the problem.

There is sufficient evidence from the psychological literature (Miles 1983, Snowling 1987) to suggest that some children clearly have particular problems which make developing literacy very difficult despite adequate intelligence, original motivation and concerned teaching. When children's assessed reading ability is significantly below what would be expected for their age and non-verbal ability then there is a major cause for concern.

Before discussing these particular children I want to mention the work of Clay (1979, 1987) in New Zealand. Professor Clay has instituted a programme called Reading Recovery in New Zealand which is aimed at avoiding reading failure. Schools which are involved in the programme screen their children after one year of reading instruction and the bottom 10–15 per cent are given specific reading recovery teaching. Each child is given thirty minutes a day of individual teaching involving reading many, many graded books and doing specific work on segmentation and spelling. The aim of the programme is to avoid the possibility of the children gradually slipping through the literacy net because of poor self image and lack of motivation through failure. Clay suggests that the programme takes on average about twenty weeks and after that the children can be taken off the programme and integrated into their class, functioning at the level of the average for that class. The programme scoops the children up at the point of failure, or really before they have failed, and gives them a boost. The concentrated, individual tuition with specialist teachers works for the vast majority of the children. The system has been tried, with modifications, in Australia and America with equal success. The reasoning behind the programme is that these children do not have specific cognitive or linguistic deficits which may be handicapping them; they are simply taking a long time to get going. Rather than let them take time, with the risk of demotivation and demoralization, as well as finding the rest of the curriculum more and more inaccessible because of their limited literacy skills, the programme aims to give them a concentrated acceleration to get them going. Through the success of the programme they do not come adrift from the rest of their peers. As Clay points out, it could appear to be an expensive programme because, in any one infant school, an extra teacher is needed so that individual tuition can be given. This teacher is, of course, only part of the time a reading recovery teacher and the rest of the time an ordinary class teacher. However, the costs at the early stage pay off handsomely later on because there are so few children with reading problems higher up the age range. In fact Reading Recovery turns out to be very cost efficient.

Reading recovery does not work for all children. She finds that some children remain with intractable problems. These children need specific individual help over a more prolonged period of time. They could be said to be *developmental dyslexics*. These are the children who may never find reading and writing an automatic activity. This does not mean that they can never read and write. It means that they will experience considerable difficulty and need specific individual teaching. The cause of the problem is as yet unknown, but since reading is an applied cognitive/linguistic activity it is not surprising to find that children with these particular reading problems do have difficulty with a number of linguistic, memory and categorization tasks (Miles 1983, Frith 1985, Snowling 1987). The underlying problems manifest themselves in reading and writing difficulties.

A study by Boder (1973) is particularly important here. She studied the reading and writing skills of a group of 'dyslexic' children and found that they showed specifically different patterns in their performance. She studied the children's sight vocabulary, word attack skills and spelling performance of words that they either could or could not read. Sixty-seven per cent of her children showed a pattern of relying on memory and visual processing of words. Word attack skills were poor and, whilst their spelling of known words was better than their spelling of unknown words, they could not use letter–sound correspondences to generate possible spellings. She called these children *dysphonetic* dyslexics to suggest that they had particular problems with the segmentation side of reading. Nine per cent of the children showed a completely different pattern. Their sight vocabulary was poor but they had good word attack skills. Though they were slow, they could work out what the words were. They showed no difference in performance when spelling known and unknown words but across all words their spelling errors tended to be phonological. This group she called *dyseidetic* to suggest that they had problems with the visual aspects of reading. The final 24 per cent of the children showed mixed patterns from both the previous types.

There were a number of methodological problems in this early research, as Snowling (1987) reports, but as a starting point for recognizing that children with reading problems cannot be seen as a uniform group it was important. Boder also recognized that the children would possibly be having problems with writing as well as reading and that this too would show different patterns of errors. If teachers integrate knowledge of these types of studies with understanding of the development of reading strategies then they may find that they can begin to make helpful diagnoses of reading problems.

The models clearly show that, in order to develop speedy, accurate word reading, children have to crack the alphabetic code. This frees them from reliance on context so that they can work out what any word is. This does not mean that they do not use their top-down skills, but it does mean that their reading is likely to be accurate. A child who finds the phonological/segmentation side of language awareness difficult is going to have particular problems with this side of reading. Such children may begin to read as successfully as any others, but they will be relying heavily on their visual recognition memory and the context. This may serve for some time, but eventually their progress will slow down and their spelling is likely to be extremely problematic. Their poor phonological skills will be very obvious when they are asked to read, spell or even repeat non-words.

There are a number of possible teaching strategies that can be considered. The children can be encouraged to use their top-down skills. This will enable them to work out meanings, but we have to recognize that, as they progress through the school, reading of textbooks will become more and more difficult for them. They can be given help with grapheme-to-phoneme matching. This means very explicit teaching about the spelling–sound rules of English. The aim of such teaching will be to try to improve the phonological skills of the children in order that they may achieve some success at cracking the alphabetic code. A third possibility is to try to teach through the children's preferred visual strategy.

If the children have an obvious, major difficulty in developing the grapheme–phoneme route to reading then the answer may be to try and bypass it and help the children to read orthographically by giving explicit teaching about patterns and groups of letters. This, combined with top-down skills, may enable the children to develop reasonable fluency in reading though they may always find it a least preferred activity. In Chapter 7 we recognized the importance of Bruner's notion that teachers should present children with material in such a way that they can use all three modes of representation. This will be particularly true for the children who are intellectually able to understand the subject matter but who cannot read textbooks of the appropriate standard. Videos and auditory tapes may be needed to supplement learning through reading. As we said above, spelling is also going to be a problem. Spelling is a more difficult task than reading in any case since it requires generation of the correct sequence of letters and not just recognition. Use of cursive script may be particularly useful here since it may enable orthographic patterns to be learned as units rather than as groups of letters.

Children who have difficulty with the visual aspects of reading, but no problems with segmentation, may start off quite slowly because they will not develop an early whole word visual vocabulary. However, once they develop their segmentation strategies their reading will become quite successful. Using a combination of top-down and segmentation, they will be reasonably fluent and able to tackle most texts of an appropriate age range, but they will be quite slow since they are not using direct access to the semantic system. Spelling on the other hand may be their distinuighing problem. Their spelling is likely to be phonic-ally based and, though the meaning will be clear, words whose spelling cannot be generated regularly from their phonological identity will be consistently mis-spelled. Since these children may appear to be reading in an adult fashion, their written performance may be a source of despair to their teachers who may label them as lazy rather than recognizing the problem. Analysis of spelling perform-ance should enable a more appropriate diagnosis to be made.

Children who have difficulty with the phonological side of reading, but who also have poor visual memories, are going to have the greatest difficulty in developing literacy. They will need a great deal of individual help to enable them to use the abilities that they do have to the best advantage. Both top-down and bottom-up teaching strategies will be needed plus a lot of emotional support to enable them to maintain a positive self image in this print laden world.

The task of primary teachers is to develop the literacy skills of all children to the best possible level. The labelling of the disability is very secondary as far as they are concerned. However, since it is in the primary schools that reading problems will become apparent, it is important that teachers take a careful diagnostic approach. They need to take account of the strategies that the children are using and their progress patterns so that they can provide the most effective learning environment within the classroom. This will also give teachers the confidence to ask for extra help when they feel it is needed in the best interests of the children.

Conclusion

A few years ago there were many cars driving round with stickers saying 'If you can read this, thank a teacher'. One of the most exciting and important accomplishments of teaching is that children are taught to read. For many children this will seem to be an almost effortless task. Teachers provide the books and the time and the children seem to do the rest. However, beneath the surface of that is the provision of the appropriate materials and the recognition of the levels of abilities that the children have attained so that they can be helped in their progress. The models of reading development provided by psychologists provide useful guidelines for monitoring progress and for recognizing when intervention is necessary.

Further Reading

Whereas many of the subjects covered by this book have a limited number of applied publications related to them, literacy is the one area where there are many, many books all about how to teach. The six books recommended here are all theoretical, but they are well written and make the theory accessible to the non-psychologist. Gibson and Levin (1975) *The Psychology of Reading* is a very comprehensive book covering all aspects of reading. You will also find Oakhill and Garnham (1988) *Becoming a Skilled Reader* useful. Clay (1979) *The Early Detection of Reading Difficulties* sets out her views on reading and provides practical advice for helping slow starters to get going. Miles (1983) *Dyslexia: the Pattern of Difficulties* and Snowling (1987) *Dyslexia: A Cognitive Development Perspective* will give you a sensible and wide ranging knowledge of reading problems.

References

ALLPORT, D. A., ANTONIS, B. and REYNOLDS, P. (1972) 'On the division of attention: A disproof of the single channel hypothesis', *Quarterly Journal of Experimental Psychology*, **24**, pp. 225–35.

ALSTON, J. and TAYLOR, S. (1984) *The Handwriting File: Diagnosis and Remediation of Handwriting Difficulties*, Wisbech, LDA.

ALSTON, J. and TAYLOR, J. (1987) *Handwriting: Theory, Research and Practice*, London and Sydney, Croom Helm.

APPEL, L. F., COOPER, R. G., MCCARRELL, N., SIMS-KNIGHT, J., YUSSEN, S. R. and FLAVELL, J. H. (1972) 'The development of the distinction between perceiving and memorising', *Child Development*, **43**, pp. 1365–81.

ATKINSON, R. C. and SHIFFRIN, R. M. (1971) 'The control of short-term memory', *Scientific American*, **225**, pp. 82–90.

ATKINSON-KING, K. (1973) 'Children's acquisition of phonological stress constraints', UCLA Working Papers No. 25.

BADDELEY, A. D. (1982) *Your Memory: a User's Guide*, London, Penguin.

BADDELEY, A. D. and HITCH, G. J. (1974) 'Working Memory', in Bower, G. A. (Ed.) *The Psychology of Learning and Motivation*, Vol. 8, New York, Academic Press.

BADDELEY, A. D. and LONGMAN, D. J. A. (1978) 'The influence of length and frequency of training on rate of learning to type', *Ergonomics*, **21**, pp. 627–35.

BADDELEY, A. D. and PATTERSON, K. (1971) 'The relationship between long-term and short-term memory', *British Medical Bulletin*, **27**, pp. 237–42.

BALL, E. (1985) Unpublished B. Ed. Thesis.

BAMFORD, J. and SAUNDERS, E. (1985) *Hearing Impairment, Auditory Perception and Language Disability*, London, Edward Arnold.

BARON, J. and STRAWSON, C. (1976) 'Use of orthographic and word-specific knowledge in reading words aloud', *Journal of Experimental Psychology: Human Perception and Performance*, **2**, pp. 386–93.

BARON, J. and TREIMAN, R. (1980) 'Some problems in the study of cognitive processes', *Memory and Cognition*, **8**, pp. 313–21.

BARON-COHEN, S., LESLIE, A. M. and FRITH, U. (1985) 'Does the autistic child have a "theory of mind"?' *Cognition*, **21**, pp. 37–46.

BERKO, J. (1958) 'The child's learning of English morphology', *Word*, **14**, pp. 150–77.

BERLYNE, D. E. (1960) *Conflict, Arousal and Curiosity*, New York, McGraw-Hill.

BETTELHEIM, B. (1967) *The Empty Fortress*, London, Collier-Macmillan.

BEVERIDGE, M. and CONTI-RAMSDEN, G. (1987) *Children With Language Disabilities*, Milton Keynes, OUP.

BIEMILLER, A. J. (1970) 'The development of the use of graphic and contextual information as children learn to read', *Reading Research Quarterly*, **6**, pp. 75–96.

BISHOP, D. V. M. (1982) *T.R.O.G. Test for Reception of Grammar*, Abingdon, Thomas Leach.

BODER, E. (1973) 'Developmental dyslexia: a diagnostic approach based on three types of reading–spelling patterns', *Developmental Medicine and Child Neurology*, **15**, pp. 663–87.

BOUSFIELD, W. A. (1953) 'The occurrence of clustering in the recall of randomly arranged associates', *Journal of General Psychology*, **49**, pp. 229–40.

BOWER, T. (1966) 'The visual world of infants', *Scientific American*, **215**, pp. 80–92.

BOWERMAN, M. (1982) 'Reorganisational processes in lexical and syntactic development', in WANNER, E. and GLEITMAN, L. R. (Eds) *Language Acquisition: The State Of The Art*, Cambridge, CUP.

BRADLEY, L. and BRYANT, P. E. (1983) 'Categorising sounds and learning to read: a causal connection', *Nature*, **301**, pp. 419–21.

BREMNER, M. W., GILLMAN, S. and ZANGWILL, O. L. (1967) 'Visuo-motor disability in school children', *British Medical Journal*, iv, pp. 259–62.

BROWN, R. and KULIK, J. (1977) 'Flashbulb memories', *Cognition*, **5**, pp. 73–99.

BRUNER, J. S. (1957) 'On Perceptual Readiness', *Psychological Review*, **66**, pp. 123–52.

BRUNER, J. S. (1966) *Studies in Cognitive Growth*, New York, Wiley.

BRYANT, P. E. and BRADLEY, L. (1980) 'Why children sometimes write words which they cannot read', in FRITH, U. *Cognitive Processes in Spelling*, London, Academic Press.

BRYANT, P. E. and BRADLEY, L. (1985) *Children's reading problems*, Oxford, Blackwell.

BRYANT, P. E. and TRABASSO, T. (1971) 'Transitive inferences and memory in young children', *Nature*, **232**, pp. 456–8.

BULLOCK, A. (1975) *A Language for Life*, London, HMSO.

CARROLL, L: *Through the Looking Glass and What Alice found there.*

CARROLL, L: *Alice's Adventures in Wonderland.*

CHAPMAN, E. K. and STONE, J. M. (1988) *The Visually Handicapped Child In Your Classroom*, London, Cassell.

CHAUCER, G: *The House of Fame II.*

CHERRY, C. (1956) 'Some experiments on the recognition of speech with one and two ears', *Journal of the Acoustic Society of America*, **23**, pp. 915–19.

CHI, M. T. H. (1978) 'Knowledge structures and memory development', in SIEGLER, R. (Ed.) *Children's thinking what develops?*, Hillsdale, NJ. LEA.

CHOMSKY, C. (1969) *The Acquisition of Syntax in Children from 5 to 10*, Cambridge, MA, MIT Press.

CHOMSKY, N. (1972) *Language and Mind*, New York, HBJ.

CLARK, M. M. (1976) *Young Fluent Readers*, London, HEB.

CLARK, M. M. (1985) *New Directions in the Study of Reading*, London, Falmer.

CLAY, M. M. (1979) *The Early Detection of Reading Difficulties: A Diagnostic Survey with Recovery Procedures*, London, HEB.

CLAY, M. M. (1987) 'Implementing Reading Recovery: systematic adaptations to an educational innovation', *New Zealand Journal of Educational Studies*, **22**, pp. 35–58.

CONRAD, R. (1964) 'Acoustic confusions in immediate memory,' *British Journal of Psychology*, **55**, pp. 75–84.

COOPER, J. C., MOODLEY, M. and REYNELL, J. (1977) *Helping Language Development*, London, Edward Arnold.

COWAN, W. M. (1979) 'The development of the brain', *Scientific American*, **241**, pp. 88–133.

COX, C. B. (1988) *English for Ages 5 to 11*, Report of the English Working Group, National Curriculum Council, London, DES.

CRAIK, F. I. M. and LOCKHART, R. S. (1972) 'Levels of processing: a framework for memory research', *Journal of Verbal Memory and Verbal Behaviour*, **11**, pp. 671–84.

CRUTTENDEN, A. (1985) 'Intonation comprehension in ten year olds', *Journal of Child Language*, **12**, pp. 643–61.

CRYSTAL, D. (1976) *Child Language Learning and Linguistics*, London, Edward Arnold.

DAY, H. E. and BERLYNE, D. E. (1971) 'Intrinsic Motivation', in LESSER, G. (Ed.) *Psychology and Educational Practice*, Illinois, Scott Foresman.

DOBBING, J. (1974) 'The later growth of the brain and its vulnerability', *Paediatrics*, **53**, pp. 2–6.

DOBBING, J. and SMART, J. L. (1973) 'Early undernutrition, brain development and behaviour', in BARNETT, S. A. (Ed.) *Clinics in Developmental Medicine, No. 47: Ethology and Development*, London, Heinemann Medical Books.

DONALDSON, M. (1978) *Children's Minds*, London, Fontana.

DONALDSON, M., GRIEVE, R. and PRATT, C. (1983) *Early Childhood Development and Education*, Oxford, Blackwell.

DORVAL, B. and ECKMAN, C. (1984) 'Developmental trends in the quality of conversation achieved by small groups of acquainted peers', Monographs of the Society of Research in Child Development, **29**, No. 206.

DREVER, J. (1952) *A Dictionary of Psychology*, London, Penguin.

EHRI, L. C. and WILICE, L. S. (1980) 'The development of orthographic images', in FRITH, U. (Ed.) *Cognitive Processes in Spelling*, London, Academic Press.

EHRI, L. C. and WILCE, L. S. (1980) 'The influence of orthography on readers' conceptualisation of the phonemic structure of words', *Applied Psycholinguistics*, **1**, pp. 339–49.

ELKIND, D. (1975) 'Perceptual development in children', *American Scientist*, **63**, pp. 533–41.

ELKIND, D. (1978) *The Child's Reality: Three Developmental Themes*, Hillsdale, NJ, Erlbaum.

ELLIS, A. W. (1984) *Reading, Writing and Dyslexia: A Cognitive Analysis,* London, LEA.

ELLIS, N. C. and HENNELLEY, R. A. (1980) 'A bilingual word-length effect: implications for intelligence testing and the relative ease of mental calculations in Welsh and English', *British Journal of Psychology*, **71**, pp. 43–52.

FLAVELL, J. H., BEACH, D. R. and CHINSKY, J. M. (1966) 'Spontaneous verbal rehearsal in a memory task as a function of age', *Child Development*, **37**, pp. 283–99.

FRITH, U. (1985) 'Beneath the surface of developmental dyslexia', in PATTERSON, K. E., MARSHALL, J. C. and COLTHEART, M. (Eds) *Surface Dyslexia*, London, LEA.

FROMKIN, V. and RODMAN, R. (1988) *An Introduction to Language*, 4th edn., New York, HRW.

GALTON, M., SIMON, B. and CROLL, P. (1980) *Inside the Primary Classroom*, Oxford, RKP.

GARDNER, R. A. and GARDNER, B. T. (1969) 'Teaching sign language to a chimpanzee', *Science*, **165**, pp. 664–72.

GIBSON, E. J. (1969) *Principles of Perceptual Learning and Development*, New York, Prentice Hall.

GIBSON, E. J. and LEVIN, H. (1975) *The Psychology of Reading*, Cambridge, MA, MIT Press.

GINSBERG, H. and OPPER, S. (1969) *Piaget's Theory of Intellectual Development: An Introduction*, Englewood Cliffs, Prentice-Hall.

GORDON, N. and McKINLAY, I. (1980) *Helping Clumsy Children*, London, Churchill Livingstone.

GOUGH, P. and HILLINGER, M. L. (1980) 'Learning to read: an unnatural act', *Bulletin of the Orton Society*, **30**, pp. 179–96.

GREGG, V. H. (1988) *Introduction to Human Memory*, London, RKP.

GRICE, N. P. (1975) 'Logic and Conversation', in Cole, P. and Morgan, J. (Eds) *Syntax and Semantics: Volume 3: Speech acts*, New York, Academic Press.

HABER, R. N. (1969) 'Eidetic Images', *Scientific American*, **220**, pp. 36–44.

HARRIS, M. and COLTHEART, M. (1986) *Language Processing in Children and Adults*, London, RKP.

HAYES, C. (1951) *The Ape in our House*, New York, Harper.

HUGHES, M. and DONALDSON, M. (1983) 'The use of hiding games for studying coordination of viewpoints', in Donaldson, M., Grieve, R. and Pratt, C. (1983) *Early Childhood Development and Education*, Oxford, Balckwell.

HULME, C. (1981) *Reading Retardation and Multisensory Learning*, London, RKP.

HULME, C., SYLVESTER, J., SMITH, S. and MUIR, C. (1986) 'The effects of word length on memory for pictures: evidence for speech coding in young children', *Journal of Experimental Child Psychology*, 41, pp. 61–75.

JARMAN, C. (1979) *The Development of Handwriting Skills*, Oxford, Blackwell.

KAIL, R. V. (1979) *The Development of Memory in Children*, San Francisco, W. H. Freeman.

KANNER, L. (1943) 'Autistic disturbance of affective contact', *Nervous Child*, 2, pp. 217–50.

KEENEY, T. J., CANNIZZO, S. R. and FLAVELL, J. H. (1967) 'Spontaneous and induced verbal rehearsal in a recall task', *Child Development*, 38, pp. 953–66.

KELLOG, W. N. (1933) *The Ape and the Child*, New York, McGraw Hill.

KINGMAN, J. (1988) *Report of the Committees of Inquiry into the Teaching of the English Language*, London, HMSO.

KINGSLEY, P. R. and HAGEN, J. W. (1969) 'Induced versus spontaneous rehearsal in short-term memory in nursery school children', *Developmental Psychology*, 1, pp. 40–46.

KOBASIGAWA, A. (1977) 'Retrieval factors in the development of memory', in KAIL, R. V. and HAGEN, J. W. (Eds) *Perspectives on the Development of Memory and Cognition*, Hillsdale, NJ, Laurence Erlbaum Associates.

KREUTZER, M. A., LEONARD, C. and FLAVELL, J. H. (1975) 'An interview study of children's knowledge about memory', *Monographs of the Society for Research in Child Development*, 40, No. 159, pp. 1–58.

LASZLOW, J. and BAIRSTOW, P. (1985) *Perceptual Motor Behaviour*, London, HRW.

LEONARD, L., WILCOX, M., FULMER, K. and DAVIS, G. (1978) 'Understanding indirect requests: an investigation of children's comprehension of pragmatic meanings', *Journal of Speech and Hearing Research*, 21, pp. 528–37.

LESLIE, A. M. (1987) 'Pretense and representation: the origins of "Theory of Mind"', *Psychological Review*, 94, pp. 412–26.

LIEBECK, P. (1984) *How Children Learn Mathematics*, London, Penguin.

LINDSAY, P. H. and NORMAN, D. A. (1977) *Human Information Processing*, New York, Academic Press.

LLOYD, P., MAYES, A., MANSTEAD, A. S. R., MENDELL, P. R. and WAGNEN, H. L. (1984) *Introduction to Psychology: An Integrated Approach*. London, Fontana.

McGARRIGLE, J. and DONALDSON, M. (1974) 'Conservation Accidents', *Cognition*, 3, pp. 41–50.

McGARRIGLE, J., GRIEVE, R. and HUGHES, M. (1978) 'Interpreting class inclusion: a contribution to the study of the child's cognitive and linguistic development', *Journal of Experimental Child Psychology*, 25, pp. 1528–50.

McKAY, D. G. (1973) 'Aspects of the theory of comprehension, memory and attention'. *Quarterly Journal of Experimental Psychology*, 25, 22–40.

MACNAMARA, J. (1972) 'The cognitive basis of language learning in infants', *Psychological Review*, 79, pp. 1–13.

MANDLER, G. (1967) 'Organization and memory', in SPENCE, K. W. and SPENCE, J. T. (Eds) *The Psychology of Learning and Motivation, Vol. 1*, New York, Academic Press.

MARATSOS, M. (1973) 'Non-egocentric communication abilities in pre-school children', *Child Development*, 44, pp. 697–700.

MARSH, G., FRIEDMAN, M., WELCH, V. and DESBERG, P. (1981) 'A cognitive developmental theory of reading acquisition', in MACKINNON, G. E. and WALLER, T. G. (Eds) *Reading Research: Advances in Theory and Practice*, New York, Academic Press.

MENYUK, P. (1988) *Language Development, Knowledge and Use*, Illinois, Scott Foresman.

MILES, T. R. (1983) *Dyslexia: The Pattern of Difficulties*, London, Granada.

MILLER, G. A. (1956) 'The magic number seven, plus or minus two: some limits of our capacity for processing information', *Psychological Review*, 63, pp. 81–97.

MOBLEY, M. (1984) 'Evaluating curriculum materials', Schools' Curriculum Development Committee, Programme 2, Longman Resources Unit.

MOELY, B. E., OLSON, F. A., HAWES, T. G. and FLAVELL, J. H. (1969) 'Production deficiency in young children's clustered recall', *Developmental Psychology*, 1, pp. 26–34.

MORAY, N. (1959) 'Attention in dichotic listening: affective cues and the influence of instructions', *Quarterly Journal of Experimental Psychology*, 11, pp. 56–60.

MURPHY, K. P. (1976) 'Communication for the hearing impaired in the United Kingdom and the Republic of Ireland', in OYER, H. H. (Ed.) *Communication for the Hearing Handicapped*, Baltimore, University Park Press.

OAKHILL, J. and GARNHAM, A. (1988) *Becoming a Skilled Reader*, Oxford, Blackwell.

ORNSTEIN, P. A., NANS, M. J., and STONE, B. P. (1977) 'Rehearsal training and developmental differences in memory' *Developmental Psychology*, 13, 15–24.

PAIVIO, A. (1971) *Imagery and Verbal Processes*, New York, Holt.

PASTERNICKI, J.G. (1987) 'Paper for writing: research and recommendations', in ALSTON, J. and TAYLOR, J. (Eds) *Handwriting: Theory, Research and Practice*, London, Croom Helm.

PETERS, M. (1985) *Spelling Caught or Taught: A New Look*, London, RKP.

PIAGET, J. (1972) *Psychology and Epistemology: Towards a Theory of Knowledge*, London, Allen Lane.

REYNOLDS, J. (1977) see Cooper, Moodley and Reynell.

ROETHLISBERGER, F. J. and DICKSON, W. J. (1939) *Management and the Worker*, Cambridge, MA, HUP.

SASSOON, R. (1983) *The Practical Guide to Children's Handwriting*, London, Thames and Hudson.

SEYMOUR, P. H. K. and ELDER, L. (1986) 'Beginning reading without phonology', *Cognitive Neuropsychology*, 1, pp. 43–82.

SHAKESPEARE, W., Henry IV part 1.

SHERIDAN, M. (1973) *From Birth to Five Years. Children's Developmental Progress*, Windsor, Nelson–NFER.

SMITH, F. (1978) *Understanding Reading*, (2nd edn), New York, Holt, Rinehart and Winston.

SNOWLING, M. (1987) *Dyslexia: A Cognitive Developmental Perspective*, Oxford, Blackwell.

STUART, M. and COLTHEART, M. (1988) 'Does reading develop in a sequence of stages?', *Cognition*, 30, pp. 138–91.

TERRACE, H. S. (1979) *Nim: A Chimpanzee Who Learned Sign Language*, New York, Knopf.

TREISMAN, A. (1964) 'Selective attention in man', *British Medical Bulletin*, 20, pp. 12–16.

TRUDGILL, P. (1975) *Accent, Dialect and the School*, London, Edward Arnold.

VYGOTSKY, L. S. (1962) *Thought and Language*, Cambridge, MA, MIT Press.

WALSH, D. J. (1976) 'The critical, but transitory importance of letter naming', *Reading Research Quarterly*, 23, pp. 108–22.

WARDEN, D. A. (1976) 'The influence of context on children's use of identifying expressions and references', *British Journal of Psychology*, 67, pp. 101–12.

WASON, P. C. and JOHNSON-LAIRD, P. N. (1972) *Psychology of Reasoning Structure and Content*, London, Batsford.

WEBER, R. H. (1970) 'A linguistic analysis of first-grade Reading Errors', *Reading Research Quarterly*, 5, pp. 427–51.

WEBSTER, A. (1986) *Deafness, Development and Literacy*, London, Methuen.

WEBSTER, A. and MCCONNELL, C. (1987) *Children with Speech and Language Difficulties*, London, Cassell.

WHELDALL, K., MORRIS, M., VAUGHAN, P. and NG, Y. Y. (1981) *Rows versus tables: an example of the use of behavioural ecology in two classes of eleven year old children'*, *Educational Psychology*, 1, pp.171–84.

WILDING, J. M. (1982) *Perception: From Sense to Object*, London, Hutchinson.

WILSON, D. (1983) *Rutherford: A Simple Genius*, London, Hodder.

Author Index

Allport, A. 72
Alston, J. 28
Appel, L. F. 101
Atkinson, R. C. 92
Atkinson-King, K. 153
Baddeley, A. D. 20, 21, 26, 93, 96, 100, 104, 112
Bairstow, P. 28
Ball, E. 72
Bamford, J. 67
Baron, J. 189
Baron-Cohen, S. 162
Beech, D. R. 103
Berko, J. 152
Berlyne, D. E. 82
Bettelheim, B. 162
Beveridge, M. 158
Biemiller, A. J. 188
Bishop, D. V. M. 157
Boder, E. 197
Bousefield, W. A. 99
Bower, T. 37
Bowerman, M. 152
Bradley, L. 184, 194
Bremner, M. W. 26
Brown, R. 98
Bruner, J. S. 47, 133, 134, 135, 136, 186
Bryant, P. E. 130, 184, 194
Bullock, A. 22

Cannizzo, S. R. 103
Carroll, L. 143, 149
Chapman, E. K. 48

Chaucer, G. 173
Cherry, C. 73
Chi, M. T. H. 105, 106
Chinsky, J. M. 103
Chomsky, C. 154
Chomsky, N. 140, 149
Clark, M. M. 72, 177, 184
Clay, M. M. 196, 199
Coltheart, M. 158, 185
Conrad, R. 101
Conti-Ramsden, G. 158
Cooper, J. C. 90
Cowan, W. M. 13
Cox, C. B. 25, 125, 165, 173
Craik, F. I. M. 99
Cruttenden, A. 153
Crystal, D. 158

Day, H. E. 82
Dickson, W. J. 84
Dobbing, J. 8
Donaldson, M. 4, 129, 130, 131, 133, 135, 137
Dorval, B. 161, 162
Drever, J. 110

Eckman, C. 161, 162
Ehri, L. C. 179, 182, 185
Elder, L. 185
Elkind, D. 40
Ellis, N. C. 108
Ellis, A. W. 179, 180, 182, 188, 191, 192

Subject Index